Computer and Web Resources
for
People with Disabilities

The production of *Computer and Web Resources for People with Disabilities* was an exciting experience that demanded a great deal of time and energy on the part of many knowledgeable people throughout the Alliance for Technology Access community. This was a dynamic collaboration of consumers, families, professionals, community-based organizations, technology companies, and funders. We are very grateful to the following companies and foundations for their sponsorship and help in making this effort a success:

The Morris Stulsaft Foundation
The Learning Company
Pacific Bell
Carlston Family Foundation

"An Outstanding Academic Book of 1995."

— *Choice* magazine

"This book on assistive technology speaks directly to people with disabilities and their families. Technology is vital for attaining independence. This book can assist you in finding out how to get it into your life."

— **Ed Roberts,** late President and Cofounder, World Institute on Disability

"This book gets beyond the jargon, beyond the commercialism, and beyond the theory to address the real needs of people with disabilities who want to use technology in their lives."

— **Vicki Casella, Ph.D.,** Professor, Department of Special Education, San Francisco State University

"The Alliance for Technology Access has produced an indispensable guide for anyone interested in using computers or assistive technology to expand their horizons in employment, education, or any other area of their lives….If you're ready to take the plunge into the world of computers, but lack the courage or the knowledge to dive into untested water, *Computer Resources for People with Disabilities* can teach anyone with any kind of disability how to scan, select, and scroll with the best of them."

— *One Step Ahead*, A Newsletter by People with Disabilities for People with Disabilities

"This wonderful new book is another example of the power of parents to change the world. Less than 10 years ago, a few parents recognized that technology could help their children with disabilities. They began a collaborative effort which became the Alliance for Technology Access. Today, these centers serve thousands of children and adults with disabilities, parents, and professionals."

— *Exceptional Parent*

"This book is a veritable clearinghouse of different technologies available and their applicability to the lives and tasks of people with various disabilities. It strives to be a sort of Whole Earth Catalog of cutting-edge and approaching technologies….[It is] informative and unusually easy to use."

— *Booklist*

"This well-organized work is an invaluable and much-needed reference tool for all types of users….In this time of universal ADA compliance, this is a highly recommended reference."

— *Library Journal* (starred review)

"Assistive technology can be liberating, creating opportunities and independence for people with disabilities. This comprehensive and clear guide through the often confusing maze of technology can inform people, and empower them as well."

— **Joseph P. Shapiro,** Senior Editor, *U.S. News & World Report* and author of *No Pity: People with Disabilities Forging a New Civil Rights Movement*

"This book takes the reader step by step through the process of setting goals, assessing needs, finding the right people to help, and getting funding, through the selection of hardware and software to actual purchase and follow-up assistance….For anyone with a disability or working with a person with a disability, this is probably one of the best starting points to consideration of adapted computer technology. As stated in the book, though, this will only be the start. Where each individual goes will be determined by his-her own needs, desires, and will to succeed and grow."

— *Kliatt*

"The authors of this book give 'non-techie' people with disabilities (and people who love and work with them) a user-friendly manual for approaching, evaluating, securing, and using computers and assistive devices—all in understandable, simple language."

— *Inside MS,* a publication of the National Multiple Sclerosis Society

"The next time someone says, 'I think a computer would benefit me (my child, my student, my client)—but I don't know where to start,' give them *Computer Resources for People with Disabilities*….If you can only afford one book, this is probably it."

— *Real Times*

Ordering

Trade bookstores in the U.S. and Canada please contact:
Publishers Group West, 1700 Fourth Street, Berkeley CA 94710
Phone: (800) 788-3123 Fax: (510) 528-3444

Hunter House books are available at bulk discounts for textbook course adoptions; to qualifying community, health care, and government organizations; and for special promotions and fundraising. For details please contact:
Special Sales Department
Hunter House Inc., PO Box 2914, Alameda CA 94501-0914
Tel. (510) 865-5282   Fax (510) 865-4295
email: marketing@hunterhouse.com

Individuals can order our books from most bookstores or by calling toll-free:
(800) 266-5592

Computer and Web Resources for People with Disabilities

A Guide to Exploring Today's
Assistive Technology

3rd edition

The Alliance for Technology Access

Hunter House Inc., Publishers
P.O. Box 2914
Alameda CA 94501-0914

Library of Congress Cataloging-in-Publication Data
Computer and web resources for people with disabilities : a guide to exploring today's assistive technologies / Alliance for Technology Access.—3rd rev. "millennium" ed. p. cm.
Includes index.
ISBN 0-89793-300-1 (pbk.: alk. paper)
ISBN 0-89793-301-X (spiral : alk. paper)
1. Computers and the handicapped. 2. Computers and the handicapped—Equipment and supplies. 3. Web site development. I. Alliance for Technology Access. Computer resources for people with disabilities. II. Title.
HV1569.5. A45   2000
004' .087—dc21   99-059323

Project Credits

Cover design: Jil Weil, Oakland
Cover illustration: Kiran Rana
Copyeditor: Lydia Bird
Proofreader: John David Marion
Indexer: Kathy Talley-Jones
Book design and production: Hunter House
Production Director: Virginia Fontana
Acquisitions Editor: Jeanne Brondino

Associate Editor: Alexandra Mummery
Publicity Director: Marisa Spatafore
Customer Service Manager:
  Christina Sverdrup
Shipping and order fulfillment:
  Joel Irons, A&A Quality Shipping
Publisher: Kiran S. Rana

Printed by Publishers Press, Salt Lake City, Utah
Manufactured in the United States of America

9 8 7 6 5 4 3 2 1   Third edition   00 01 02 03 04

Contents

Contents (continued)

Foreword

This book is about problems of expression and communication and how to solve them. I am dumb, in the literal sense of not being able to speak. Maybe I'm dumb in the more figurative sense, but we won't go into that here. I, and thousands like me, have been helped to communicate by modern technology. Indeed, the fact that I have been asked to write this foreword is a sign of what technology can do.

This book offers something no other does: a guide to maneuvering the growing world of computers, both the mainstream and the assistive technology, to find what is right for you. Evaluating your needs and finding the technology to fill them is a process. My methods of communication are an example.

The main problem of communicating without being able to speak is what is called the baud rate, the rate at which information can be conveyed. Normal speech is between 120 and 180 words a minute. By contrast, a reasonable typist can produce 40 to 60 words a minute. Thus, if people were equipped with keyboards to communicate, they could do so at half to a quarter of the speech rate.

However, many people like me who cannot speak also have other disabilities. They cannot use a keyboard. Instead, they can use one or more switches, operated by a head or hand movement. This is where a person is really confronted with the rate of information flow. If you take an average word to be five characters and assume that any character can follow any other character, normal speech has an information flow rate of between 50 and 75 bits a second. By contrast, a person might be able to operate a switch at two or three bits a second.

The real information flow in human communication, however, is much less than this. (In the case of political speeches, it is practically zero.) This is because spelling out a sentence letter by letter is inefficient. Most sequences of letters don't make recognizable words, let alone meaningful sentences. It takes a handful of these bits of information (letters) to create meaningful communication (a word). So, communicating by specifying every letter is a lot of redundant effort.

For someone who can use a switch to communicate, it is much more efficient to pick words or even whole phrases from a list of likely ones. Computer technology makes this possible. To translate the press of a switch into letters, words, or sentences requires computers. The development of microprocessors in the last 15 years has meant that virtually unlimited computing power is available at a reasonable cost.

The next step is to find efficient software to translate the input from the

x

——

Computer
and Web
Resources
for People
with
Disabilities

switch into phrases and sentences. With the Equalizer program that I use, I can manage about 15 words a minute. That is not too bad, since an information flow rate of three bits a second corresponds to 25 to 30 words a minute. But obviously there is scope for improvement. And the promise of computer technology is that improvements are always in development.

Having decoded the signals from some input devices, such as a switch, one then has to broadcast it in a form people can understand. This could be visually, with text or diagrams on a screen. But if you want to communicate like others, which is what people in my position would like, you need to be able to speak. Computerized speech synthesizers have improved a great deal in recent years, and this is important: not only does one want to be understood, but one also does not want to sound like Mickey Mouse or a Dalek. My voice may be a bit tinny and American, but it is almost human.

The process I have just described is what this book is all about. I hope others find in this book the inspiration and the technology, hardware and software, that can help them to communicate better—to express their human-ness.

Stephen Hawking
Cambridge University
Cambridge, England

Stephen Hawking is perhaps the best-known modern physicist since Einstein. When he was 21, he was diagnosed with ALS, a degenerative nerve disease. With the use of a voice synthesizer and other computer technology, he has been able to communicate his genius to the world. He is the author of *A Brief History of Time* and *Black Holes and Baby Universes and Other Essays*.

Preface

The work of redefining human potential and creating a world of access to opportunity through technology has only just begun. It must continue until technology is a regular part of the lives of all individuals with disabilities who can benefit from it. The nonprofit Alliance for Technology Access exists solely to promote this mission, which encompasses millions of people directly and every one of us indirectly.

This book would never have come to be without the vast expertise and boundless passion of the children and adults with disabilities and their families, the professional service providers, and the forward-thinking businesses who make up the Alliance for Technology Access and who contributed so generously and unselfishly to the writing of this book.

We need your help. Please think about joining this terrific and enthusiastic group of people dedicated to improving access to technology for people with disabilities. There are many ways for individuals and organizations to support this compelling mission:

- By volunteering time
- By contributing financially
- By providing in-kind donations
- By establishing new Alliance Technology Resource Centers
- By becoming ATA Affiliate or Associate members

To find out more about how you can become part of the mission, vision, and work of the Alliance, or to be added to our mailing list, please call or write us today at:

The Alliance for Technology Access
2175 East Francisco Blvd., Suite L
San Rafael CA 94901
phone: (415) 455-4575   fax: (415) 455-0654
email: ATAinfo@ATAccess.org
website: www.ATAccess.org

xii

———

Computer
and Web
Resources
for People
with
Disabilities

Important Note
to the Reader

The material in this book is intended to provide an overview of the hardware, software, and other considerations surrounding computer resources for people with disabilities. Every effort has been made to provide accurate and dependable information and the contents of this book have been compiled in consultation with a variety of computer professionals and users. The reader should be aware that professionals in the field may have differing opinions and change is always taking place. Therefore, the authors, publisher, and editors cannot be held responsible for any error, omission, or outdated material.

The authors and publisher disclaim any liability, loss, injury, or damage incurred as a consequence, directly or indirectly, of the use and application of any of the contents of this volume.

If you have any questions or concerns about the information in this book, please consult your local Alliance for Technology Access Center.

Many of the designations used by manufacturers and sellers to distinguish their products are claimed as trademarks. Where those designations appear in this book, and the authors were aware of a trademark claim, the designations have been printed with initial capital letters. The inclusion of a product in this book does not imply endorsement or recommendation.

The people and events described in the personal stories in this book are real. In all but the first chapter, their names have been changed to respect their privacy and that of their families.

Acknowledgments

This book was produced through a collaborative effort of the Alliance for Technology Access, its staff, board, volunteers, friends, and families. The effort that created this book models the Alliance way of doing business. It involves children and adults with disabilities, parents and family members, educators, technology developers, medical professionals, advocates, and friends, all working together to bring the best information and most complete access to interested people everywhere.

The Alliance lovingly acknowledges the invaluable and essential contribution to this book by Jackie Brand, the Founder and first Executive Director of the Alliance for Technology Access. Not only did she see the big picture and keep the vision for this work, and all the work of the Alliance, she also kept a focus on the little picture. It was her continuous hands-on support of the team, in writing, editing, fact checking, and proofreading, that dramatically strengthened our effort. It was her dedication and devotion that motivated each of us to give not only our skill but our heart to making *Computer Resources for People with Disabilities* more than just a book. It is also a reflection of the talent within the Alliance, and a tribute to the passion and commitment to our mission, that Jackie has inspired in us all.

The book grew under the loving guidance and tireless efforts of our editor, Mary Lester. Without her skill, leadership, and patience, this book would not exist. While many people provided her with individual stories, perspectives, and expertise, she translated them into a meaningful whole with clarity, passion, and truth.

The Alliance also wishes to especially thank the following people for their significant writing contributions, starting with Bob Glass, without whose help this effort would not have been possible. Although many people participated and are acknowledged in later sections, this group contributed the major writing for the book: Jackie Brand, Amy Dell, Donna Dutton, Bob Glass, David Grass, Joyce Hakansson, Melinda Harrington, Donna Heiner, Russ Holland, June Isaacson Kailes, Jane Lee, Steve Mendelsohn, Bridgett Perry, and Lois Symington. We also thank Mali Apple for her clarity, knowledge, and expertise, which improved this effort so dramatically.

We are particularly indebted to Bridgett Perry, who played a crucial role in making sure that the technical information in Part II was accurate and complete. She coordinated a vast network of contributors, making a tough task seem easy.

We acknowledge with great appreciation the wonderful work of graphic designer Sherry Stoll, who developed the charts in Part II.

xiv

Computer
and Web
Resources
for People
with
Disabilities

Third Edition

The Alliance acknowledges the enormous contribution of Bob Glass, the staff, board of directors, and volunteers of the Bluegrass Technology Center in making this third edition a reality. Without their dedication, hard work, and leadership, this edition would not exist.

We also wish to thank and appreciate Russ Holland and Mary Lester for their support and expertise which was invaluable in bringing this work to completion.

Original Concept Team

Jackie Brand, Greg Burkett, Vicki Casella, Pat Cashdollar, Lynn Chiu, Lisa Cohn, Donna Dutton, Suzanne Feit, Bob Glass, Mary Ann Glicksman, Ann Grady, Hod Gray, Melinda Harrington, Anita Harris, Donna Heiner, Russ Holland, Jane Lee, Helen Miller, Caren Normandin, Bridgett Perry, Dave Salkever, Mary Salkever, Dave Schmitt, John Schweizer, Sherry Stoll, Lois Symington, Lisa Wahl, Alice Wershing

Technical Team

Carol Adams, Francia Baily, Michael Baruch, Jane Berliss, Greg Burkett, Pat Cashdollar, Terri Chastain, Lynn Chiu, Donna Dutton, Charlie Farkas, Suzanne Feit, Pam Frost, Janice Fouard, Ken Funk, Mary Ann Glicksman, Lana Gossin, David Grass, Elaine Hackett, Pam Harnden, Melinda Harrington, Kirsten Haugen, Donna Heiner, Ginny Heiple, Robert Hill, Russ Holland, Roger Holt, Jean Isaacs, Gary King, Patricia Kenyon, Cindy Mathena, Helen Miller, Sue Murn, Charlotte Nelson, Steve Obremski, Janet Peters, Melody Ram, Dave Salkever, Helen Schneiderman, Cindy Storm, Judy Timms, Leslie Todd, Randy Tompkins, Sally Townsend, Lisa Wahl, Edie Weintraub, Alice Wershing, Peggy Whitworth, Sherrill Williams, Jean Wunder

Fact Checkers for Second and Third Editions

Marge Adams, Michael Baruch, Deborah Bauder, Judy Bias, Kathy Bradford, Roxanne Cortright, Janice Fouard, Patricia Furner-Nolan, Margaret Gallaway, Dierdre Geraci, Lana Gossin, Anthony Griffin, Kathy Griffin, Elaine Hackett, Nancy Johnson, Cheryl Klein, Theresa Lupo, Jan Michelson, Tom Morales, Kathy Reed, John Schweizer, Gloria Stuart, Lois Symington, Judy Timms

Other Contributions

Carol Adams, Marge Adams, Glenda Anderson, Mike Birkmire, Craig Boogaard, James Francis-Bohr, Michelle Brand, Pat Cashdollar, Diane Coleman, Tony Compton, Amy Dell, John Duganne, Mary Ann Glicksman, Ann Grady, Joyce Hakansson, Kim Hall; Kirsten Haugen, Paul Hendrix, Dee Hoban, Paul Jakab, Darrell Jones, June Isaacson Kailes, Cheryl Klein, Laura Leininger, Jeff Loving, Mary Male, Steve Mendelsohn, Sue Milburn, Laura

Payne, Susan Pompa, John Schweizer, Bob Segalman, Debbie Sharon, Tom Shworles, Peter Soloman, Karen Spurrier, Pat Steinke, Marie Stepp, Pat Stewart, Lois Symington, Cathy Synyders, Mary Ann Trower, Terry Trzaska, Lisa Wahl, Richard Wanderman, Rachel Wobschall, Gregg Vanderheiden, Mike Young, Adrian Zackheim

Reviewers

Eric Averson, Michael Baruch, Jane Berliss, David Clark, Donna Dutton, Bob Glass, Ann Grady, David Grass, Kathy Griffin, Joyce Hakansson, Donna Heiner, Russ Holland, Don Johnston, Linda Judeich, June Kailes, Arjan Khalsa, Jane Lee, Sue Murn, Bridgett Perry, Janet Peters, Jenny Sanders, Dave Schmidt, Sheila Sondik, Lois Symington, Judy Timms, Alice Wershing.

Most of the people listed above are staff and board members of Alliance for Technology Access Centers. The following Centers have participated in the writing, editing, or reviewing of this book:

Technology Assistance for Special Consumers, Huntsville AL; Technology Resource Center, Little Rock AR; Center for Accessible Technology, Berkeley CA; Computer Access Center, Los Angeles CA; Sacramento Center for Assistive Technology, Sacramento CA; SACC* Assistive Technology, Simi Valley CA; Team of Advocates for Special Kids, Anaheim CA; CITE—Center for Independence, Technology and Education, Orlando FL; Tech-Able, Conyers GA; Aloha Special Technology Access Center, Honolulu HI; United Cerebral Palsy of Idaho, Boise ID; Northern Illinois Center for Adaptive Technology, Rockford IL; Technical Aids & Assistance for the Disabled Center, Chicago IL; Technology Resources for Special People, Salina KS; Bluegrass Technology Center, Lexington KY; Enabling Technologies of Kentuckiana (enTECH), Louisville KY; Learning Independence Through Computers, Baltimore MD; Michigan's Assistive Technology Resource, St. Johns MI; PACER Computer Resource Center, Minneapolis MN; Technology Access Center, Saint Louis MO; Parents, Let's Unite for Kids, Billings MT; Center for Enabling Technology, Whippany NJ; Techspress, Utica NY; Carolina Computer Access Center, Charlotte NC; Technology Resource Center, Dayton OH; TechACCESS Center of Rhode Island, Warwick RI; East Tennessee Technology Access Center, Knoxville TN; West Tennessee Special Technology Resource Center, Jackson TN; Technology Access Center of Middle Tennessee, Nashville TN; Computer Center for Citizens with Disabilities, Salt Lake City UT; Tidewater Center for Technology Access, Virginia Beach VA

We are very grateful to Libbie Butler for painstakingly reviewing the corrections for Part III to ensure that the resource and references lists are current and accurate. We are also grateful for the important contribution made by Maggie Morales.

xvi

———

Computer
and Web
Resources
for People
with
Disabilities

The Alliance is especially and deeply grateful to Lisa Lee, our first editor at Hunter House and our supporter. Without her vision and energy, this book would never have been started. Without her belief and trust in us, we would not have had this tremendous opportunity to share with you what we have learned. And without her patience, persistence, hard work, and commitment, this book would never have been finished.

We would also like to thank Kiran Rana, Paul Frindt, Corrie Sahli, Lydia Bird, Alexandra Mummery, and Jeanne Brondino of Hunter House for believing in this work and for promoting access to it for consumers, family members, and professionals everywhere.

Our work, though utterly fascinating and truly compelling, has rarely been confined to a mortal's time schedule, as all of our wonderful and significant others will unanimously agree. Among the most important contributors have been and continue to be our own families, who often and gracefully handle the personal loads that allow us to follow our dreams.

Most importantly, we thank those people we meet everyday in every center who have taught us so much and who have, in countless ways, contributed to the richness of this book.

Computer and
Web Resources
for
People with Disabilities

Introduction

Imagine having a keyboard that changes effortlessly from a standard lay-out to one that includes only the keys you need for a specific task, such as creating a budget, working on an English assignment, or exploring music composition. Imagine a computer that talks to you, that reads messages sent to you from all over the world. Imagine having the ability to make choices by simply touching a picture on your computer screen. Imagine having the ability to type without using your hands by simply looking at the right letter on a keyboard pictured on the screen. Imagine going to the Library of Congress to gather materials for a research project without leaving your home.

These scenarios are just a few examples of what you can do today with computers. For a person with a disability, today's applications offer new promise and excitement. These new abilities level the playing field for all of us.

Why This Book Was Written

If you are a person with a disability or a parent, other family member, teacher, employer, or friend of a person with a disability, we want to share with you what we have learned about the ways assistive technology is literally chang-ing lives by creating new abilities for children and adults with disabilities—sensory, cognitive, learning, or physical disabilities.

Everyday, in the course of our work, we are asked questions about avail-able technology and its applications. "I have a vision impairment. Which computer should I buy?" "My son has a learning disability, and his teacher said a computer might help him do better in school. Which should I buy?" "I have a girl in my sixth-grade class with cerebral palsy, and the school has agreed to provide her with a computer. Which is the best?" Your questions may be similar.

The goal of this book is to help you begin answering your questions for yourself and to allow you to take advantage of the incredible new tools on the market today. We won't teach you about the insides of the latest com-puters or list every computer product ever developed. Our intention is to help you create a purpose and a framework for approaching technology so you can make initial decisions about the role it can play in enhancing your life. We have included many stories about real people who are using tech-nology successfully—people of all ages and all disabilities who use technol-ogy for different reasons.

This book is written for a community that has not yet discovered the power of technology. This community includes people with disabilities, but it also includes family members, advocates, and friends of people with disabilities. It encompasses thousands of professionals in the fields of education and rehabilitation who are concerned about quality-of-life issues and options for children and adults with disabilities. It includes the technologists, engineers, and designers who will be the developers of tomorrow's technology. This broad group represents a huge constituency that will be dramatically impacted by technology in this and the next century. We believe this constituency will demand nothing less than a revolution in expectations, making more options available for people with disabilities everywhere.

Throughout the book, we address the audience as "you," in recognition of the important decision-making role played by individuals with disabilities in defining their own futures. Supportive family members, friends, advocates, and professionals should translate the wording as needed, but always remember that choices about technology should be, to the greatest possible degree, dictated by the user.

A Word about Us

We, the authors, are a diverse group of people who have become connected and interrelated by our search for technologies to support our dreams. We are people with disabilities, children and adults, family members and friends, teachers and therapists, employers, service providers, technology vendors, professional organizations, and community agencies. We come from all over the United States, from small towns and urban centers. We cross age, ethnic, and ability/disability lines. We represent a growing community of people across the country and around the globe who are employing the tools of technology and reaching new levels of satisfaction. We did not choose technology because we were intrinsically interested in it; we became users of technology because it allowed us to become what we wanted to be: teachers, communicators, artists, composers, students, engineers.

We are connected by a strong belief in the vast potential of people with disabilities to use technology to achieve their dreams, and by a profound commitment to bring the benefits of technology to people who have historically been excluded from the American dream. We have been through the process of trying to understand a bewildering and complex field. We have searched for expertise and support. And we have created an organization that bonds us to each other and to all people looking for similar answers and support.

The Alliance for Technology Access is a collaborative, energetic community of people redefining what it means to have a disability. Having a

4

———

Computer
and Web
Resources
for People
with
Disabilities

disability no longer has to mean that things cannot be done—it means that we can find new ways to get them done. The Alliance is made up of expert advocates dedicated to pushing the limits of convention—people who ask not whether something can be done, but how it can be accomplished. We share your challenges and your frustrations. We believe in every person's right to be productive and independent and to achieve his or her desired quality of life. And we believe the most noble application of technology is to support those rights. The Alliance is a network of assistive technology Resource Centers, affiliates, associates, and technology vendors whose members share a common vision—an uncommon commitment to improving the quality of life for children and adults with disabilities through the imaginative application of assistive technology.

The Alliance was created to demonstrate how technology can transform limitations into opportunities. We work toward this goal by providing access to assistive technologies and related services that enable people to achieve productivity, independence, and success according to their needs and interests. Services available at Alliance technology resource centers include:

- Guided exploration and consultations

- Hands-on computer demonstrations

- Information and resource services

- Workshops and user groups

- Technical support services

- Professional development

The Alliance has rapidly grown from a small group of parents, consumers, professionals, and vendors to become one of the nation's most effective efforts devoted to enabling people with disabilities to gain access to the full benefits of technology. And public demand for services continues to grow at a rapid rate; the number of individuals crossing resource center thresholds, for example, went from 20,000 in 1987 to over 100,000 today.

People with disabilities must be at the center of the learning and decision-making process. We take a new approach to service, both at our centers and in this book, that varies from the standard, professionally driven model that assumes the "experts" know what's best for you. We believe that we as individuals know what we need; that a team that includes professional resources can help guide us in the right direction; and that, in the end, we must make our own decisions and direct our own lives.

Navigating through This Book

This book, like the Alliance, represents a collaborative effort, with many voices lending richness and texture to the content. We represent a great diversity of approaches and solutions, each with its own purpose and validity. We will introduce you to a broad and growing community of technology users who are excited and eager to share what they have learned.

You'll find the arrangement of this book somewhat unusual. Many books relating to people with disabilities are arranged according to disability. You can usually turn to a chapter on "visual impairments" or "physical disabilities," and you are likely to read about a particular tool that was designed for a specific disability.

We find that approach restrictive and inappropriate and prefer to focus on a functional look at a person's needs rather than looking at deficits. If the goal is to have a screen display large letters, it doesn't really matter if you need it because you have a visual impairment, a learning disability, or some other requirement. The question is not what does a person with X disability require, but what are the ways in which we can enlarge print on a computer screen. The assistive technology field is about giving people better access to the environment—through a better-designed environment or a set of tools that navigates around barriers.

The Structure of This Book

The book is divided into three parts. **Part I, The Search for Solutions,** will guide you through the process of defining your needs, developing a technology plan, building a supportive team, and making technology-related decisions. It offers strategies, first steps, and resources, and it should help you become more confident in your exploration.

Part II, The Technology Toolbox, focuses on the technology itself, offering examples of various assistive technologies. Several guides will inform and direct your search, helping you to zero in on the technologies most likely to match your abilities and goals. Part II can be read selectively as you narrow your search. It is not a compendium of every product on the market, but through it you will learn enough about the categories of products on the market today to feel comfortable taking the next steps.

The search for technology solutions is a lifelong process. As your life changes and as technology evolves, you'll find yourself continuing your search. This is one of the most exciting aspects of this field: realizing that the technology is constantly evolving. Changes are so rapid that information is often out-of-date before it is printed. We can't predict your needs or the products that will be available in the future, but we can provide

6

Computer
and Web
Resources
for People
with
Disabilities

you with a plan and appropriate resources for starting and continuing your search.

Part III, Helpful Resources and References, contains lists of resources, references, and organizations that we have found valuable in our personal and professional study of assistive technology. Keep in mind that as quickly as the technology changes, so does the information regarding the players in this newly emergent field.

This third edition of our book includes a great deal of updated information, much related to the Internet, the Information Age, and the critical issue of ensuring that all have both equal access to it and input into the nature of its development. As a powerful vehicle for the delivery of ever-changing information, we plan also to utilize the Internet to maintain the currency of what we are sharing here. We encourage you, as you develop your own access, to continue to pursue your search via our website at http://www.ATAccess.org.

Much of what we offer are the right questions and some key resources. You will learn how others have faced similar challenges and have developed effective strategies. If you find that, after reading this book, you have a goal in mind, some easy first steps to take, and a range of supporters to help; if you are armed with enough information to talk comfortably with your local computer dealer; or if you are inspired or excited by someone's story, we have accomplished our goal.

In the following pages, you'll hear a lot about journey, process, pursuit, quest, direction, search, exploration, routes, dead ends, travel assistance, places to seek out, places to avoid, rights, and community. We will go over what you should know, where to go, and what to do next; how to handle disenchantment and how to persevere until you find a friendly voice. Do the concepts of pioneering and journey sit well with you? Fortunately, we make every effort to positively reward your pioneering spirit with sound advice and guidance.

Part I:
The Search for Solutions

Chapter 1

A Millennium Vision

People have a great desire to predict the future. During an election, a sporting event, or the roll of the dice we focus our thoughts and sometimes our money on predicting the results. However, some people say it is futile to spend our time and efforts on prediction. In the words of Alan Kay, "The best way to predict the future is to invent it." This active posture is much more appealing to those of us who will not just wait patiently to see if the changes we deem necessary do occur. As we witness the dawn of a new century, we find it more appropriate to focus on what role each of us will take in determining how technology will be best fashioned to meet the needs of people, particularly those with disabilities.

One way to shape our future actions is to build knowledge of the present and the past. In the following chapters you will read many stories describing how individuals currently use adaptive devices connected to computers to enhance their own abilities.

Looking at the history of computers, we can see that each year they become dramatically smaller, faster, and less expensive. Therefore, it is realistic to think that much more technology can be developed and put into use in years to come. Technology can help children, who might be isolated and removed from childhood learning environments because of what they cannot do, to experience a full childhood with other children, developing confidence in what they *can* do. Through the use of technology, adults—who because of age, disability, chronic conditions, or other functional limitations become temporarily or permanently disabled—will be able to continue to function effectively.

It is a time of rapid change, and the changes we promote can provide expanding opportunities for the empowerment of people. Change, however, does not always produce the desired results. In China they understand the dual nature of change and represent it in their language with a character created by combining two other characters—opportunity and danger. Currently, in the area of accessible technology, the Internet best represents the two faces of change. It offers the positive opportunity of immediate, worldwide access from home to commerce, information, communication, and employment. Much of what you need or want to know, buy, or learn can be found right on your computer. People who do not want to or cannot go to all the libraries, archives, meetings, and conferences they are interested in visiting or attending can get there via access in their own homes.

The danger is that the Internet will not be accessible to everyone who wants to use it. If inability to see the screen, hear the sounds, use a keyboard, or pay fees become barriers to access to the Internet, we, as a society, will lose the talents and contributions of a large part of our population. We will create a two-tiered society in which a substantial number of people will be kept out of the mainstream. The technology is powerful and growing. It must be created in a manner that makes it accessible to all.

All individuals have the right and the responsibility to define the roles they will play in shaping the future for themselves and others. There is no right way to proceed. The actions each of us choose may be big or small, affect many or just one person. The important thing is to realize that we have a choice, that we can make change happen, and we do not have to be passive observers.

Here are some ideas that will help and inspire you to organize your own thinking. June Isaacson Kailes, a disability policy consultant in Los Angeles, California, and a member of the ATA Board of Directors, is a very successful advocate of positive change. June shares with us her method for focusing her thoughts and one of her visions for the future:

No time better than the present to think about the future! We need to put some quality time and effort into thinking about our individual and collective millennium visions!

After all, for most of us, this is the only turn of the century we will see. So, do this:

- On a piece of paper—or in your head if paper doesn't work for you—draw a line

- On the left end of the line put "0" and date you were born

- On the right side put the age of your oldest living relative

- Put an "X" for your current age at the appropriate place on this line

- Put an "X" at the age you think you may retire

- Compute the number of years between now and your estimated retirement year. These are the peak years you hopefully have to accomplish your goals—to make a difference!

Of course, there are no guarantees! What are your goals? Think about this for a minute!

- Where do you, and you as a part of the disability community, want to see us put our energies?

- Where are you going? What does the preferred future look like?

10

Computer
and Web
Resources
for People
with
Disabilities

- What's the most meaningful future you can create?

- How do you stretch beyond what is, to create something far better, the best that can be?

I ask you to consider using my 3B filter! It works like this....

You should always ask yourself at the end of the day, the week, the month, the year, the decade...how have you made a difference? Have you achieved the 3Bs?: BIGGEST BANG FOR OUR BUCK!!!!

A way to begin to think about your biggest bang for the buck is to imagine your preferred future. Sometimes it is freeing to really stretch and exercise your creativity. Here's my stretch:

I'm a selective Techno-Luster—I can't get the latest technology fast enough! I want it all yesterday.

I see my days of using erasable bond paper and electric typewriters as slower than the horse-and-buggy days. I lust for powerful, robust, lightweight, ubiquitous and seamless technology that I can operate any way I like...by voice, or just by thinking what I want to happen.

Here's one of my millennium visions for technology!!!

Before going to bed I turn on my all-in-one "La Maid Clothes Care Time Saver," which sorts, washes, dries, irons, folds, and packs my laundry for the next trip. It's 11 P.M. and my "robo personal assistant" gives me a 30-minute massage while I watch some "on-demand TV" by keying in the programs I want to see and deleting all commercials, except for the techie ones, by using by my commercial zapper.

The next thing I hear is the 6 A.M. alarm. The pink glow of the sky signals that the hot summer sun will soon be intense. I voice-activate the news and my computer begins to read me the morning headlines in the order of interest priority that I have programmed into it:

"The Americans with Disabilities and The IDEA Restoration Acts are again under serious attack!"

"Airline delays are expected for those flying today due to flow control into Dulles and strong air turbulence midcountry."

In the bathroom my "expert health system" embedded in my "smart toilet analyzer" indicates all is well, except for the usual stern message: "Cut down on the salt and fat and increase the fruit, vegetable, and calcium intake!" So I press "vitamins for the day," knowing that the correct tailor-made vitamin pill concoction will be next to my OJ at breakfast.

I activate controls in the bathroom indicating what I want for breakfast: "Toasted bagel lightly buttered with lox and Muenster cheese, one extra-large orange juice, vanilla bean coffee latte with extra foam and one-quarter teaspoon of sugar." No personal assistant services needed!

I activate my personalized exercise-intelligent CD and do my exercises while continuing to listen to morning news sequenced in the order of my interest. I fast-forward the story regarding Los Angeles' latest earthquake-predicting scheme, because it's a pipe dream that bores me, to a story about vacationing on the moon. Summer round-trip ticket fare wars to the moon have started. Advocates are protesting moon pollution by flooding elected representatives with Internet-based voice and video mail.

I do a closet scan and choose my old, red power suit. My intelligent agent takes care of everything else I'll need to go with it, shoes, belt, underwear, etc.

I do a quick computer check to see if any income has come in from my clients and note that the University of Vermont still hasn't paid. All other outstanding invoices have been paid, and the balance on my smart card is adequate to see me through this trip.

I toss my under-two-pound hovercraft, which replaced my 125-pound scooter 20 years ago, into my smart car and give the car a voice command to take me to the United Airlines loading area at the airport. I flip the car switch to electric power since it's a short trip to the airport. I sit back and admire the view. It's another typical smog-free day in Los Angeles: sun, sun, and more sun! I activate my hands-free video car phone for a quick call to Don, a colleague in New York who is deaf, to finalize a few meeting agenda items for tomorrow. Don's phone converts my speech to text automatically.

My smart car lets me off at the door of the plane, loads my bags into the plane's belly, and parks itself. I flash my airline debit smart card and board. I find my workstation aboard the plane, easily slide my collapsible hovercraft under the seat, and activate, via an infrared port at the seat, my five-ounce computer with its 14-inch screen, full-size keyboard, built-in microphone, and headset. I proceed to do my client billing for the month. I then spend time on assignments and class discussion for a course I'm taking online at Harvard's John F. Kennedy School of Government.

Upon arrival in DC, my rental smart car, which has already retrieved my gear from the plane, picks me up at the plane's door and zips me to my hotel in the District. I'm lucky to get my favorite corner room at The Floating Hyatt Potomac, four floors under water with two huge windows and a great accessible work area. I stare at the fish for a while and look for my favorite shark, then I....

June's vision seems like a stretch indeed. Clearly we're not there yet—in some cases we are not even close, but in other cases we are much closer than you think. Technology is changing so rapidly that we can be almost wherever we want to be. We are truly beginning to realize a world in which we are only limited by our imaginations. So, the first challenge is imagining where you want to go and having the expectation that you can get there.

Chapter 2

Real People and Their Success Stories

The success of technology has more to do with people than machines. All the right parts and pieces together won't work miracles by themselves. It is people who make technology powerful by creatively using it to fulfill their dreams.

The evolution of the field of assistive technology is more about the evolution of people and their expectations than it is about circuitry. The story is about challenges, barriers, and solutions; about people wanting to do things and finding more creative ways to get them done. It is about the inclusion of people with disabilities in every aspect of society and how technology can serve as a tool to facilitate that process: in school, at home, on the job, and in the community. From the elementary school classroom to the labs at NASA, people with disabilities are taking their places as full and participating members, and technology is helping to make that happen.

The stories that follow illustrate how a few people have found and used technology to accomplish their goals.

Victor

Victor had a vision. To him it was simple: go to school with his peers, graduate from high school with a New York State Regent's Diploma, go to college, get a job, be independently mobile, and live independently.

Victor had cerebral palsy and was nonverbal. In 1984, at the age of seven, his only reliable physical control was his eyes and a single switch he could activate with his head. For most of his younger years, no technology was available to help him. While watching *Sesame Street*, Victor had developed a technique of spelling with his eyes that enabled him to communicate with family, friends, and others willing to take the time to learn his system. Victor had become an effective self-advocate with a vision of what he needed.

The first use of assistive technology Victor encountered was a system that enabled him to communicate by scanning a series of choices as the computer cycled through them and then making a selection by pressing a switch. The system printed out Victor's message on a narrow ticker tape.

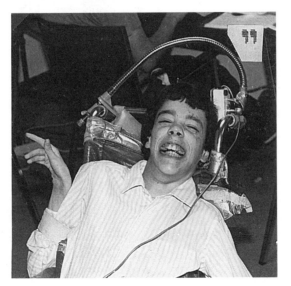

Victor

In 1984, with the support of the local Optimist club, Victor procured an Express III (Prentke Romich Company), a row/column scanning device activated by a single switch. Using the device was laborious, and little support was available in Victor's community for its programming and use, so Victor continued his search.

He advocated for the development of his own technology support team, which included a counselor in the New York State Office of Vocational Rehabilitation; a technology resource person to assist with programming the scanning device, adding computer components to the system, and helping Victor learn the technology; a high school counselor willing to help make classes and materials accessible; and a tutor to assist Victor in developing his writing skills. In 1989, Victor became the first student using augmentative communication in New York state to receive a Regent's Diploma. Victor received his diploma not because of the sophistication of the technology, but because he had expectations, vision, and the determination to pursue them.

Victor was empowered far more by his vision than by the technology. He *expected* that the technology was there or would be developed. When he went camping, Victor expected to be able to fish. He assembled a team on the spot and had them develop technology consisting of a fishing pole attached to an old helmet. And when it came time to toast marshmallows around the campfire, Victor had the team make a few technological modifications to the fishing pole that soon had flaming marshmallows flying across the campsite.

14

Computer
and Web
Resources
for People
with
Disabilities

Ben

Ben came to the Technology Assistance for Special Consumers (TASC) Resource Center of the ATA in Huntsville, Alabama, after hearing a presentation by Pam Harnden at a meeting of the local chapter of the National Federation of the Blind. Not a lover of the computer age, Ben decided to come just to see what all this ado about a "talking computer" was about.

"I knew nothing about computers, and really didn't want to know," Ben says. "My experiences with computers had not been not very good—I felt that man was becoming a slave to the computer, instead of the computer being man's slave."

His experience at TASC has changed Ben's mind. During the fall and winter of 1993, Ben visited the Resource Center once or twice a week to learn both Vocal Eyes, a screen reading program (GW Micro), and a word processing program. "It really opened up a new world for me," Ben says. "I realized that before becoming familiar with the talking computer I was lost in darkness."

After retiring from the military, Ben had worked as a news director for WAHR Radio 99, an FM stereo adult contemporary music station in Huntsville. Then, in 1987, he discovered he had glaucoma, and his world crashed around him. "You see, I'm a journalist by profession," Ben recalls, "and blindness really puts a crimp on your ability to write, edit, and—in my case—be a newscaster."

At the insistence of his family and friends, Ben became active in community volunteer work to keep busy. He has edited a magazine, planned banquets, and still does public relations work for a nonprofit organization.

Ben

Ben has become very proficient at using the computer. He was able to borrow a computer from TASC to use at home and more thoroughly study Vocal Eyes and the tutorial for the computer's operating system. "I've changed my mind," Ben mutters. "The technology is fantastic. It has allowed me to do the things that I did before losing my sight."

With assistance from the Department of Rehabilitation Services, Ben was able to purchase a computer; scanner; Braille and Speak, a portable notetaker (Blazie Engineering); and a printer to use at home in preparation for his new job as a talk show host with WEUP, another Huntsville radio station. Ben uses his equipment to print and send preshow letters to the individuals who will be appearing on his show. They respond with printed information that Ben then scans into his computer and reads with the assistance of his screen reader, Vocal Eyes. He uses his Braille and Speak to make notes to use during the actual interview on air.

To keep up with changing technology, Ben is currently training with staff at the Technology Center operated by the Alabama Institute for the Deaf and Blind in Huntsville. He is learning both the Windows 98 operating system and JAWS for Windows, a screen reading program (Henter-Joyce), to use with a new computer he will be purchasing. He also intends to get online with his new computer to "communicate effectively with my prospective guests, because email and the Internet are the wave of the future, and will probably replace the telephone soon."

John

I was born with cerebral palsy in 1971, and my first public school program was a development center for children with severe disabilities. I couldn't control my movements and couldn't talk like other kids. Teachers said to my parents, "He's not learning." The school psychologist tested me and said that I had mental retardation.

Lucky for me, my parents didn't believe it. They believed that I needed friends and support to be able to do things that my body wouldn't allow me to do. My stepfather began making gadgets and switches, and my mother began to advocate for me to be included in everything with kids my age: in school, in play group, at playgrounds, at church. I left public school and went to a community play group and then to a private alternative school where I was the only kid with a disability and was included in everything.

However, I was still having trouble learning, and after two years the teachers suggested that I return to public school where there were special education teachers to help me. But my IQ test followed me, and people saw my wheelchair and my inability to talk before they saw me. I was again in a class for students with severe disabilities.

16

Computer
and Web
Resources
for People
with
Disabilities

John

Then in 1978, when I was seven years old, I got my first computer. This was the beginning of real life for me. There were no adaptive devices at that time, so my family's first invention was plastic wrap over the keyboard so I wouldn't drool on it, and a pencil taped in my hand to touch the keys. We saw the computer as a learning and communication tool. We have been working at making it perform for me ever since.

With the help of my computer, my family, and my friends, I finished high school and was exhausted. After a year's rest, I went on to junior college, and after three years there I was accepted at California Institute of the Arts. There I did animation and experimental videos using my nose, a micro switch on my lip, and a HeadMouse [see Part II for pointing devices]. I graduated in 1998 with a Bachelor of Fine Arts in film and video. I am presently doing 3-D animation and hoping to get my first job and film credits.

John makes presentations regularly to large audiences in the hope that, by sharing some of his story, he will have demonstrated "how technology, great expectations, and a support network have helped one person to get around some of the stereotypes and prejudice that block off connections with real life for children who are growing up with disabilities."

Dusty

In 1981, when Dusty was just six years old, she visited her friend John (who told his story above) and was amazed at all he was doing with his Apple II+ (an early Apple computer). Dusty saw immediately what power John had. Control was an issue for Dusty, as she had Down syndrome and very little control over things in her life at that time. With John's computer, she could push a button and make things happen. Her parents had to drag her home from that first technology encounter.

Dusty was in a regular kindergarten at the time. Her parents were told that she did not attend well and wouldn't stay on task. Her mother knew the trick would be to find a task that would engage Dusty.

Through her research, Dusty's mother learned that children with Down syndrome tend to be good visual learners. This clinched it for her. At Christmas her parents bought Dusty an Apple II+ and some intriguing early learning software programs which explored the alphabet and numbers. Dusty learned the keyboard quickly and began practicing counting without even being invited.

Dusty's mother had had no prior experience with computers and wasn't mechanically inclined. She and Dusty learned together. As a way to get her

Dusty

18

———

Computer
and Web
Resources
for People
with
Disabilities

daughter access to a computer at school, she volunteered to help the teacher and work with the other students. As the children used the software, it became clear to the teacher that Dusty could be included in activities using the computer, just like everyone else.

Dusty attended her local high school and took many classes with her nondisabled peers, including a computer class. A word processing program with large print, speech output, and word prediction gave her the support she needed for writing. Using these tools she wrote children's books in her English class, which she then read to the babies in the daycare center where she worked one period a day.

Dusty is now 24. She has completed four years at her local community college, earning 60 units. She enjoyed classes in keyboarding, using a computer for personal and business purposes, and using the Internet. Screen magnification software was provided by the college's Disabled Students Program. She enjoys volunteer work and is about to start her first paying part-time job.

Visiting her favorite places on the Internet is an enjoyable pastime for Dusty. She and her mom have built a Web page with picture icons representing links to her favorite spots. Her own Web page serves as a support for her.

Independent living (with support) is one of Dusty's goals. Currently she is focusing on cooking. Each week, she and her mom or helper add a new recipe to the electronic cookbook she is building. Luckily, her standard database software, FileMaker Pro (FileMaker Inc.), includes a large-print option, so the support she needs is built-in.

As her mother says, "Technology gave Dusty confidence in her ability as a learner. She began to feel good about herself. Her self-esteem improved.

"Technology is highly motivating and it can bring out the best in a person. As a parent, I think it can help you find out how your child learns best, because it gives you so many exciting avenues to explore. It's a feel-good thing, plus it's a focus for the whole world these days."

Chase

Chase uses computer technology and the Internet every day, not only for his job, but to pursue many other personal needs and interests. Watching him work in his government office today, it's hard to believe he was ever resistant to using technology and other electronic tools. "I have to strive for simplicity, dependability, and flexibility in all my tools," he says, as someone who must rely every day on mechanical and electronic devices like van lifts, power wheelchairs, eating utensils, door openers, and speakerphones. "When I was younger, electronic devices would break easily and repairs could take up to six or eight weeks," he recalls. "The more complex electronic devices became, the less I wanted to depend on them."

Chase has been a very determined and inventive person ever since he was eight years old and became quadriplegic from polio. Despite his initial hesitancy, when one considers the expectations and personal goals he had set for himself, it was inevitable that he would become a passionate and competent technology user. After graduating from college, he went to law school. "Back then, I could only write using my mouth stick and a typewriter. I would have to place a chess piece on the shift key to hold it down, while I pressed on another key with my mouth stick. I was a terrible speller, too. Later, I had to start finding people to take dictation, type papers for me, take me to the law library for many late evenings, and read very dry and boring law books to me. Now I can do all that by myself with a laptop computer!"

It was not until Chase was in the midst of a four-month stay in intensive care, recovering from spinal surgery, connected to a respirator, with tubes running in and out his mouth, able only to do "the winking and blinking thing," that he discovered computer technology with the help of his friends and family. The Macintosh computer he used at that time had several built-in accessibility features that were incredibly important to him: 1) Sticky Keys (Apple Computer), which allowed him to perform tasks in which two or three keys had to be pressed simultaneously; 2) Mouse Keys (Apple Computer), which allowed him to move a pointer to different places on the screen by pressing just one key at a time; and 3) a spell checker. "Good grief," he remembers thinking, "I can do anything I want to!" Soon afterward, he discovered that there was an ATA Center in his city, and he connected with them right away.

Chase

20

Computer
and Web
Resources
for People
with
Disabilities

Today, Chase is the executive director of a federal program in his state. He uses both PC and Macintosh computers, in both their desktop and portable laptop models. Using only his mouth stick, he operates his four different types of computers with only two basic kinds of modifications: 1) the current equivalent of the Sticky Keys utility he first discovered many years ago in ICU (see Part II for Keyboard Access Utilities); and 2) the appropriate kind of trackball for each computer (see Part II for trackballs and other alternatives to the mouse). Recently he acquired a speech input program, Dragon Dictate (Dragon Systems), which he is now setting up to provide him with the ability to dictate to the computer and bypass the keyboard altogether.

Via the Internet, Chase uses email to communicate with project staff and contractors in other locations within the state, with state directors in other states, with federal program officers across the country, and with a wide variety of colleagues, advocates, and friends around the world. He also uses the Internet extensively to research legal, medical, and policy issues and to share the information throughout his organization. On a personal level, he can use the same technology to explore and express his creative talents in graphic arts, music, and writing, as well as to independently manage many of his household affairs such as budgeting, banking, and bill paying. "This technology opens the whole world to me. I can go anywhere and do anything I am interested in."

Tammy

Tammy was mainstreamed into the neighborhood school where she was the only student with a physical disability. But, by the time she was seven years old, school was becoming harder and harder because she could not see to read the board, books, or even her own handwriting.

As computers grew more commonplace, it became obvious that if Tammy could use one in school, it would make a tremendous difference in her ability to participate and learn. Her father brought a computer home and started using it with Tammy. Like most children, Tammy wasn't fearful of or intimidated by the computer.

After elementary school, Tammy enrolled in the state school for the blind—where there also were no computers. Her parents knew that Tammy could benefit from them, but convincing the school to start using them took quite a while. Using a computer for administrative purposes was one thing; making them available to students, it seemed, was a fairly radical notion.

Even when computers were finally introduced, they were mostly kept in a separate room that students could only access once or twice a week and rarely in the evenings. The school had not anticipated that the students might want to use the computers to do their homework. Compounding this

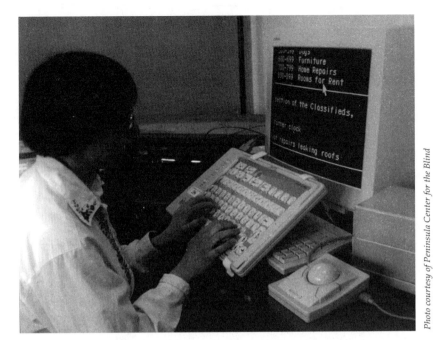

Tammy

Photo courtesy of Peninsula Center for the Blind

lack of access was the fact that none of the teachers or evening staff knew how to use the equipment themselves.

In spite of the fact that the school had no expectations of Tammy's being able to pass the exams for her high school diploma, she gained her diploma by taking all the required functional tests on a computer.

Early on, Tammy's mother had low expectations for technology because it was difficult to think very far ahead. She knew that computers could assist her daughter in school, but it wasn't until Tammy was out of school that her mother realized the impact technology could have on Tammy's career options. "I have high expectations of computers in terms of her career. In the right environment, technology can really work for my daughter."

Tammy, now in her twenties, works as a telephone receptionist at the Museum of Industry. She uses a computer with speech output (JAWS). When she needs to record a written message, she types it into her computer where she can then email it to a recipient or print it out. Without the computer, she would not be doing this job, which is a source of much enjoyment, pride, and income (!) for her.

Tony

Tony is an athlete, but he is no longer able to compete professionally in his sport because of progressive vision loss. Just when the world told him his

Computer
and Web
Resources
for People
with
Disabilities

Tony

options were narrowing, he told himself that in order to have more options he was going to have to create them for himself.

Tony was in his forties when he went to his rehabilitation counselor with the idea that a computer might be worth exploring. His counselor agreed to enroll him in a local community college where he could take a computer class. Tony started with only an understanding that technology would give him new skills. "Once I was introduced to voice output [the ability of a computer to read text aloud with a synthetic voice], I knew that with a computer I could be employable. I had no real idea of what job I might do, because I didn't know what was out there that I would be capable of doing with technology. I just knew it was the key for me."

Tony's first surprise was that he not only had to learn how to operate his IBM computer, but also how to use a screen reader, a software program that tells the user what is on the screen and vocalizes every keystroke the user makes. "Use of a computer requires a nonvisual individual to use his or her memory a lot more in the beginning, during the learning process. I have to know what is going to be produced on the screen when I call for it, as well as know how to call for it. It required some real retraining for me, because I hadn't exercised my brain that way in a long time. I wasn't really intimidated; I always thought it was exciting, something to have fun with as much as something to use to get work accomplished."

With a computer using a speech synthesizer and a screen reading program, Tony is able to attend writing classes and build his communication skills, critical preparation for reentering the work world as an equal. "Technology has given me higher goals and hope for greater achievements. It has allowed me to find my creativity and express it through writing—a whole new form of communication for me. Communication is going to be the key for me in any job, and technology is my most critical tool."

Tom

Over 25 years ago, Tom was exploring the possibility of getting a grant to figure out how to employ home-based people with disabilities using technologies then emerging at the beginning of the Information Revolution. His fellow rehabilitation professionals were discouraging, but Tom is not one to tolerate negativism, and he was on a mission to assist a man who had sustained a major spinal cord injury in finding a new occupation. Tom wrote the grant and got it federally funded. As a result of Tom's effort, the man became a computer programmer with a terminal installed in his home (personal computers were not yet on the scene).

Tom and his son

24

Computer
and Web
Resources
for People
with
Disabilities

Tom's project ran successfully for six years. It employed occupational therapists and rehabilitation engineering students in helping to match home-based people with disabilities for the first time with information handling occupations such as computer programming, data entry, and microfilm equipment operations.

Tom's own use of technology did not come until later, when he purchased a TRS-80 (an early Radio Shack computer) to be able to play with his children. The computer gave Tom a growing feeling of empowerment, as it allowed him to play with his children on equal terms and to be less dependent on them to perform physical tasks for him. It changed what it meant for him to have a disability. And it compelled him to look for other people with disabilities in his city who were using technology.

Tom found three other people, and together they founded a self-advocacy organization focused on increasing access to technology by people with disabilities. This small group felt strongly that if people with disabilities let technology pass them by, they were going to lose out in a very big way. Before long, they had six hundred members in their group using technology in new and innovative ways.

Tom, now almost 70, has a well-equipped office in his home, as well as a Macintosh laptop computer in the backpack of his motorized wheelchair, which allows him to carry on his activities as an advocate for people with disabilities regarding their right and need to access personal computer technologies.

He reflects on the many roles and "hats" he has taken on just before and during the upheavals of the Information Age and how his use of the quickly changing tools of this industry affected the many roles he fulfills.

As a husband, father, student, volunteer, community activist, and church member, I remember many occasions when the availability of personal computer technologies kept me in the ball game—helping the kids with homework, maintaining personal and family finances, researching and producing social issue documents for public debate, and fully joining in Bible study groups.

In job performance, my best nonhuman ally was—and still is—the personal computer, which I now use with voice input, an on-screen keyboard, and a mini trackball controlled only by my weak right thumb. I have found much fulfillment when I joined these tools to my personality, aptitudes, and interests and met the test...getting the job done in the work world as a counselor, an R and D project director, a teacher and lecturer, and an education administrator. My computer hard drive, along with scores of shelved diskettes, holds files and records of telephone calls and faxes made and received by the hundreds, graphics, letters, agendas, lists, and reports. Because I use the personal computer and the assistive technologies that make the computers accessible to me, I am empowered and enabled to do many jobs!

My use of the Internet over the years is constantly spiraling upward and leads me not just to the world's libraries, but to the world itself. I am not a chat room person who converses regularly with strangers via computer, modem, and telephone lines, but I eagerly use these tools to communicate daily with distant family, fellow board members, and colleagues with similar interests.

Liberation comes in surprising ways. I used to wait for someone to take dictation, fold and insert mail into envelopes, address, stamp, and then carry my mail to the post office. And when mail arrived at my office—forget it! One more helper needed to open it and lay it on the desk, where soon another document or book or whatever else was set on it, to create, alas, another communication not read or readily taken care of by me. It is liberating for me today to create, forward, receive and respond to correspondence independently and in a timely manner.

I am not a technocrat, but an ideologist. I am aware of the unemployment, pollution, depersonalization, and other evils associated with technology. But information tools combined with my personality and social factors are defining me, positively and satisfactorily. Social and personal fulfillment through wonderful experiences and sustaining high-esteem—these are my rewards.

Tom ends his thoughts with a personal confession.

I feel an agony knowing the wondrous impact of ATA Centers, and knowing people firsthand with disabilities gaining advantages from the use of these technologies. I know their liberation. But the pain is to know also that millions of persons with disabilities won't have access soon enough to the amazing freedoms these technologies bring—for empowerment, for personal and social growth, and for advancement. Sometimes, memories of the coal miner's tears and the good that grew from them buoys me up. And so does the work of my ATA colleagues and others respectfully bringing access to my sisters and brothers with disabilities. At least, it isn't as hard as it used to be. There is so much more to be done, and wondrous results are guaranteed. This eases the pain that only a person with a disability can feel.

Jumping In

If you spend enough time around seasoned users of assistive technologies, you will pick up on an important perspective about incorporating technology into your life—it's a process. It is a journey with a definite starting point for every individual, but it's also a journey with a destination that can be vague at times. You may know which direction to head. It could be a short

26

Computer
and Web
Resources
for People
with
Disabilities

trip or a long one. You have some expectations. All that you may be really certain of at this point is that you are ready for a change. And, though you may not be sure exactly where you will end up, you realize that you, yourself, will be the greatest determinant of what happens to you.

No one goes into the search for technology access knowing exactly what to expect or fully understanding the power or potential of technology. Everyone just jumps in. And that's what we are inviting you to do.

Chapter 3

Setting Your Goals

The Power of Expectations

From day one, you may hear about realistic expectations. It may come first from the medical community telling you that because of an identified medical condition, you must lower your expectations to avoid disappointment. At a kindergarten screening, you may be told that your child does not conform to the norms for her age and that you should reduce your expectations for her academic success or even her participation in mainstream education. At a parent-teacher conference, a teacher may suggest that you be more realistic, that you accept your child's placement in a classroom designed for children who are autistic, along with the teacher's notion of the appropriate expectations for autistic children. After a spinal cord or traumatic brain injury, you may be told that you will need to accept that there are things you will just not be able to do any longer. Or, as you grow older, you may be told that you can no longer participate socially or live independently at home.

We have all been told to be realistic in our expectations of ourselves (or others) based on someone else's best guess as to our ability and potential. Every expert has education and experience on which to base an opinion, yet none necessarily knows you or your child well. An expert may know about a physical or cognitive condition, but know little of who you really are: your personality, ambitions, goals, and drive. Experts are aware of some barriers to goal attainment and may recommend that you modify your goals. If you accept their recommendations for lowering your expectations, those diminished expectations may prove correct.

Henry Ford once said, "Whether you think you can or think you can't— you are right!" Most of us perform to the expectation level we and others set. If you are told that your reading level will never exceed fourth grade and you are placed in a classroom where the expectations for students are just that, your reading level will likely be fourth grade. Your achievement often has more to do with the expectations and environment than with your real potential. We have seen far too many examples of the negative consequences of lowered expectations.

Jennifer came to our Resource Center in rural upstate New York at the

28

Computer
and Web
Resources
for People
with
Disabilities

Photo courtesy of Don Johnston, Inc.

*Discover:Switch allows this child to do anything you
could do with a standard keyboard and mouse.
(Don Johnston, Inc.)*

age of 18. She was minimally verbal and had been placed in a local
developmental center at age two at the recommendation of the family
physician. Jennifer's family was now exploring community living
options because the developmental center was closing. Jennifer was
learning the skills of daily living but had few opportunities for learning
academic materials. She had written very little because of her poor fine-
motor skills. In the course of her visit, she played with a talking word
processor on a computer with a speech synthesizer (see Part II for more
about talking word processors and speech synthesizers). She was ecstatic at being able to make the computer speak and within a few minutes
had demonstrated the ability to make it communicate whatever she
wished. Eventually, Jennifer was moved to a foster home and attended
special education classes, and in three years she was reading at an
eighth-grade level.

Most of us aspire to similar goals: to reach our maximum potential, to
participate in many aspects of community life, and to pursue gainful
employment. Each of us puts different twists on these expectations and generally is free to do so. There are constraints—finances, academic achievement, prior experience—but our society affirms the right of most citizens to
aspire to whatever they choose. It is that freedom that lets us think big and
achieve big. It is also that freedom that enables us to decide to start all over
again, to adopt new goals, to set new expectations, and to follow some paths
many times over. The same freedom must apply to people with disabilities.

"Unrealistic" expectations may carry the dangers of disappointment, failure, or lack of fulfillment, but they enable us to apply all of our abilities in reaching our maximum potential. It is in our best interest to encourage them.

Conventional and assistive technologies empower children and adults who have disabilities with new abilities to communicate without speech or sight, to manipulate the environment with little or no physical dexterity, and to demonstrate cognitive abilities in nontraditional ways. The future holds even more promise and excitement for expanding the potential of all individuals. The following sections will help you examine the specific areas around which your expectations are soaring and help you define in greater detail those goals that can be supported by access to technology.

Having a Vision

To have and nurture a vision, we must see beyond externally imposed constraints and give ourselves permission to think freely. This is the key to developing goals to which we want to apply our abilities and to setting our sights high enough so that we are unwilling to settle for expectations based on a limited understanding of our abilities and the available tools.

For a person with a disability, the most difficult part of this process is often feeling free and able to envision a preferred future. How do we give ourselves or others this freedom amidst all the voices of realism? Person-centered planning is one of the processes by which we receive permission to do what everyone else is allowed to do: to develop grand expectations, then employ all possible abilities and tools in their pursuit. In person-centered planning, an individual brings together a group of people to help in imagining a preferred future and thinking through the supports needed to realize that future. This process, like the one described in this book, places the individual with a disability at the center, hence the term *person-centered.*

Setting Goals

Whether or not you are a planner or a goal-oriented person, establishing some specific personal goals and a plan for yourself with technology will be helpful for making the technology discovery process manageable. There is much to consider, and having a plan will help insure that nothing important is forgotten, such as budgeting for training.

Goals provide the foundation upon which you will establish your personal technology plan, which will be examined in subsequent chapters. A technology plan should include the following elements:

1. Goals

2. Resources

30

Computer
and Web
Resources
for People
with
Disabilities

— Knowledge of pertinent legislation
— Community resources

3. Supporters and advisors

4. Budget

5. Technology tools and vendors

6. Sources of funding

7. Implementation and training

8. Ongoing self-evaluation

Many people begin with very broad goals like "I want a better job" or "I'd like my son to do better in school" or "I want to be more productive." These are fine goals, but technology can only play a supporting role in reaching such broad goals. For example, using a computer for writing is one way technology might help a child to do better in school. Good attendance, a healthful environment, and appropriate related services—such as physical therapy—are also essential. Making good personal choices about assistive technology requires asking the right questions and specifying the tasks and activities in which technology can play a part in helping you attain your broader goals.

Getting specific

The reasons for using technology are as varied as the equipment options themselves. Many adults purchase computers for such tasks as writing letters or email messages, keeping up with personal finances, and developing a database of addresses and phone numbers. Parents often purchase computers to help their children in school. For example, access to the Internet brings a vast library into the home, where interests can be freely explored; word processors can assist with writing, doing a research project, or designing a school newsletter; software can improve skills in reading, math, or spelling. Computers can also provide entertainment and recreational opportunities such as sports simulations and outlets for creativity through music and art programs. Computers can help people develop social skills by connecting them with others via the Internet, where they can correspond with people around the world.

Some people buy technology because it exists. Some believe it will make life easier. Some recognize its potential. Some people just don't want to be left behind—they want to know what dot com means. Some realize it is the only way certain tasks can be done. For example, a person with a physical disability can use environmental controls to turn on lights, radios, and other electrical devices; a person with a learning disability can use a computer rather than a pencil and eraser as a writing tool. Computers sometimes provide the only means a person with a disability has for reading, writing, or speaking.

Increasingly, computers will be the way people learn, work, vote, shop, receive, and send information. Among hundreds of other uses, you can already use the Internet to electronically file your taxes; book and purchase airline tickets; apply for college loans and scholarships; check bank balances and pay bills; trade on the stock market; attend college classes without leaving home; and post your family photo album and vacation pictures on your own website for friends and family to enjoy.

You should develop goals that will guide the decisions you have to make, whether you plan to use technology for pleasure, school, work, recreation, communication, learning, or activities of daily living. Important questions to answer in developing goals for the use of technology include the following:

1. Who will be the primary user, and who else will be using it?

2. What do you want to do? What do they want to do?

3. What do you need to do? What do they need to do?

4. What are the personal issues of each user, such as hearing and vision levels, cognitive ability, physical ability, and mobility?

Multiple users often pose interesting challenges.

Sarah, a young woman with autism, used a Macintosh PowerBook (a portable laptop computer) as her communication device. However, other family members wanted to use the PowerBook when Sarah was not using it. Sarah protested vehemently: This equipment was her voice and should be available for her at all times; use by others was an invasion of her privacy.

Multiple users can also be an issue in schools. When a student needs access to a computer for writing or other schoolwork, the computer might become a dedicated machine for that student, off-limits to other students. If the family has purchased the equipment, it has some control over who uses it and when; if the school or others purchased it, the school would probably have more control over its use.

Identifying Your Goals

Among your expectations for technology, you can probably categorize your goals into five areas:

32

———

Computer
and Web
Resources
for People
with
Disabilities

1. Education

2. Employment

3. Communication

4. Living more self-sufficiently

5. Recreation

An individual may have technology-related interests in all five areas. In which area or areas do your interests lie? In a specific area of interest to you, what are your immediate goals? Near-future goals? Long-term goals? The following sections discuss each area and give examples of immediate, intermediate, and long-term goals.

Education

Technology can help you achieve success from preschool to graduate school.

What are your education goals?

- Full inclusion for your child in your neighborhood elementary school?

- Attending a university and majoring in math?

- Vocational training to help you reenter the workforce?

Can you imagine ways in which technology might help you to accomplish those goals?

- Using a computer, could your child complete homework assignments?

- With a low-vision aid, could your child read the same textbook the rest of the class is using?

- Could the computer serve as your pen and paper if you cannot use your hands?

- By using the Internet, could you finally gain access to the research resources of the library which has always been architecturally inaccessible to you?

- Could you use software to simulate your frog dissection?

- Could you read instrumentation if it were magnified or produced audible feedback?

- Could you complete your college education using your computer and the Internet to participate in online courses?

James was a six-year-old with cerebral palsy, and the ultimate goal for him was inclusion. An early step toward this was a simple game—Red Light/Green Light—that involved his entire classroom. Using Ke:nx (Don Johnston, Inc.), a special interface device, we set the computer to alternate between a large square on half of the screen, labeled Red Light, and a square on the other half, labeled Green Light (for more information on Interface Devices and Switches, see Part II). These squares lit up one after the other. When James made his selection by pressing his switch, the computer would say either Red Light or Green Light. The class, assembled in a circle, responded to James's commands by walking or stopping. (In the traditional Red Light/Green Light game, students line up and try to reach the finish line first. The computer version was designed to be noncompetitive so students of all abilities could enjoy it.) The simple game soon had everyone laughing, and James was ecstatic. The computer had empowered him as a leader. Red Light/Green Light was particularly successful for James because it was something he really enjoyed doing, it made technology part of the curriculum rather than a separate activity, and there were no wrong answers since the class responded to whatever choice James made.

Education is a lifelong series of learning opportunities, including postsecondary education, continuing education, informal education, self-improvement, and professional development. The common theme in educational endeavors is that an individual acquires and demonstrates new learning. Technology can be used for instruction; for written, artistic, and verbal expression; for reading, calculating, and simulating inaccessible or dangerous activities; for gaining basic reasoning and higher-level thinking skills; and for making the transition from school or from the ranks of the unemployed to the workplace.

Technology can play an important part in your education goals. In a post-secondary program, using assistive technology to earn a degree in architecture might be a long-term goal. A short-term goal might be having an instructor make reasonable accommodations to computer-aided design (CAD) courses, permitting a person with a disability to have access to the technology and materials used by the rest of the class.

Employment

Technology is redefining the workplace for everyone. The possibilities today are limitless.

What are your employment goals?

34

Computer
and Web
Resources
for People
with
Disabilities

- To reopen your accounting firm after sustaining a spinal cord injury?

- To attain an entry-level position in a local bank?

- To get a job as a research assistant to a fund-raiser for a local nonprofit organization?

- To start a home-based business on the Internet?

- To return to work after being on leave with a repetitive stress disorder (such as carpal tunnel syndrome)?

Can you imagine ways in which technology might help you to accomplish those goals?

- Could a computerized address book and automatic dialer help you place calls?

- Would the capacity to send and receive faxes from your computer reduce your physical exertion in a helpful way?

- Could a handheld, closed-circuit television system that enlarges print enable you to read instruments?

- Would a portable computer with wireless access to the Internet allow you to work away from your office desk?

- Would a computer that "talks" provide you with access to customer account records?

Photo courtesy of IntelliTools

The world is becoming more accessible since products like IntelliKeys, originally designed for people with disabilities, are increasingly used by others as well. (IntelliTools)

- Would access to the publications and resources available on the Internet help in doing research?

Perhaps you tend to think of employment in terms of a career, such as investment broker, lawyer, small business owner, printer, public servant, broadcast announcer, accountant, journalist, engineer, poet, or teacher. Even from such a career perspective, there are specific job-related functions to be performed and that can be identified.

With the advent of the Americans with Disabilities Act, jobs are frequently described in terms of the functions required of the employee. This functional perspective is particularly well suited to identifying specific tasks in which conventional and assistive technologies can play an important role. For example, a particular job might require placing and answering telephone calls, accessing a computer database, visually inspecting an assembly line product, or manipulating a set of controls at a power plant. Setting goals for employment involves selecting the job and identifying the essential functions required to perform it. Once the functions have been specified, technology can be identified to help support them.

Shenita is a social worker who needs to type many reports. She is a one-handed typist because of her cerebral palsy. The trouble is she now has developed carpal tunnel syndrome. Surgery had been ruled out for her so she needed to find another solution. She tried an alternate keyboard and IntelliKeys (IntelliTools) (see Alternate Keyboards in Part II for more information). The angle and the sensitivity of the keyboard now allows her to type without pain. She has also added a word prediction program that allows her to type using fewer keystrokes (see Word Prediction Programs in Part II). These accommodations are making it possible for her to go about her business.

The strategy for achieving an employment goal consists of developing a list of essential job functions and developing access to those functions using technology where appropriate.

Nick is an engineer, recently retired from the Army Corps of Engineers. His job involved monitoring flooding and protecting homes, commerce, and traffic along the river. While attending a training seminar, he contracted Legionnaire's disease. He developed multiple sclerosis and became legally blind within a year. Keeping the job he loved and remaining productive required him to find some new ways of doing business.

Working with his state department for the blind and later with his local Alliance for Technology Access Center, Nick gained screen access

36

Computer
and Web
Resources
for People
with
Disabilities

to the IBM computers and software used at his previous position. He needed access to the Lotus 1-2-3 spreadsheet program to monitor readings and to perform calculations and to a word processor to report findings. With access to technology, Nick was able to remain a fine engineer and to reach retirement with the Corps after nine more years, and he has established an engineering consulting business in his home.

Communication

Everybody has something to say. Technology offers new ways to communicate when the old ways are not effective.

What are your communication goals?

- To establish a more effective written communication system?

- To communicate with your health practitioner and others about your needs?

- To express your thoughts in class about a current event of importance to you?

- To expand your oral communication in a work environment?

- To improve your social interactions with friends?

Can you imagine ways in which technology might help you to accomplish those goals?

- Using a spell checker and a word prediction program to speed up the process of typing, could you write more effectively?

- If important phrases are programmed into a portable communication device to "speak" at work, would communication with colleagues be enhanced?

- With specialized presentation software and a voice synthesizer, could you make training presentations?

- Could you share information with sighted colleagues using a printer that prints both letters and braille dots on the same page?

- Using the Internet, could you find people with similar interests around the world with whom you could communicate?

The ability to communicate is a worthy goal for assistive technology, which opens channels of communication through print, symbols, and synthetic speech. For example, devices are now available to allow individuals with severe hearing impairments to converse over the telephone (see the section on TTYs in Part II).

Technology can also provide a synthetic voice for individuals who are unable to articulate their thoughts verbally. This application is often referred to as employing augmentative or alternative communication (AAC) aids, which range widely in complexity and price. An augmentative aid supports existing voice capabilities while an alternative aid replaces them (see Augmentative and Alternative Communication Products in Part II for more information on these devices). If access to these aids is part of your technology goals, we recommend finding a qualified speech therapist with experience in this technology to assist you in selecting the right solution for you. Together, you will consider many important factors, such as hearing characteristics, cognitive abilities required to use the device, and the ability to connect the device to a computer.

People who have lost their ability to communicate in either print or speech due to degenerative physical conditions or diseases can benefit from alternative forms of communication.

Sidney has multiple sclerosis and no longer has the ability to control any movement from his neck down. He lives in a nursing home around the corner from the church where he is a visiting minister. The church wanted to take up a collection to help Sidney realize more independence and gave him a choice between a motorized wheelchair and a computer. Sidney chose the computer.

Writing to friends around the country and even in town was not possible until he received his computer. Now he "surfs the net," plays everything from Wheel of Fortune to bridge, and feels that the computer has saved his sanity. Turning the pages of books was not possible for Sidney. The CD-ROM collection that he has now accumulated includes the Bible, an encyclopedia, and a wide range of books on great works of art and even how to learn Spanish. Before getting his computer, Sidney used to wait for someone to bring him the phone and hold it for him while he spoke. Now he easily communicates online. No more answering machines, busy signals, or waiting for assistance. Sidney is able to carry on private communications when and how he wishes.

Sidney uses a HeadMaster system (Prentke Romich Company) and an on-screen keyboard developed with Ke:nx. He uses a puff switch to replace the mouse click. The keyboard was custom designed by Sidney. If he needs a new key, he adds it. The camera key in the middle of the keyboard was added so he can take snapshots of the screen and import the graphics into his letters to his grandchildren. He uses a Macintosh Power PC with a built-in CD-ROM. The monitor is on a hospital table and is wheeled in front of him on the bed. The main unit of the computer (CPU or central processing unit) stays on the dresser next to the bed.

Living in a nursing home generally means access to a very limited

38

Computer
and Web
Resources
for People
with
Disabilities

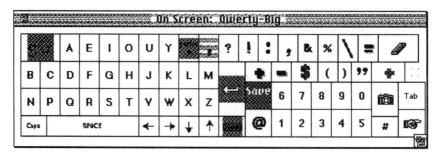

Customized keyboard layout

amount of space. Technology has afforded Sidney a level of independence that he had thought he would never retrieve.

Ben, a seven-year-old with autism, was trying to use a regular keyboard
with the assistance of his teacher. He was not having success. He was
bouncing around a lot, missing the keys, and making too many mistakes
for his meaning to be communicated. The standard keyboard was
replaced by the IntelliKeys keyboard (IntelliTools). An overlay was used
on the keyboard that had large letters, providing targets big enough for
Ben to strike. His pointing suddenly became much more accurate and
his communication was clearly understandable.

Julia is 14 years old and very suddenly lost her hearing because of a drug
she was taking to treat her cystic fibrosis. This quick and dramatic
change in her life was difficult for her, so her mother started investigating technology and went to her local Alliance for Technology Access
Center to see what they had. She borrowed a text telephone (TTY) and a
closed-caption decoder so that her daughter was again able to talk on
the phone and watch TV. Julia is now excited about investigating other
possibilities so she can carry on private conversations with her boy-
friend without having to use the phone company's relay service.

Finding technology solutions is an ongoing process as your goals and
needs change.

Living more self-sufficiently

Many goals consist of performing tasks that facilitate more independence,
such as reading mail with an optical device that converts text to large print
or synthetic speech. An environmental control system can manage a home
security system, control thermostats and lighting in the home, operate an
intercom system and front door lock, place and receive telephone calls, send
out an alert for help, and run a home entertainment system. Other goals for

daily computer use might include the ability to keep a database of favorite recipes, monitor some aspect of a health indicator, use an alarm clock, or shop and bank from home. To apply assistive technology to living more self-sufficiently, create a list of the specific, essential functions you require, and identify those that may be made accessible with the proper tools. (For more information on environmental control units see Part II.)

Technology does extraordinary things. It can also do very ordinary things like open the door, turn on the lights, and dial the phone.

What are your living goals?

- Do you want to be able to live alone?

- Do you want to move into a shared living arrangement?

- Do you want to be able to function more independently within your family?

Can you imagine ways in which technology might help you to accomplish those goals?

- Would an environmental control system that is operated by a single switch and controls kitchen appliances, the lights, the television, and the automatic door opener enable you to live more independently?

- Do you need an emergency alert system?

- Would a closed-circuit television help you to read and write messages and pay your bills?

- Would using a computer to do your shopping over the Internet increase your independence?

- Could you use the Internet to keep current with all the latest improvements in assistive technology that could enhance the quality of your life?

Jim sustained a spinal cord injury over 16 years ago and, using his computer, writes, "Because of the high level of my injury, I am unable to use my hands and arms in a functional manner. A few years ago I learned of a person who could help me in getting a voice operated system to control my environment. What he did was to customize my computer system using a Dragon Systems voice input card and X10 Powerhouse environmental control module that allows me to turn lights on and off, answer and originate phone calls, control a television set, open and close my garage door, and unlock my back door, all by voice commands. A microphone is mounted on my wheelchair, as well as a speaker through which I get voice feedback from the system. In this way, I can

40

Computer
and Web
Resources
for People
with
Disabilities

Photo courtesy of Prentke Romich Company

*Vanessa accesses the computer as well as online services with a
Delta Talker augmentative communication device from Prentke Romich.
(Prentke Romich Company)*

be anywhere in my home and still can use the voice input system to control my environment. There is also a microphone and speaker mounted by my bed, so that I can respond to any emergency during the night. This particular aspect has given me a much greater peace of mind than I have ever had since my injury. I greatly enjoy the independence I have gained from this environmental control system." (See Environmental Control Units in Part II.)

Recreation

Computer technology holds great promise for hobbies, entertainment, and other forms of recreation. Hundreds of popular games, such as poker, chess, television game shows, and board games, have been adapted for computers, providing access to games that may otherwise be inaccessible. Many commercial Internet services and websites allow users to enter into games with people in other locations or to follow sporting news around the world. Using a computer for an environmental control can also provide access to common electronic entertainment devices and appliances like the television, videotape recorder, and CD player.

Virtually every hobby interest can be explored and enhanced because of the millions of individuals and businesses now using the Internet. For example, would you like to find specialized tools for gardening and meet other gardeners who use wheelchairs? Would you like to know where the accessible fishing sites, bass boats, and nature trails are in Kentucky or North Carolina? Would you like to explore archives of photographs and the memories of specific individuals in order to put together a multimedia presentation for an upcoming special event? Are you a Star Trek fan? Do you enjoy comic books? Would you like to go shopping for magic tricks or the equipment you might need to try your hand at making your own home-brewed beer? All these hobbies and countless more have their enthusiasts and suppliers to be discovered and explored on the Internet.

Determining recreation goals consists of identifying the activity or functions in which one wishes to participate and then selecting the devices, software, or technology services required to support the goal. For example, a young adult may wish to learn to play chess with a live opponent. Once the software for the game is identified, the next task would be to identify any additional devices needed to allow each player access to the software program.

Just because you might not be able to get down on the floor with your kids doesn't mean you cannot play with them. Technology can help make the games accessible to everyone.

What are your recreation goals?

- Do you want to play music with some friends on weekends or holidays?

- Do you want to be able to play games with your children?

- Does your child want to be able to play with the children next door?

- Would you like to collect and repair dolls or build and operate a model train layout?

Can you imagine ways in which technology might help you to accomplish those goals? Can you think of ways the Internet might assist you in your search for tools and resources?

- Would your neighbor be interested in learning to play computerized chess or cards with you?

- Could access to your child's adapted computer enable you to play a favorite video game together?

- Would a talking computer be fun for kids, whether or not they needed the speech device?

- Would you like to plan a summer vacation and use the Internet to search for the best airfares, locate hotels, and print out maps?

- Would you like to be able to search the Internet for the newest challenging versions of your favorite computer games?

At the Center for Accessible Technology, the ATA Center in Berkeley,

42

———

Computer
and Web
Resources
for People
with
Disabilities

California, parents brought their children to the playgroups with the goal of developing social and other skills. Children came with the goal of having fun with their friends. Of course, they also learned. With battery-operated cars attached to large, brightly colored switches, they developed switch skills that they could later use to operate a computer. By attaching marking pens to these cars and running them over huge sheets of butcher paper and watching them crash into each other, they experienced the joy of creating and playing together.

Setting New Goals

Just as your reasons for purchasing different items change with your personal circumstances, experience, and budget, your technology needs will change over time. Six months or a year after your computer purchase, you may be anticipating a career change that would require number crunching, recalling huge amounts of information, creating multimedia presentations, or networking with other agencies via a telecommunications system, and you might want a machine with a faster processing speed. You may be dealing with a disability that will require a different configuration in the future: addition of speech recognition, alternate keyboards, or screen enlargement programs. Or you may find that your growing technology experience allows you to develop more sophisticated skills and requires more sophisticated tools.

Technology is continually changing: becoming faster, more powerful, and more versatile. It is often hard to decide when to purchase. What if I buy this computer today, and tomorrow they drop the price or discontinue this machine? Technology is an investment in the future, and no one can afford the luxury of putting the future on hold. Future achievements depend on planning, practice, and finding the right tools to work toward chosen goals.

Chapter 4

A Review of the Technology Tools

Much of what individuals with disabilities want is simply access to conventional technologies. You want to be able to write with a word processor. You want teachers to be able to read your writing. You want to find out for yourself what the Internet is all about. You want to publish a newsletter. You want your child to be able to draw and experience the process of creating pictures. You want to be able to create and perform music on a synthesizer. You want to play the latest computer games. You want to work a cash register. Your daughter needs access to a patient tutor for learning her multiplication facts. Your search for technology will have much in common with the process everyone goes through to become proficient in using technology—assistive or conventional—for a specific purpose.

The similarity of assistive and conventional technologies revolves around aspects common to both. That is, all computing involves three things: input, processing, and output. *Input* refers to how you give information to a computer. *Processing* relates to the electronics that operate on, or process, the information you provide. *Output* refers to the way you perceive what the computer is doing and producing with your information.

The ways in which assistive technologies are different from conventional technologies involve these same three aspects. In the pages ahead, you will have an opportunity to determine in what ways your search will be similar to the process everyone goes through because you are selecting some conventional technology components, and in what ways your search is unique because you have some unconventional considerations.

As you put a computer system together, individual needs—your own or those of someone you know—will determine if selections will be made from conventional or assistive technologies. Individuals with disabilities who venture into technology will usually select a combination of conventional and assistive technologies and rely heavily on the conventional, especially when universal access features are part of the product's design.

The jargon of technology can make a discussion about the specifics of input, processing, and output sound intimidating, but don't worry if some terms don't mean much to you at this point. You will gradually learn more of them in the pages ahead and in the experiences you will have during your quest for technology.

44

Computer
and Web
Resources
for People
with
Disabilities

Conventional Technology

The term *hardware* is used to refer to the computer components—the actual pieces of equipment—such as the computer box or CPU (central processing unit), the monitor, and the disk drive. The term *software* refers to the electronic instructions that tell the computer what to do. *Application* and *program* are other common words that refer to software.

The following list organizes categories of conventional hardware and software by function.

Input:

- Keyboard
- Mouse
- Trackball
- Joystick
- Microphone
- Disk drive (external and internal)
- CD-ROM drive
- Modem (telephone, cable, or office network for Internet or telecommunications input)
- Scanner
- Digital and/or video camera

Processing:

- Computer or central processing unit (CPU)
- Disk operating software (or system software)
- Microprocessors (such as Intel or Motorola processors)
- Memory or RAM
- Software program (or application program)
- Graphics cards or processors
- Sound cards or processors
- Accelerators

Output:

- Monitor

- Printer
- Speakers
- Modem—Internet and telecommunications output

The Internet and the World Wide Web

The Internet is a special technology that has moved from chiefly academic, business, and military use to being an integral part of our lives. It differs from the hardware and software mentioned above because it is not located inside a computer, but rather outside of it. In fact, the Internet can be thought of as a vast network that links a huge body of data and programs contained on thousands of computers worldwide. The World Wide Web, or just the Web, a subset of the Internet, is a collection of files, called websites or Web pages. These files are identified by unique addresses called uniform resource locators (URLs) that start with the letters http or www. Computer programs called browsers retrieve these files. For more detailed information about accessing the Internet, refer to Chapter 11.

Conventional input

Conventional input devices—devices that give information to a computer—include the keyboard and mouse. Keyboards are usually patterned after traditional typewriter keyboards in terms of key size and placement, and they contain several additional keys that make a computer do operations traditional typewriters never could. They may also contain a separate or attached numeric keypad that makes entering numbers and performing calculations easier.

The mouse, invented long after the computer keyboard, made computers easier to use because it allowed the user to point to things seen on the screen. By pointing to icons and words, you can make a computer do many things without ever touching the keyboard or memorizing commands. The mouse contains a ball that rolls around inside a small device with a button or buttons and is usually connected to the computer by a short cord. A trackball is like an inverted mouse with a large ball that is moved to control the cursor on the screen. A joystick is much like a mouse in that it causes a cursor or other object on the screen to move in the direction the user is tilting a vertical handle, rod, or "stick." Joysticks are most often associated with playing computer games, but they have other uses, too.

There are many other ways to provide input to a computer. Storage devices such as hard disk drives and CDs contain large volumes of information that can be accessed by the computer as directed or needed. Conventional peripheral—or add-on—devices such as scanners, cameras, and

46

Computer
and Web
Resources
for People
with
Disabilities

external modems carry information through cables that are connected to ports (small plugs or outlets) on the back of the computer. Nearly every computer built since the mid-90s also contains a built-in microphone. Scanners are something like photocopying machines. They put an image of the page you are scanning into your computer, and the image can then be seen on the computer screen. With the appropriate software, most scanners have the ability to decipher and read the print that appears on the scanned page. Once you have scanned the page into your computer, you can change or add to the text. Similarly, cameras can place still or moving images on the screen. Modems are devices that allow you to connect your computer through telephone lines to the Internet and other computers and information services around the world. These technologies have opened the door for an almost unlimited breadth and depth of information to be input into any computer.

Conventional processing

Processing, in conventional terms, refers to the electronics commonly used to process, or operate on, the information you provide to the computer. The key to processing is the *operating system.* The operating system is the complex programming that tells your computer system millions of mundane—but extremely important—things every minute. It tells your computer what to do when a key is pressed, what kind of electronic dots to put on the screen, how to save a piece of information, when to access the disk drive to retrieve data, and all of the other functions your computer must perform when it is turned on. The operating system gives different brands of computers their different characters.

Computer companies invest millions of dollars in developing operating systems they think will appeal to you. Which devices and software you want to use will help you determine which operating system and computer you should purchase. All of these components must be compatible with one another for your system to work.

There are many computer manufacturers in the world, but in the United States the majority of personal computers can be divided into two basic groups: PCs (personal computers) and Macintosh computers.

In a Macintosh computer (made by Apple Computer, Inc.), the operating system is referred to as the Macintosh OS. Apple originally pioneered and pushed the limits of the intuitive, graphic user interface (GUI), which allows the user to point at menus to select commands and to click on pictures to open files. This interface eliminates the need for the user to remember and type in a series of complex commands, as is usually the case with older text-based operating systems such as MS-DOS (Microsoft Disk Operating System).

For PCs, the most popular operating system is Microsoft Windows, although many older PCs operate on MS-DOS. Microsoft Windows is an operating system program that actually runs along with MS-DOS and gives the user the option of operating the computer with either system. Windows creates a graphic user interface—much like that of Macintosh computers—that makes the machine much easier to navigate for those using visual access. Microsoft later developed Windows 95, Windows 98, and Windows 2000 as operating systems designed to replace both Windows and MS-DOS. There are many other developers of operating systems in the world, but Microsoft is by far the largest, with Macintosh being a very distant second. The exploding consumer electronics industry is also using operating systems such as Windows CE (consumer electronics version) in an increasing array of CPU-based, stand-alone devices from electronic books to automobiles, microwave ovens, and home heating systems.

The way a user interacts with a computer is very different in the graphic user interface (GUI) and the text-based operating system models. With the emergence of Windows software, it appears that the world of personal computing has moved toward GUI as the common model. Many people welcome this change because it simplifies computer use. But for many other people, especially those with visual impairments, this change presents significant challenges.

Operating systems are continuously being upgraded (revised and improved) and released in new versions. Numbers after the program title often indicate which version it is, such as Macintosh System Software 9.0 and Microsoft Windows 2000.

The computer you choose will most likely be a PC or Macintosh. Your choice will reflect your opinion of which operating system you find easier to use or which is required for the software and assistive technology you need. We don't recommend one manufacturer over another, because the choice is a personal one and depends on a great many variables. The fans of each type tend to be loyal and vocal in their praise of their particular brand and model. You will probably develop the same devotion after you make your choice.

ROM (read only memory) and RAM (random access memory) are two more acronyms you will frequently encounter. The terms have to do with computer memory—how much and what kind of information it can work with at one time. Both ROM and RAM store information in computer chips. ROM is built into your computer and contains information that tells your computer what to do when it is turned on. RAM is short-term storage and holds information that is being currently processed and manipulated, like your database application when you are entering new data. When you turn off your computer, RAM is completely cleared. ROM is not affected by turning off the computer. *Storage* relates to how you can save the information that you have processed in RAM when you turn the computer off.

48

Computer
and Web
Resources
for People
with
Disabilities

Disks or diskettes are made of magnetic material—much like recording tape—on which you can store and retrieve information. You insert disks into the disk drive. A common term for disks that are 3.5-inch and made of hard plastic is "floppy" disk. There are now several different types of disks and disk drives. Hard disk drives (which are solid units) are for storage and are also made of magnetic material that can hold hundreds or thousands of times as much information as a single removable disk. Hard disk drives are often built into computers, but can also be purchased and connected to your computer separately or in addition to a built-in drive. Compact disks or CDs are based upon laser—rather than magnetic—technology and can contain much more information than magnetic-type diskettes, though not as much as hard disk drives at this time. Other types of storage devices are commonly used in business environments.

RAM and storage capacity are measured in kilobytes (K), megabytes (MB), and gigabytes (GB), commonly called "Ks," "megs," and "gigs." To give you a sense of size, 1 K equals approximately 170 words. One meg is 1024 K, so one gig (1024 megs) is a relatively large amount of storage. By way of further comparison, in 1989 few computers had 1 MB of RAM and 20 MB hard drives. Ten years later, though, most computers were selling at comparable prices yet with 64 MB of RAM and 4–6 GB hard drives.

How much storage space and RAM is in a computer is significant information and will be included in any advertising. As a general rule, the prices of computer systems increase with the speeds of their processor chips, their RAM memories, the size of their hard disk drives, the speed of their CD drives, and the speed of any built-in modems. (How to select your equipment is discussed in Chapter 9.) An ad in the Sunday paper for a PC might read something like this: "Features a Pentium 350 MHz processor, 4 GB HD, 64 MB RAM, with built-in 4X CD-ROM." What this means is that the computer processes information at a speed of 350 megahertz, the hard drive will hold 4 gigabytes, and there are 64 megabytes of RAM.

Connections

All of the components of the computer system are connected with cables between various ports. There are many different types of cables and connectors. Keyboards, mice, monitors, and printers are all connected to the CPU. Assistive technology devices are also added to the system in this manner. Many use keyboard, serial, parallel, ADB, IEEE 1394 (sometimes referred to as FireWire), IrDA (wireless infrared), or SCSI ports, depending on the type of machine. Most recently, the Universal Serial Bus (USB) has been coming into common use for all peripherals across computing platforms. As more devices adopt this type of connection, it is anticipated that customizing computer systems with either conventional or assistive technologies will

Photo courtesy of Edmark Corporation

*This young girl is making a direct selection using the Touch
Window in place of a mouse. (Edmark Corporation)*

become easier. It is important to make sure you get the right type of cable
for each of your computer components.

Software

A computer can do nothing without some kind of program telling it what to
do. These programs can be short and simple or huge and sophisticated and
are commonly referred to as *software*—electronic instructions, stored on
computer disks or computer chips, that tell the computer what to do after
you turn it on.

Computers are different from any tool you have ever owned because of the
software developed for them. Unlike a toaster—which is always a toaster—a
computer can become any tool a particular piece of software tells it to become: a
typewriter, an encyclopedia, an alarm clock, a paintbrush, a stock broker, a musi-
cal instrument, your mail and message system.

Software programs provide the instructions that make the hardware do
the work you need done. Software is created by programmers and, as you
might expect, has a cost that reflects the time and effort that went into creating the program. A program that lets your computer behave like a stopwatch may cost little or nothing; a program that allows you to produce an
animated, full-length cartoon feature or the special effects used in *Star Wars*
may require a second mortgage!

You must consider the cost of software in your planning. An individual
may well spend more on software in the first couple of years of computer
ownership than was spent on the computer hardware itself. Most new com-

50

Computer
and Web
Resources
for People
with
Disabilities

puters come with a variety of popular programs preinstalled, and these may be quite adequate for many of your needs. For example, most new computers will have some word processing program preinstalled which may be perfect for your writing needs. However, if you want to dictate—rather than type—words into this word processing program, you may incur significant expense in acquiring the voice input software you will need in addition to the word processor that came with your computer.

Furthermore, there is no "best" piece of software—or for that matter, no "best" piece of hardware—for someone with a disability, just as there is no best book or best vehicle. Your individual needs and resources will determine your software options, just as they do your choice of books and vehicles.

A note about copyright: If you are going to use a piece of software, you must be licensed to use it. Every program on your computer should be registered in your name. Unauthorized copying of commercial software is theft. For software publishers to remain in business, they must be properly compensated for their products. If you are unsure about the rules, check the manuals and other documentation. Software companies always make the laws clear. There are programs called *shareware* that you may try for free before you decide to use them. They always include information on how to pay the developer should you decide to keep and use them. *Public domain* software programs are free to anyone who wants to copy and use them.

The range of software titles is phenomenal and constantly growing. The following list, which is not exhaustive, is one way to group the types of software tools available. These programs are all available through local computer and software retail outlets, through certain Internet sites, and through good mail-order sources.

Education and training:

- Early language skills building
- Early learning
- Keyboarding
- Reading
- Writing
- Math and science
- Problem solving
- Language arts
- Social studies
- Encyclopedias and other references

Business applications:

- Word processors
- Presentation software
- Databases
- Charting, graphing, and statistics
- Spreadsheets
- Desktop publishing
- Finance and accounting/statistics
- Project planners

Hobbies, games, and recreation:

- Genealogy
- Sports simulations
- Chess and other board games
- Mysteries and adventures
- Interactive novels

Graphics and design:

- Computer-assisted design or engineering (CAD/CAE)
- Clip art
- Digital photography
- Drawing
- Animation
- Painting

Communications:

- Web browsers
- Internet email
- Online services

Music and sound:

- Training
- Composing and scoring
- Recording

52

Computer
and Web
Resources
for People
with
Disabilities

Utilities:

- Security/antivirus

- Diagnostic/troubleshooting tools

- Screen savers

- Backup

- Macros

- Printer drivers

Conventional output

Conventional output devices—devices that let you know what the computer is doing and producing with your information—include monitors, speakers, and printers. Although they may resemble them, computer monitors are more sophisticated than television screens and produce a higher-quality image. Some color monitors can produce millions of different colors. Monitors are available in many different screen sizes. Some computer systems include built-in monitors, but most are separate from the CPU. Many computers with built-in monitors—laptop models, for example—may allow you to attach an additional, larger monitor when you are at home, at work, or making a presentation to an audience.

Printers generally fall into two categories: ink jet and laser. Ink-jet printers print well-defined letters and images that are almost the quality of those produced by laser printers. Laser printers use a laser beam to form characters and images. They produce the highest quality printing and, as might be expected, are more expensive. Both types of printers can print in color, although color printing on a laser printer significantly increases its cost. A third type of printer, dot matrix, forms letters and graphics from a pattern of dots created by small pins striking an inked ribbon. Although dot matrix printers still have some usefulness in some business situations, they are generally obsolete for most personal applications.

It is standard for computers to play sounds that have been incorporated into software programs. Some computers require added equipment to play sounds. Some computers also have the capacity to record and play back sounds, while others require additional equipment and software to accomplish this.

Modems enable the computer to send as well as receive information. Modems connect computers to the Internet and to other computers. Modems allow the user to send email, share all types of computer files, put documents up on the World Wide Web, and retrieve information from the Web.

Assistive technology

The distinction between assistive and conventional technologies is becoming less clear as the concept of universal design is incorporated into conventional technology. Universal design is an approach to the design process that results in products that are usable by the greatest number of people. Both assistive and conventional fields are broadening and converging. What is a necessity for some is a convenience for all. Touch screens, for example, are used as alternatives to the mouse for people with disabilities and in tourist-information booths at airports and theme parks. Voice recognition systems, which allow you to control a computer through verbal commands, are used by people who cannot use a keyboard to provide input and, in many parts of the country, by telephone users calling directory assistance. Eventually, voice recognition may become the most common form of input for everyone, and keyboards may become obsolete.

As the plea from the community of assistive technology users has gone out for universal access, companies have responded. The worlds of assistive and conventional technology are blending, and a new generation of products is emerging—products designed to be used by all people. A number of companies are aware of the need and are designing products with universal access in mind. Brøderbund Software, for example (now a division of The Learning Company), recognizes the need for designs that provide the greatest function for the greatest number of users. Brøderbund, a successful educational software publisher of such popular and acclaimed products as Kid Pix, Print Shop, and the Carmen Sandiego games, has become educated in access issues for individuals with disabilities through training and consultation.

Brøderbund contracted with the Alliance for Technology Access to test

Photo courtesy of CITE

*This man uses the enlargement capabilities of a CCTV
to read a pamphlet.*

54

Computer
and Web
Resources
for People
with
Disabilities

the compatibility of their products with assistive technology devices and has published the data in product catalogs. By assessing the needs, addressing the issues, and identifying the steps that need to be taken, Brøderbund is making its products universally accessible and leading the way for other mainstream software developers.

Several companies are now working together to achieve greater accessibility and applicability of their products. Especially in the area of alternate keyboards, software developers such as Edmark, Brøderbund, and Hartley/Jostens Learning are teaming up with hardware developers. Together they are developing overlays (customized keyboard layouts that slip onto the surface of the alternate keyboard) for specific software programs so they can be easily accessed with alternate keyboards like IntelliKeys (IntelliTools) and Talking Keyboard 2000 (Don Johnston, Inc.). These are important collaborations in furthering the goal of increased access by making both conventional and assistive technology products that are clearly designed to work together.

The following list categorizes assistive technologies in the same way conventional technologies were categorized: according to input, processing, and output uses. Part II describes in detail dozens of products in each category. The page number following each item indicates where you can find more information about each category in Part II. In the remainder of this chapter, we will briefly discuss a few representative items in each category and help you formulate disability-related questions relevant to your needs.

Input:

- Alternate keyboards (p. 173)
- Access utilities (p. 179)
- Keyboard additions (p. 181)
- Switches and switch software (p. 184)
- Interface devices (p. 188)
- Voice recognition (p. 192)
- Optical character recognition and scanners (p. 196)
- Electronic pointing devices (p. 198)
- Pointing and typing aids (p. 200)
- Touch screens (p. 202)
- Joysticks (p. 204)
- Trackballs (p. 206)
- Arm and wrist supports (p. 208)

Processing:

Output:

Assistive-style input

Everyone needs an input method. If standard methods don't work, you must find an alternative. For example, someone with a learning disability or with complete blindness can usually use a conventional keyboard. But what if you need to protect the keys from being pressed accidentally? Someone with limited dexterity may benefit from one of the many keyboard devices available, such as a clear plastic keyguard that is placed over the keyboard, with holes over each key to help guide and support the fingers. One option for people with little or no ability to move their fingers is an electronic pointing device with an on-screen keyboard. An on-screen keyboard is a software program that displays an image of a keyboard on the computer screen. Using an electronic pointing device, you point to the key you want and activate it by pressing a switch. Someone with use of only one hand may prefer to use a miniature keyboard designed for use with a single hand; another person may benefit from a very large keyboard with picture symbols in place of letters.

56

Computer
and Web
Resources
for People
with
Disabilities

Photo courtesy of IntelliTools

*Adults with disabilities may find programmable keyboards
useful for a variety of purposes—employment, productivity,
communication.*

Arjan Khalsa from IntelliTools, the company that produces the IntelliKeys keyboard, explains how modern-day keyboard layouts came about: The QWERTY (and most common) keyboard was developed in the 1860s and first sold by a small-arms manufacturer, E. Remington & Sons, in 1873 as a typewriter. "The keyboard was designed to slow down the typist so the keys would not jam," he says. "We say that computers are great for youngsters, but they use keyboard technology developed in the 1860s. Computers feature 21st century data processing, 21st century graphics and sound, and 19th century keyboard input." The IntelliKeys keyboard, a touch-sensitive customizable keyboard, was designed to be more flexible and appropriate for all children and adults and is especially useful for people with disabilities.

It is time to discard your preconceptions about keyboards. Do you want a keyboard with eight-inch-tall keys? With tiny keys that you can operate with very small movements? With keys arranged in alphabetical order? With large keys today and small keys tomorrow? All of these options and more are possible. Why should each keystroke give you only one character? Why not assign whole sentences to a single key?

Switches and scanning are a tremendous input option for many individuals. With scanning, the computer automatically and repeatedly cycles through the alphabet and other common characters on the screen. As the computer highlights the desired letter or character, the user selects it by clicking a simple switch, then moves on to selecting subsequent letters.

Many things can be scanned, such as word lists, pictures, arrow keys, and menu choices.

Mouse modifications and alternatives provide access to conventional computer functions normally controlled with a mouse. A mouse requires the user to point to, click on, and/or drag objects seen on the screen; mouse alternatives accomplish the same tasks in other ways. An electronic pointing device is one mouse alternative that enables people who cannot use their hands to fully operate a computer system.

Assistive-style processing

Processing considerations deal primarily with how you plan to use your computer and how you can interact more effectively with the machine to best accomplish your goals. For example, an individual with a disability may require a computer that is small, lightweight, portable, impervious to constant vibrations, and has a number of important built-in applications that are available whenever the computer is turned on.

Other assistive technologies related to processing are designed to speed up the computing process or to make it more effective. For example, if you hold down a letter key on most keyboards, the letter will repeat itself until you release the pressure. For people with dexterity problems, this key-repeat feature of conventional technologies can be terribly annoying. A small program or option can tell the operating system to ignore sustained pressure on the keys.

Assistive-style output

Access to technology for individuals with disabilities must include access to computer output. What is needed for an individual to reliably perceive output from the computer? Conventionally, the individual views print or images on a monitor or on a printout. Several options provide output when these conventional methods are inadequate.

People with visual impairments or learning disabilities may benefit from specialized software and speech synthesizers that read aloud characters appearing on the screen. (Many of these products are classified as screen readers and are discussed in Part II.) People with vision impairments may benefit from options that enlarge characters on the screen or allow color and contrast adjustments to the text and background. Braille displays constantly translate what is happening on the screen into tactile output, and embossers can be connected to computers to produce brailled documents.

By using a combination of conventional output methods and assistive technology options, you can easily work with technology in a typical environment, such as an office or classroom.

58

——

Computer
and Web
Resources
for People
with
Disabilities

Roger speaks about being an adult with dyslexia:

I can remember being measured and typecast by my relative ability to use language. It was frustrating, upsetting, and humiliating because I knew that there was intelligence inside, I just couldn't share it in a way that other people understood and accepted. There is an assumption that the sophistication of one's written language is a window on one's intelligence and that people, especially adults, who have problems expressing themselves in writing are lacking in their ability to think. Before I got a computer, I struggled with writing to convince people of the fallacy of this idea, but I ran into a brick wall—my writing wasn't clear enough to be convincing, and no one could read it anyway. Finally being able to write about my disability has been an incredibly significant event in my life. Now I can attempt to explain what I was struggling with for so many years. Yes, just like the blind person who gets vision, I now have a voice, a means of expression that I lacked when I was growing up.

Typewriters helped me read my own writing and allowed me to share it with others for the first time without quite the humiliation that I felt when I shared my handwritten writing. Writing with a computer goes further. A computer-aided writing process separates composition from printing. I can edit freely without committing anything to paper. I can move words around, change the order of sentences, insert new ideas, check spelling, and proofread to my heart's content, before anything is printed on paper. I can work and rework a single page of writing for days, yet the finished printed piece has no whiteout on it, and I've only produced one draft.

All of this allows me, the writer, to concentrate on what's really important: what I am trying to say. And now that I've been writing for a while, I am beginning to believe that I have important things to say and that people find my writing easy to read. I now have an image of myself as a writer. This is why computers are so important to me.

A word about other technologies

Some stand-alone products on the market involve all three functions: input, output, and processing. Many of these helpful devices are described in Part II and include products such as handheld, closed-circuit television (CCTV) systems, which aid individuals with low vision in reading print and instruments. Reading machines use synthetic speech to read books or other print materials fed into the system. Other devices in this category include text telephones (also known as teletypewriter devices), which provide telephone access for individuals who are deaf or require printed communication.

Augmentative and alternative communication (AAC) devices, also called assistive communication products, provide speech for people unable to communicate orally. Some are designed for a single use and thus are

Photo courtesy of Don Johnston, Inc.

*Products such as Co:Writer, a word prediction program, and
Write:OutLoud, a talking word processor, make the writing
process easier for all kinds of learners.
(Don Johnston, Inc.)*

called *dedicated systems.* They may be as simple as a board with word choices
that a user selects or as complicated as an elaborate computer system. The
computer devices usually include voice synthesizers that vocalize what the
user chooses to say. Depending on the type of device, voices may sound
very real because the sound is recorded (digitized) or robotic because the
sound is synthesized. The AAC field has expanded enormously over the
last decade, and interested individuals should thoroughly investigate the
options and consult with a speech and language therapist skilled in AAC
devices before making an investment (see Part III for more references and
resources) (see Augmentive and Alternative Communication Products in
Part II for product information).

The following is a description of one individual's transition into effective communication through the use of AAC devices:

Melinda is a different young lady today than she was three years ago.
When we first met Melinda, she was a youngster with a lot to say, but
no way to express herself. She had learned in her short life that scream-
ing in frustration was the quickest way to get attention. Unfortunately,
this method of communication had become her biggest barrier, and her
family, friends, and the professionals who worked with her were as
frustrated as she was. Fortunately, Melinda's family devoted themselves
to exploring alternative means of communication for her.

Melinda first visited an augmentative communication clinic when
she was nine. She had begun to use sign language and gestures as her

60

Computer
and Web
Resources
for People
with
Disabilities

main form of communication. During this visit it was suggested that she use a portable communication system, consisting of a book of picture symbols. The occupational therapist and speech therapist suggested that the pictures in the book be color coded and provided ideas for how to use the book. Melinda's mother took these ideas and improved on them, attaching the book with suspenders, laminating it, and personalizing it for Melinda. Teachers and staff at her school added their ideas as well. At first, Melinda didn't use the book and the challenge became one of how to facilitate her interest in this method of communication. Again, more frustration.

One night Melinda was very upset and could not calm herself down. Her mom lay in the bed next to her and tried to help by asking Melinda what she wanted for breakfast the next morning. As she listed her daughter's favorite foods, Melinda became increasingly upset. She had a specific food in mind, but she couldn't communicate what it was. They went to the kitchen to try and find what Melinda desired, but she indicated it wasn't there. Then suddenly, Melinda remembered her communication book. She quickly retrieved it and pointed to the picture of a person eating a donut. They went out and got the donuts that night and Melinda slept peacefully, as did her mom.

What resulted from these efforts was an enjoyable and functional method of communication. Melinda began actively communicating with her peers, friends, and family and showed much less frustration. Using her signs, gestures, and verbal expressions along with her new book, Melinda became excited about communication and began making tremendous gains in school as well as at home.

Melinda returned for a follow-up appointment to see the augmentative communication specialists. School personnel, family, and the team believed it was time to add speech output to her communication repertoire. A school visit was made to survey the school setting and talk to relevant professionals and friends of Melinda in her new inclusion setting. In the end, several different devices, all with voice output, were loaned to Melinda for trial periods of one to three months. She and her family determined the appropriate device. "The Wolf has a voice that her classmates do not understand but we like the overlays; the Cheaptalk 8 doesn't have enough space for messages but we like its ease of use." Finally, a device called the EasyTalk (The Great Talking Box Co.) was tried. It had portability, lots of spaces for messages, and was easy to use.

Mom reports that Melinda is enjoying her EasyTalk but that the learning process is never ending. She explains it is difficult to keep on top of the programming because Melinda's communication needs are dynamic and always changing. She says she often feels frustrated by not being able to identify all the messages her daughter might need, and

Melinda sometimes cannot find what she needs on her board when she needs it. But, we all laugh as we discuss this because we know that it is the *process itself* that has transitioned Melinda from a very unhappy girl to one who enjoys communication. We also know that no device is the only means of communication and that Melinda will continue to rely on the total communication approach.

Setting Off in the Right Direction

The questions that follow will help you specify some of your general areas of interest and disability-related considerations. The questions are grouped around issues related to the input-processing-output technology model. By answering the questions, you will begin to focus on many of the specific options and solutions described more fully in following chapters and in Part II that will be important in your particular quest for access to technology.

Questions about input:

- What parts of your body and what abilities can you use consistently?

- Is there at least one set of muscles you can move reliably? For example, can you blink, move your chin, use your fingers, use one hand, or turn your head whenever you wish?

- Do you think you can use a regular computer keyboard very well, OK, somewhat OK, poorly, or not at all?

- Do you think you can use a regular computer mouse very well, OK, somewhat OK, poorly, or not at all?

- How might input devices be positioned to make the input process as comfortable as possible?

Some input solutions:

- By using a switch with scanning, you can operate a computer with any reliable muscle movement.

- There are keyboards that can be altered to create keys of any shape, position, size, and color.

- There are devices that replace the mouse, and there are ways you can use the keyboard instead of the mouse to accomplish the same tasks.

Questions about processing:

- Would it be difficult for you to hold down more than one key at a time?

62

Computer
and Web
Resources
for People
with
Disabilities

- Are you aware of any aspect of using a computer that could be annoying to you, such as the key-repeat feature of many keyboards?

- Do you have difficulty finding the cursor on the screen? Would a significantly enlarged or magnified cursor save you time?

- Will your computer need to run several kinds of applications simultaneously, such as email, voice recognition, word processing, and environmental controls?

Some processing solutions:

- There are access utilities that allow you to press keys sequentially rather than simultaneously.

- You can turn off the key-repeat function with a software access utility.

- Word prediction programs allow the computer to finish words that you start.

- Increasing the amount of RAM will improve your computer's ability to operate several programs simultaneously.

Questions about output:

- If it's not possible for you to see the screen, do you know that a speech synthesizer can be used to read the screen for you? Would speech output interest you?

- Do you want to be able to produce output and materials that can be used by people both with and without disabilities?

- Do you need brailled output?

- How might output devices be positioned to make their use as comfortable as possible?

Some output solutions:

- Words you create with a computer can be spoken with synthetic speech, translated and embossed in braille, seen on the screen, and printed on paper.

- There are several devices that can pass braille dots beneath your fingertips.

These questions and answers, and the information proceeding them, provide a framework in which to think about technology, both conventional and assistive. At this point you should begin to see, at least in a broad sense, how technology can help you fulfill your goals.

Chapter 5

Current Laws and Legislation

Many people have taken this journey before you and have forged the way. The most significant trails blazed have been through the United States Congress. What follows is a review of the pertinent legislation enacted through the hard work and persistence of people with disabilities and their families across the nation who understand the growing importance of technology.

This legislative summary will give you a sense of the rights and protections afforded individuals with disabilities. The passage of these groundbreaking laws clearly indicates that technology is gaining recognition at every level of our society and that advocates for its use are developing more clout in every arena.

Legislative Mandates: A Brief Overview

Congress has passed several important laws that have the potential, when enforced, to greatly improve the civil rights of people with disabilities. Among many other benefits, the following pieces of legislation provide access to assistive and conventional technologies for individuals with disabilities in certain situations. The mandates are:

- Individuals with Disabilities Education Act of 1990 and 1998 (P.L. 101–476 and P.L. 105–17)

- Americans with Disabilities Act (P.L. 101–336)

- Assistive Technology Act of 1998 (P.L. 105–394) and the Technology-Related Assistance for Individuals with Disabilities Act of 1988 (P.L. 100–407), which was also amended in 1994 (P.L. 103–218) and is commonly referred to as the "Tech Act."

- Rehabilitation Act of 1973 as amended in 1992 and 1998 (P.L. 102–569 and P.L. 105–166)

- Telecommunications Act of 1996—Section 255 (P.L. 104–104)

By contacting the office of your congressional representative or senator, you can obtain copies of these laws and related background materials. Call

64

Computer
and Web
Resources
for People
with
Disabilities

(202) 225-3121 for the U.S. House of Representatives or (202) 224-3121 for the U.S. Senate, and an operator will connect you to the right office. Materials on all of these laws are available in braille, large print, audio tape, and as computer files from the appropriate government agency. If you have access to the Internet, legislation can be located and reviewed through the website operated by the Library of Congress (http://thomas.loc.gov/). You can identify and contact your congressional representatives at www.house.gov and your senators at www.senate.gov. There is a list of additional selected resources on pages 67 and 71–72. In this section, we briefly summarize each law.

Individuals with Disabilities Education Act (IDEA)

IDEA is the amended version of the Education for All Handicapped Children Act of 1975 (P.L. 94–142). The law encompasses and expands upon several earlier education initiatives and guarantees four basic rights and three protective assurances for infants, toddlers, children, youth, and young adults with disabilities:

- All children with disabilities are entitled to a free public education appropriate to their needs.

- To the maximum extent possible, children with disabilities should be educated with students without disabilities, as close to home as possible, and in the least restrictive environment.

- Children with disabilities must be provided supplementary services that permit them to benefit from their education, such as physical therapy and assistive technology services.

- With the parents' informed consent, a fair assessment must be completed to determine the student's educational needs.

- Due process rights require prior notice be given to parents before changes are made in the child's program and a method provided for resolving disagreements.

- Students who have been identified or who are perceived as having difficulty learning in school must have an Individualized Education Program (IEP) prepared annually for them by a team that includes the child's parents. The IEP must clearly spell out what services a student will receive and how and where the student will receive them and set forth specific educational goals and the tools to be used. An example of a specific goal would be, "John will write a well-organized, grammatically correct paragraph, free of spelling errors, using word pro-

Photo courtesy of Don Johnston, Inc.

*Discover:Board is an alternate keyboard that works like
a standard keyboard and mouse. (Don Johnston, Inc.)*

cessing software on a Macintosh computer equipped with IntelliKeys and a large-print overlay."

- Assistive technologies and technology access to the curriculum being used in the classroom must be addressed in the IEP. If a request for assistive technology is denied, the rationale must be presented in writing and is subject to appeal.

In addition to provisions for the school-age population, the law includes the preschool level of ages three to five years and provides for the Early Intervention State Grant Program for infants and toddlers from birth to age two. For infants and toddlers, assistive technologies may be specified in the individualized program and include toys and other devices that develop readiness for computer-based technologies that the child will need to participate in the environment and to learn. IDEA also mandates the inclusion of transition services in the IEP beginning no later than age 16. Assistive technology can serve a vital role for youth with disabilities who are making the transition from secondary school to higher education, the workplace, or greater community involvement.

Once assistive technology has been included in a student's IEP, the school system must provide it, as is true of any services included in an IEP. The Office of Special Education Programs (of the U.S. Department of Education) has issued a series of administrative letters over the years interpreting IDEA. One such letter stated that a school district or other local educa-

66

Computer
and Web
Resources
for People
with
Disabilities

tion agency may not maintain a flat policy barring the inclusion of assistive technology in IEPs. Rather, it must make a determination based on the facts of each case. Other letters have upheld the student's right to use assistive technologies purchased with school funds at home and away from school, when the IEP specifies that the devices are needed to maintain educational goals and learning.

Americans with Disabilities Act (ADA)

Modeled after Section 504 of the Rehabilitation Act of 1973 and the Civil Rights Act of 1964, the ADA provides civil rights protection against discrimination for individuals with disabilities similar to the protection provided in other legislation on the basis of race, gender, age, nationality, and religion. The ADA defines disability functionally as any condition that impairs major life activities such as seeing, hearing, walking, or working, and it covers nearly 900 specific disabilities. Under separate sections, it mandates accessibility and accommodation requirements in public facilities, employment, state and local government services, transportation, and communication. For example, one of the protections afforded by the ADA that is not commonly discussed covers parents and guardians with disabilities wishing to participate in their child's school environment. PTA meetings, parent-teacher conferences, and other school events are required by law to be accessible. The law intends to break down the barriers that exist in all of these areas and to provide equal opportunity for individuals with disabilities.

Among the many important rights and protections addressed in the ADA is the requirement that an employer with 15 or more employees may not discriminate against an individual with a disability because of the disability when the person is qualified to perform the essential functions of the job, with or without a reasonable accommodation. The ADA defines *reasonable accommodation* as some modification in a job's task or structure, or in the workplace, that will enable the qualified employee with a disability to do the job. The modifications or changes, which can include the use of assistive technology and technology access, must be made, unless the change creates an undue hardship for the employer. Many employers and consumers (before doing their research) make the assumption that most modifications are going to be very costly and therefore qualify as undue hardships. This is not proving to be the case.

Preliminary findings of the President's Committee on Employment of People with Disabilities indicate that the majority of accommodations cost less than $500 and many have little or no cost at all. This committee, a small federal agency, is working with businesses and groups representing people with disabilities to promote the successful implementation of the ADA.

Through the Attorney General's Office and the Office of Civil Rights, the U.S. Department of Justice places a high priority on fair, swift, and effective enforcement of this landmark civil rights law. Contact the following agencies to receive lists of publications, location of the state or regional office nearest you, and information about people's rights and responsibilities under the law. They can also provide information about how and where to file a complaint.

Disability and Business Technical Assistance Centers
(see list in Part III for locations) (800) 949-4232
website: www.adata.org

U.S. Equal Employment Opportunity Commission
1801 L Street NW, Room 9405 (800) 669-3362, voice
Washington DC 20507 (800) 800-3302, TTY
website: www.eeoc.gov

Access Board
Architectural and Transportation Barriers Compliance Board
1331 F Street NW, Suite 1000 (800) 872-2253, voice
Washington DC 20004-1111 (800) 993-2822, TTY
website: www.access-board.gov

Office of Program Management of Federal Transit Administration
U.S. Department of Transportation
400 Seventh Street SW (202) 366-4020, voice
Washington DC 20590 (202) 366-4567, TTY
website: www.fta.dot.gov or www.ftanet.gov

U.S. Department of Justice
Civil Rights Division
Public Access Division
PO Box 66738 (800) 514-0301, voice
Washington DC 20035-6738 (800) 514-0383, TTY
website: www.usdoj.gov/crt/ada/adahom1.htm

The Assistive Technology Act and the Technology-Related Assistance for Individuals with Disabilities Act (Tech Act)

The Assistive Technology Act, the 1998 amended version of the earlier Tech Act, provides federal funds to assist states in developing easily available,

68

Computer
and Web
Resources
for People
with
Disabilities

consumer-responsive systems of access to assistive technology, technology services, and information. First signed into law in August 1988, the Tech Act was the first piece of U.S. legislation ever to use the term *consumer responsive*. The law requires that state-developed systems must, at a minimum, have in place a process for evaluating and responding to the concerns and suggestions of citizens with disabilities.

The Tech Act provides a definition of assistive technology that became the standard definition used in all subsequent federal legislation and regulations. In the Tech Act, assistive technology includes devices that are not necessarily computer-based. The definition is broad enough to include "any tool or item that increases, maintains, or improves functional capabilities of individuals with disabilities" in such areas as seating, mobility, daily living, and environmental control. In addition to "high-tech" devices, it includes "low-tech" and "no-tech" devices such as mechanical page turners, custom-molded seats, single-switch-activated toys, and handheld magnifiers.

All states are funded to implement the Tech Act. States have primarily used their federal funds for providing technology services such as information and referral and for creating statewide programs that provide access to assistive technology to individuals with disabilities. The Tech Act focuses on eliminating barriers in state government systems of service that prevent consumers of disability services from gaining access to assistive technology. In each state, the Tech Act agency should also be able to inform you of the available resources for funding the purchase of equipment. You can obtain information related to the Tech Act from the lead agency in your state (see Part III for a list of State Tech Act projects).

Rehabilitation Act Amendments of 1992 and 1998

In 1973 the Rehabilitation Act was passed. It was enacted to prevent discrimination against people with disabilities and covered employment and government services. The 1973 act primarily constituted a reauthorization of existing federal aid programs for people with disabilities. The act provides a statutory basis for developing and implementing comprehensive programs of vocational rehabilitation and independent living through such means as research, training, services, and the guarantee of equal opportunities.

In general, the Rehabilitation Act and subsequent amendments cover both public and private employment. The basic goals of sections 501, 503, 504, and 508 are to prohibit discrimination against individuals with disabilities and to increase the employment opportunities within society.

The Rehabilitation Act amendments represent a dramatic departure from the practices that evolved in the rehabilitation system under earlier laws. Particularly for individuals with severe disabilities, the 1992 amendments abolish many barriers to gaining access to rehabilitation services. The former system evaluated individuals for their "employability," "feasibility of employment," and "rehabilitation potential." It served in many ways as the gatekeeper of opportunity for hundreds of thousands of people with disabilities. The 1992 law is built on the presumption of ability to achieve employment and other rehabilitation goals regardless of the severity of disability.

Under the 1992 law, "individuals with even the most significant disabilities should be presumed capable of gainful employment and provided the needed supports to do so." Vocational rehabilitation agencies are now required to focus on solutions and the attainment of employment outcomes. In a 180-degree shift in perspective, vocational rehabilitation agencies must provide services unless the agency can "unequivocally demonstrate" that no possibility of employment exists for a particular individual, even after careful consideration is made of every option for training, assistive technology, reasonable accommodation, and other supports.

Additionally, all state vocational rehabilitation agencies are required to provide a broad range of technology services on a statewide basis, and the technology needs of every client of a vocational rehabilitation agency must be addressed in the Individualized Written Rehabilitation Program (IWRP). Conceptually similar to the IEP required in educational settings, the IWRP for every client must contain "a statement of the specific rehabilitation technology services to be provided to assist in the implementation of intermediate rehabilitation objectives and long-term rehabilitation goals." (Minnesota Star Program, ADA/ADR Pilot Program 1996)

The 1998 amendments strengthened the law further by requiring the federal government in Section 508 to make the technology it uses accessible to persons with disabilities. Section 508 is a part of the Rehabilitation Act of 1973, which requires that electronic and information technology developed, procured, maintained, or used by the federal government be accessible to people with disabilities. On August 7, 1998, the President of the United States signed into law the Workforce Investment Act of 1998, which includes the Rehabilitation Act Amendments of 1998. Section 508 was originally added to the Rehabilitation Act in 1986; the 1998 amendments significantly expand and strengthen the technology access requirements in Section 508.

When federal departments or agencies develop, procure, maintain, or use electronic and information technology, they shall ensure that the electronic and information technology allows federal employees with disabilities to have access to and use of information and data that is comparable to the access to and use of information and data by federal employees who are not individuals with disabilities, unless an undue burden would be imposed on the department or agency.

70

Computer
and Web
Resources
for People
with
Disabilities

Section 508 also requires that "individuals with disabilities, who are members of the public seeking information or services from a federal department or agency, have access to and use of information and data that is comparable to that provided to the public who are not individuals with disabilities." The legislation exempts only national security systems from coverage of Section 508.

The 1998 amendments to Section 508 directed the Architectural and Transportation Barriers Compliance Board (Access Board) to develop and publish standards by February 7, 2000, setting forth a definition of electronic and information technology and the technical and functional performance criteria necessary for achieving accessibility to such technology and information by individuals with disabilities. The new legislation also instructed the Access Board and General Services Administration (GSA) to provide technical assistance to federal agencies and consumers once the standards are implemented on August 7, 2000 (for more information and updates, Internet users see http://trace.wisc.edu/docs/eitaac/).

Telecommunications Act of 1996— Section 255

Very much related to the goals of Section 508 of the Rehabilitation Act, the Telecommunications Act of 1996 requires all telecommunications systems and services to be accessible to members of the public with disabilities and to federal employees with disabilities as well. In a rapidly changing telecommunications environment, Section 255 contains specific language about how the telecommunications industry must change to enable people with disabilities to enjoy more of the benefits of new telecommunications technologies. It mandates that all telecommunications products and services be "accessible to and useable by individuals with disabilities, if readily achievable." If that is not readily achievable, the products are required to be compatible with the assistive technologies and other adaptive equipment used by people with disabilities.

The Access Board and the FCC are responsible for making sure these provisions have meaning and are enforced. The Access Board has issued specific guidelines to industry in its Final Rules. The FCC's Final Rules on Section 255 were released on September 29, 1999. This document also includes a Notice of Inquiry on the accessibility of computer telephony and Internet telephony. (For more information on the ongoing work in this area, telephone numbers and mailing addresses are listed earlier in this chapter. Internet users can contact the Access Board website at www.access-board.gov/ and the FCC website at www.fcc.gov/.)

More References and Resources

In addition to copies of the laws and related supporting materials, which are available from your congressional representative, other resources are available at the community and national levels. Parent training and information centers, as well as consumer groups and independent living centers, can be especially helpful (see Part III for a list of these organizations).

Parent centers can fully inform you about your options under IDEA and assist you in advocacy efforts. Consumer groups and independent living centers can furnish you with a great deal of information related to ADA and the Rehabilitation Act amendments. Your state's department of vocational rehabilitation can provide materials related to the Rehabilitation Act amendments, and public schools are required to distribute information on IDEA to families who have children with disabilities. Some other resources are:

Partners in Policymaking
c/o Minnesota Governor's Council on
   Developmental Disabilities   (651) 296-4018, voice
300 Centennial Office Building, 658 Cedar Street   (651) 296-9962, TTY
St. Paul MN 55155
email: admin.dd@state.mn.us
website: www.partnersinpolicymaking.com

Partners in Policymaking was created in Minnesota by the Governor's Council on Developmental Disabilities in 1987. Partners is an innovative, competency-based leadership training program for adults with developmental disabilities and parents of young children with disabilities. The purpose of the program is twofold: to teach best practices in disability and to teach the competencies of influencing policy and communication.

Since 1987, Partners programs have been implemented in 40 states. More than 4,000 Partners graduates are part of a growing national network of community leaders serving on policy making committees, commissions, and boards at local, state, and national levels.

U.S. Department of Justice
950 Pennsylvania Ave. NW   (202) 305-8304, voice
Washington, DC 20530-0001   (202) 353-8944, TTY
email: sec508.questions@usdoj.gov   (202) 307-1198, fax
website: www.usdoj.gov/crt/ada/adahom1.htm or
www.usdoj.gov/crt/508/508home.html or www.usdoj.gov

The Department of Justice maintains offices specifically designated to promote the implementation of ADA, as mentioned earlier, as well as Section

72

Computer
and Web
Resources
for People
with
Disabilities

508 of the Rehabilitation Act. They are a resource for requesting additional information and for exploring complaints you may have with the ways the laws are being implemented in your community.

National Association of Protection and Advocacy Systems
900 Second Street NE, Suite 211   (202) 408-9514, voice
Washington DC 20002   (202) 408-9520, TTY
email: napas@earthlink.net
website: www.protectionandadvocacy.com/

Protection and Advocacy, Inc. (PAI) is a federally mandated system in every state that provides legal assistance and information to individuals with disabilities and their families. PAI is also included in the Tech Act as amended in 1994 to provide information and assistance in the area of assistive technology. For the PAI office in your state, contact the national office.

The Internet is a growing source of information on these issues. Many online resources are currently available that can provide you with the text of laws, legislative updates, and alerts. Internet resources and how to locate them change on a regular basis. But, with that in mind, here are a few places that can provide valuable information, as well as point you toward additional resources on the Internet. More references are included in Part III.

The Alliance for Technology Access
website: www.ATAccess.org

The Library of Congress
website: http://thomas.loc.gov

The Arc
website: www.thearc.org/

Justice For All (provides alerts about pending legislation)
website: www.jfanow.org/access.html

StartSpot Mediaworks ("government information portal to the Web")
website: www.govspot.com

There Is More to Be Done

Much has been accomplished, but there is still much to do. These laws form a good foundation for including technology as a regular part of the lives of people with disabilities, but none guarantees access to technology.

Laws are only as good as we make them. They need to be enforced. If laws are being violated and complaints are not filed with the authorities responsible for enforcement, the violations will continue. Learn more about how the law applies to you or your child. Follow up on the resources presented here. If you feel your rights have been violated and you need advice on how to proceed, there are many community-based advocates who can help figure out what next steps to take.

In spite of what the law says, there is still a strong tendency in these days of budget cutting for technology to get dismissed as a costly luxury rather than an essential tool for education, employment, and independence. It is everyone's responsibility to make sure that this does not happen. We all need to take action to help ensure that the new generation of technology products will be designed with universal access in mind. We all need to assure that people will have lifetime access to technology.

Chapter 6

Exploring Your Local Resources

Assistive technology is still a new enough field that it can be difficult at first to discover working partners in your area. Geographic isolation has been a formidable barrier for years; overcoming it is one of the primary reasons this book was written.

Part III covers many types of information resources that you may contact by telephone, mail, email, or a personal visit. Information resources are also available in more common community settings, such as the public library. Developing natural supports in the community will do more than anything else to ensure your success with assistive technologies.

Your First Steps: Where You Can Go to Learn More

Conventional and assistive technologies can be very seductive, appealing to your impulsiveness to purchase immediately. If possible, identify a place where you can get hands-on experience with computers and assistive devices before making purchase decisions. Be patient. It is easy to overbuy or underbuy assistive devices when you are operating with incomplete information. We frequently hear stories that speak to this. One father spent a great deal of money on a sophisticated computer system that tracks eye movements, when a simpler touch screen would have been the more appropriate tool for his child. A family that bought a secondhand TRS-80 (an ancient Radio Shack computer) at a yard sale because they heard it say "Die Earthling!" had assumed that, because the computer had some speech capability, it could function as a talking word processor for a child with complete blindness. At the time they did not understand the nature of the technology, the task, or the options. This is where community-based technology resources can help.

Many types of places and groups can be good resources in technology and disability, and some may be in your community. As you make your initial contact with them, here are some questions you might ask:

- Is there anyone in your group or on your staff who knows about assistive technologies for children or adults with disabilities?

- Would this person know about specific assistive technologies for people with particular needs?

- What computers and assistive devices are you using now? How are you using them?

- Would it be possible to see your equipment?

- Do you know, or can you recommend, anyone else in the area who can show me more about assistive technologies?

When you contact information sources, don't be afraid to ask questions and to keep asking them until you feel you know what you need to know. Most people in this field love to share what they know with others.

The Alliance for Technology Access

One of the most important resources is the directory of Alliance for Technology Access Centers (see Part III for more information). Call, write, or visit one of them as soon as possible. The staff and volunteers provide hands-on opportunities to explore assistive technology in an environment free of architectural and attitudinal barriers. There are no eligibility requirements, and everyone seeking assistance is served. Alliance Centers take an approach that places the potential technology user at the center of the process as the evaluator of the equipment and software, rather than as the object of evaluation. The Centers are committed to helping you develop the expertise you will need to make the best decisions.

Alliance Centers are dedicated to serving people of all ages with disabilities of all kinds and have comprehensive, multifaceted programs that reflect community needs and local talents and resources. Although each Center is unique, all provide services that help parents, teachers, employers, children, and adults with disabilities explore computer systems, adaptive devices, and software. Once connected to an Alliance Center, you are in touch with a large network of individuals with disabilities, parents, educators, friends, and vendors who are glad to share their expertise.

Libraries

Every library has a number of resources that will be useful to you. Libraries stock a wealth of books and periodicals that cover conventional computing, and you will find reference books cataloged under the topic of computers. The reference librarian can suggest current periodicals such as *MacWorld, PC Magazine, T.H.E. Journal (Technology Horizons in Education), Electronic*

76

Computer
and Web
Resources
for People
with
Disabilities

Learning, and *Technology and Learning.* A bit technical for the novice, these periodicals are still useful sources of new product information. Most of these publications are also available at local bookstores and computer stores.

In the beginning of your search, avoid books on computer programming. It is a common misconception that everyone who uses a computer must know how to program one. That's a little like thinking you can't ride on an airplane unless you know how to fly one. The fact is, you can use computers every day and never need to write a single line of computer code. If you later find yourself interested in computer programming, you may decide to learn programming in order to create tools that do not currently exist.

Check out the journals, available in college and some public libraries, that regularly discuss aspects of assistive technology and that can refer you to other sources. Some of these journals are *Closing the Gap, Exceptional Parent Magazine, Journal of Special Education Technology, Journal of Vision Impairment and Blindness,* and *Assistive Technology Journal.* They contain a variety of articles on new products, strategies for using assistive technology in the classroom, resources, and personal stories (see Part III for a listing of these publications).

Libraries can also be a good source of information about local organizations, as libraries are often on mailing lists to receive newsletters and brochures. Many libraries also provide free public access to the Internet.

Computer dealers

Visit a local computer dealer just to begin learning about conventional technology. Keep in mind that dealers generally have not been exposed at all to

Photo courtesy of CITE/Florida

A keyboard personalized with muppets provides an exciting alternative for kids.

the field of assistive technology and will probably not be able to answer your questions related to access and assistive technology, especially if the end user has a moderate to severe disability

Parent groups

Parent groups provide information and support to family members of children with disabilities. The types and strengths of parent groups vary greatly.

In the mid-1970s, a federal program to establish a national network of community-based parent training and information centers (PTI) was created. These centers inform parents of their child's educational rights and assist them in their advocacy efforts. Parents and family members are always welcome to join an environment in which they can share and contribute from their own experience. Some of these centers are good resources for assistive technologies.

General information about parent training and information centers in your area can be obtained from the Federation for Children with Special Needs (voice/TTY (617) 236-7210, or at www.fcsn.org). The parent training and information center in Billings, Montana, called Parents, Let's Unite for Kids (PLUK, (406) 657-2055) is the federally designated source for parent and family information specifically related to assistive technology in public education. PLUK is also an Alliance for Technology Access Center and maintains a website (www.pluk.org).

Many communities have parent support groups focused around specific disabilities or early intervention. Families of children with disabilities can be rallied and reinvigorated around the banner of assistive technologies. Consider joining the effort and introducing technology into programs and groups that have not yet given the issue the attention it deserves.

Consumer groups and independent living centers

If you enjoy individualism and taking personal responsibility for making your life all it can be, you will find many kindred spirits at independent living centers (ILCs) and in other groups that are led primarily by adults with disabilities. ILCs and other consumer groups have many missions, but they primarily exist to support individuals with disabilities in reaching self-defined goals. Like parent groups, ILCs and other consumer groups have many levels of knowledge about assistive technologies. Some are disability specific; some are open to any adult with a disability. Since they are community-based programs, they reflect the needs and resources of the individual community.

Independent living philosophy upholds certain beliefs and values:

- A person with a disability has the right to self-determination.

78

Computer
and Web
Resources
for People
with
Disabilities

- A person with a disability has the right to access and to participate fully in the environment.

- A person with a disability has the right to tools that enable full participation.

- A person with a disability has the right to direct the process through which tools are procured.

Consumer-driven groups and models of disability services such as ILCs have emerged as important alternatives to the traditional medical model of disability services. You can obtain a directory of independent living programs by contacting ILRU (Independent Living Research and Utilization), 2323 South Shepherd, Suite 1000, Houston TX 77019; (713) 520-0232, voice; (713) 520-5136, TTY). The cost for the directory is about $10. The ILRW also maintains a website at www.ilru.org, where the information is available at no charge.

Disability agencies

Most communities have several agencies serving children and adults with disabilities. Some are government agencies, such as the Department of Vocational Rehabilitation (which may have a different name in your state, such as the Department of Rehabilitation Services or the Department of Rehabilitation); some are private for-profit or not-for-profit organizations, such as Easter Seals, United Cerebral Palsy, and The Arc (formerly Association for Retarded Citizens); some may provide opportunities for hands-on computer demonstrations and explorations. Disability agencies usually have restrictions regarding who they can serve, which may vary by age, disability, and geographic service area. Although they may not usually serve people with your disability or zip code, they may be happy to discuss or share with you the assistive technologies they are using or refer you to some other resources.

Many disability organizations operate time-limited projects on technology under grants from the government or foundations. For example, United Cerebral Palsy Association in Washington, DC, is operating the Family Center on Technology and Disability which is focused on providing technology information to organizations serving families of children and youth with disabilities. For more information, see its website at www.ucpa.org/fctd/.

Persevere in your search through the bureaucracy. Some agencies are staffed by highly trained professionals and are extremely well equipped with assistive devices, software, and hardware; others have yet to discover technology.

Public schools

Infants, toddlers, children, youth, and young adults with disabilities, up to the age of 22, are entitled by law to a free public education. Every public school system in the U.S. has a special education department or some cooperative arrangement for providing special education and related services. You may find teachers, therapists, or other individuals in your special education department with expertise to share. You may also find many regular educators who are well versed in technology and able to provide assistance.

A school system will often have only one individual who coordinates all or most of the assistive technology resources for the entire district. Although these people may be busy and difficult to contact, they can often provide you with valuable information. You may be able to schedule time to explore their equipment and to observe students using it. Call the special education department to identify the people on the staff who are most knowledgeable in assistive technologies.

Teachers' colleges and university schools of education

The college of education at your local university trains educators. Teacher preparation programs for special education and related services often have a faculty member who is knowledgeable in assistive technologies and who may be able to provide you with access to equipment and information resources. You may want to inquire about taking an introduction to assistive technology class.

University services

Most colleges and universities have an office dedicated to coordinating services for students with disabilities and to providing access to college life through technology. Facilities and expertise may be located on campus, or you may be referred to local community resources such as ILCs. These offices have many concerns—housing, transportation, physical access to facilities, curriculum adaptations—and so may not be completely knowledgeable about assistive technology. However, with so many legislative mandates in place, colleges and universities are moving closer to becoming models of access with each passing year.

User groups

Many communities have well-developed user groups of computer enthusiasts who enjoy getting together to share new technologies and practical tips to improve their performance with existing technologies. Some groups are so large that they are subdivided into special interest groups, such as educators, accountants, and dentists. Some groups are dedicated to specific disabilities, as well. User groups are usually focused around a particular type

80

Computer
and Web
Resources
for People
with
Disabilities

of computer or operating system such as Windows, MS-DOS, or Macintosh.

To find out how to contact user groups in your area, call the User Group Connection in Ben Lomond, California, at (831) 336-4508 or visit its website (www.ugconnection.com). You may find announcements of user group meetings in the computer section of your newspaper's classified advertisements or in computer magazines.

The main benefit of connecting with user groups is learning about conventional technologies. For example, if personal financial management software is of interest to you, a user group member can probably teach you everything you need to know about the topic. Members of user groups tend to be knowledgeable, helpful, and enthusiastic. What they may lack in assistive technology experience, they will make up for with motivation, commitment to helping others, and ingenuity.

User groups are outstanding places to obtain public domain software, demonstration programs, and shareware programs. Public domain software is free; shareware requires you to send a small fee to the programmer if you decide to keep and use the program. Demonstration programs are copies of software that the publisher has made available for people to test out to see whether the software is suited to their needs. They are usually missing a crucial function, like the ability to print or to save work, or are fully operational but only for a limited period of time. In addition to user groups, a number of online computer services have forums focused on the use of technology by people with disabilities. The people who participate in these forums and use online bulletin board services can also provide good and up-to-date information. For more about online services and telecommunications see Part III.

Friends and neighbors

Don't overlook friends and neighbors who are computer users in your quest to become one yourself. They can be valuable resources for keeping you current and for good advice. Technology can be so energizing and contagious that you may discover a new friend or two. Friends who use technology at work or at home should be able to advise you about places to shop and things to avoid. They can be enlisted to help you carry boxes, hook up your computer, or help make telephone calls to your local resources for support and follow-up.

Disability newspapers and newsletters

Like mainstream newspapers and newsletters, those related to disabilities contain both articles and advertisements that may offer valuable information. Many disability newspapers have regular features on conventional and assistive technologies, plus space for vendors of conventional and assistive technologies to reach their markets. In the classified advertisements and small print, you may find components you need at a lower price or announcements of meetings and events to help in your networking efforts (see Part III for a list of publications).

Lead offices of the Tech Act

Part III lists, by state, the lead offices coordinating the implementation of the Tech Act. By contacting the lead office in your state, you can obtain information about devices and funding options. Your state may also have demonstration centers established for technology exploration. Be sure to inquire about placing your name on the mailing list to receive newsletters and publications.

Vendors of assistive technologies

When you contact some of the resources above, such as an Alliance Center, state Tech Act office, disability newspaper, special education department, or independent living center, you can gather names and addresses of vendors of assistive technologies, services, and information resources (a list of vendors is included in Part III). Vendors can provide you with information about their products and may be able to furnish names and phone numbers for additional resources or upcoming events in your area. The vendors listed in Part III also can be contacted through their websites and email addresses.

Making sense of it all

If you have been talking to friends, neighbors, parent or consumer groups, your Tech Act office, dealers, and a few users, you have no doubt heard differing viewpoints on the best computer, the best software, the best place to shop, and the best people with whom to work. It is natural to be confused by all this input.

You may be able to reduce confusion by realizing that technology decisions are very personal. There is no one best computer, no one best software title, no single universal access device. There are only tools to be found that work well for you in your circumstances. The decision-making process is analogous to a personal automotive decision: pickup trucks are the most popular vehicle in the nation, but they are not right for everyone.

Take time to interpret what you find, read, and hear and to seek additional advice from the helpful people you have discovered. You are exploring tools that have changed what it means to have a disability, and you are going places and doing things that have been inaccessible to people with disabilities throughout history.

Take a moment now to record the next three to five steps you need to take, the types of questions you have, and who in your community you think can help you answer them.

Chapter 7

Building a Circle of Support

Once you have identified key resources in your community, it is time to enlist their help in your personal search. You need to find a few good thinkers, people who can work with you on imagining a preferred future. In this chapter we present a range of individuals who represent the kinds of people you might want to involve in your effort to help you solve problems and explore potential solutions.

We take a collaborative approach to the subject of technology exploration, knowing from experience that the most effective efforts are those tackled by a team, a circle of support made up of people who can help you think through all of the possibilities. Your personal support team might be informal, including only one or two trusted friends, or it might be formal, like an Individualized Education Program (IEP) team, including parents, teachers, therapists, and school administrators.

Whatever its size, at the center of the team is the person who will eventually use the technology: you, your son or daughter, or your student or client. Even if an agency will be funding your technology, you—regardless of your age or the nature of your disability—are the ultimate authority on what is the most useful for you. We all have preferences and can express them in a variety of ways: through speech, gestures, actions, attitudes, or a twinkling in the eye. In any case, it is the ultimate user who must be heard by all others involved in the process.

Choosing technology is a complex process. Working collaboratively with a team of supportive people with various types of expertise is the most effective and comfortable way to proceed.

The Talent Pool

In building your team, you might want to start with a generalist, someone you trust who has a broad knowledge of assistive technology. This person may help you identify a few other people to involve in your effort.

You will find plenty of people who want to help you once you start to look for them. Some will have more time and energy than others. You need not necessarily ask people to make a major time commitment; it may be that you only need someone to attend one meeting, to make a couple of fact-finding phone calls on your behalf, or to refer you to a community agency or an advocate. Use the resources discussed in the previous chapter to locate help in areas you haven't yet covered. Here are some of the people you might want to consider to be a part of your personal support team:

- Parents
- Partners
- Friends
- Advocates
- Professional service providers
- Other people with disabilities or their parents
- Computer-using children
- Computer and Internet enthusiasts
- Rehabilitation counselors
- Job coaches
- Employers
- Teachers
- Funders

Consider people with a good knowledge of:

- You
- Your environment
- The Internet and online resources
- Funding resources
- Relevant legislation
- Community resources
- Assistive technology and the vendor community

Your parent, partner, or friend

This team member is someone who is already a support in your life and who knows you well enough to offer sound advice. He or she can help you consider all the areas in which you might benefit from using technology in your life and can also help you sort through your financial position.

84

Computer
and Web
Resources
for People
with
Disabilities

Someone who knows your environment

You may spend most of your days in a classroom, on the job, or at home. Someone familiar with the environment in which you will use your technology—a teacher, job developer, job coach, employer, or someone with whom you live—may be very helpful.

Someone who knows about funding resources

If you are hoping to secure funding from an outside source—for example, a school district, the Department of Rehabilitation, Social Security, or medical insurance—you will want to involve someone who can advise you about such resources.

Someone who knows the law

Provisions in federal legislation—Americans with Disabilities Act (ADA), Individuals with Disabilities Education Act (IDEA), the Rehabilitation Act, and the Tech Act—regarding assistive technology and the rights of people with disabilities may be helpful to you. You need to know how they can directly benefit you, and a person who knows about the law as it relates to the provision of assistive technology will prove very useful (see Chapter 4 for more information on these laws).

A trained advocate

If you are concerned about challenges from a potential source of funding, you may want to use the services of a trained advocate. This person may be a member of an organization that frequently deals with the implementation of laws and public policy relating to people with disabilities, such as a self-advocacy group, a parent advocacy center, or a disability-related organization. In extreme situations in which there is concern regarding a person's rights, you might want to seek counsel from an organization that specializes in disability rights, such as Protection and Advocacy (P&A). P&A is a system of federal programs mandated to provide legal and other advocacy services in each state to protect the rights of individuals with disabilities (see Part III for additional information on the National Association of Protection and Advocacy Systems).

A professional with relevant expertise

An occupational therapist or physical therapist who can help with seating and positioning may be of benefit to you. A speech pathologist can help if augmentative, alternative, or facilitated communication is needed. Other professionals can provide assessments and evaluations when needed. If you anticipate the need for customized equipment, you may want to consult an engineer. Rehabilitation engineering centers around the country provide formal evaluations and specialized service.

Other consumers or parents with similar interests or experiences

It is often extremely helpful to ask someone ahead of you on this journey to act as your mentor. The person may be a current user of assistive technology or have had experience working with one of the organizations involved. It is wonderful to be able to call someone to ask whether you are on the right track or if you are considering all of your options.

Children who are accomplished computer users

Some of the most remarkable mentors we have encountered are young people who are avid computer users. This especially applies to youngsters with disabilities who use assistive technology effectively in their daily lives.

Joshua, age 15, has a learning disability and has found energy, excitement, and academic success with his Macintosh computer. His computer has changed his life and empowered him as a leader. He has become a model and a mentor to many young people he meets. He is programming with sophisticated multimedia tools and creating programs on disability awareness. He is focused on the issues of access and making sure that every student's needs for access are considered.

Photo courtesy of IntelliTools

*Combine IntelliTalk with IntelliKeys, Overlay Maker,
and your computer to create a powerful and flexible
communication and learning system. (IntelliTools)*

86

Computer
and Web
Resources
for People
with
Disabilities

Someone who can provide technical support

It may be helpful to include a friend or acquaintance with technical expertise at the beginning of your search. Computer user groups can be good sources of people you might need to get your computer up and running.

Jerome, a parent of a son with cerebral palsy, knew he would need assistance with setting up his son's new computer. He involved a staff member from his local Alliance Center in his plan right from the beginning, so that when he was ready to connect the cables he would have the help he needed. When the time came to open the box, set up the machine, and install the software, the staff member was there to assist.

Your state's office of rehabilitation

If you are seeking employment with the support of assistive technology, you may wish to work with your state vocational rehabilitation agency. Counselors can assist you with your job search and the acquisition of the assistive technology.

Angela brought her rehabilitation counselor with her to her local Alliance Center to try out equipment and software so they both could begin to construct a mental image of Angela working in a business office with a computer. Prior to this experience, the counselor had ruled out several potential positions in offices because she had assumed Angela would not be able to see the screen well enough to do the necessary tasks. After their visit, she and Angela both had ideas about how to magnify images on a computer screen so Angela could adequately see the text. They left with more clearly defined goals and the information they needed to meet with an employer to discuss with confidence specifics of job accommodation.

An agency providing supported employment

Agencies that provide support for employment for people with developmental disabilities can help with employment needs.

Andre needed his job developer and his job coach to see that he could enter data accurately and quickly using a computer. At a community center, Andre copied information from cards into an electronic database with almost compulsive accuracy. Seeing this, the job developer was able to convince a community college library to hire Andre in a data entry position. In the library, Andre's job coach knew what to expect and was able to tailor support strategies and eventually turn over his supportive role to Andre's employer and coworkers.

An employer

Potential and current employers can be valuable resources.

> *Ron,* who has autism and was unemployed, holds a degree in math. A public agency serving people with developmental disabilities wanted to hire someone with a disability to run a complex database using the Windows operating system. Ron got the job. His new employer needed to learn what accommodations Ron needed to use the necessary software and sought assistance in the planning process from his community resource center. Working together, the team—Ron, the employer, a coworker, and a technology access specialist—determined what computer equipment and software was needed.

School or school district personnel

A teacher, administrator, special education program specialist, or technology coordinator from a district might be of tremendous assistance to a family planning for classroom technology for a student. It is not uncommon to discover that there is one overworked technology expert for many schools, with little or no budget. A lack of understanding about technology on the part of many administrators, combined with ongoing budget dilemmas, have led some administrators to allot zero dollars for assistive technology purchases. When district or school staff are resistant, cautious, or apprehensive, it is important for you to involve them from the start and to work on convincing them of the wisdom of what you are doing. It won't be easy, but it will be worth it.

When working with a school, it is helpful to have basic information about the school:

- What kind of computers are used at the school?

- Are they in the classroom or in a lab?

- Will a portable computer be necessary to meet the needs of a student who moves from classroom to classroom during the day?

- Is a printer available?

- In what ways is the IEP team willing to provide support and follow-up for the student if assistive technology is purchased?

- Will the school provide a computer for use at home?

- Is compatibility an issue?

- Will disks be shuttled between home and school?

88

———

Computer
and Web
Resources
for People
with
Disabilities

With older students, the issues can be somewhat different.

Gloria is about to finish high school and move into a transition program that her district provides for students 18 to 22 who are not going to become full-time college students and who need special education services as they move to adult life. Gloria has been using a laptop computer and switch access hardware and software in lieu of a pencil and paper to complete work in high school. The equipment and software were provided by the district through the IEP process. Gloria's current goal, articulated in her Individual Transition Plan (ITP) as mandated by IDEA, is to have a full-time job by the time she is 22. She wants to work in an office and would use a computer system similar to her current setup. As she moves into the transition period, these questions must be addressed:

- Will the laptop computer she has been using work in the transition program?

- Will she use it in the workplace?

- Will she need to consider new equipment?

- Who will help her find a job?

- Who will provide support in the workplace?

- Who will help the employer understand her needed accommodations?

- Will she have a job coach?

- Will the Department of Rehabilitation play a role?

- Will other agencies be involved?

- At what point should they become involved?

- Will independent living skills be an issue?

- Who will provide help?

- What are Gloria's long-range dreams, and what nightmares does she seek to avoid?

- Who will be a part of her circle of support as she moves into adulthood?

At this point in her life, technology is playing an integral role in Gloria's transition process. Her technology support people will need to advise the rest of her transition team to ensure that technology is integrated into Gloria's life where appropriate.

A dreaded scenario is one in which Gloria is forced to leave her computer at high school because it was purchased by the school district and belongs to them. Separated from her writing tool, she enters into a limbo transition period. No one understands that she is capable of writing well and can use her skill capably in a job if she has the right tools. Gloria starts to spend most of her days at home and becomes more and more socially isolated. No one knows whom to contact for help.

A brighter projection is that Gloria is allowed to bring her computer with her into the transition period. A job developer works with her over time to find her a wonderful job where she can use her assistive technology. A community agency provides job coaching and links her with the supports she needs within the company. The Department of Rehabilitation commits to providing an upgrade to her hardware and software along with training in their use. Gloria links with an independent living center to help her in finding her own apartment. Gloria meets regularly with her circle of support to iron out problems and takes her place as a contributing member of her community.

Who might Gloria enlist for her technology team? Members might include her high school English teacher, who fully understands her current use of the computer; the counselor from the school district's transition program, who has an interest in and responsibility for continuing the use of assistive technology; Gloria's prospective Department of Rehabilitation counselor, who will help with employment planning; a staff person from a supported employment organization, who can explore emerging technology with Gloria and help her envision herself using it in her future; the technical resource person from the local Alliance Center, who can provide Gloria with opportunities to try out new technology before choosing what she wants to use; and her sister, who will help coordinate the process and advocate for Gloria. With all or some of these people included, Gloria has a much better chance of achieving her goal.

Private organizations

Representatives from the following agencies might be helpful to you in your journey: your local Alliance Center; your local center for independent living; a disability organization to which you belong, such as United Cerebral Palsy or your Retinitis Pigmentosa Support Group; a parent training or advocacy center; a self-advocacy group; and a service organization. If you have close ties with anyone from any such group, they might play an advocacy role for you or help you to sort through all of the information you will uncover along the way.

Mabel just completed her GED using computer technology for all of her

90

Computer
and Web
Resources
for People
with
Disabilities

written work. Mabel is 93. She is a participant in a social model day program in an independent living center, which is designed to assist individuals to live independently. She became interested in the technology program at the center at the same time she became determined to finish her high school education. With support from a peer-mentoring program at the center, she learned word processing and used a computer for all of her written schoolwork.

Song is the leader of a self-advocacy group for young adults with developmental disabilities who are learning how to stand up for themselves and to be full participants in their communities. At one of his monthly meetings, Song learned from a fellow member that he could visit his local Alliance Center and use a computer to work on his agendas and print them out for the meetings. He began making regular visits and brought his independent living coach along to help him. His coach works with him several times a week as he acquires the skills he needs to become an independent adult living on his own. Together they are becoming proficient at using word processing software and are beginning to think about how Song might acquire a computer for use at home.

A potential funder

If you will be seeking funding from an outside source, you will want to learn all you can as early in the process as possible. You may want to turn to someone with a good understanding of funding resources who can help you assess your financial resources and make optimal use of your options. Perhaps someone from Social Security, Medicaid, or your private insurance company will figure into the equation. Consult with these experts throughout your process, and make no assumptions about what they will or will not be able to do for you.

Gary is a pediatrician and has been a dedicated scientist all of his adult life. A traffic accident and spinal cord injury were not going to stop him. After his initial rehabilitation, it was clear that Gary would not be able to use his hands, but he was determined to continue his work, perhaps with the assistance of a computer and an aide to help him physically. He had read about devices just coming on the market that would provide computer access for people with little or no hand use. The team he assembled included a staff person from the local Alliance Technology Resource Center, a counselor from the Department of Rehabilitation, and himself. He brought to the table an excellent knowledge of emerging technology, gained through his personal efforts. The Alliance Center staff person brought a variety of devices Gary could try out. The rehabilitation counselor brought the ability to provide funding by negotiating a complex system. After Gary made his choices, the stressful process of securing funding began. Various agencies turned him down, as is often the case, until finally one agreed to provide him with a portable computer, a HeadMaster (a head pointing system by Prentke Romich Company), and an on-screen keyboard. Patience and perseverance had been extremely important, as were the people that helped Gary negotiate the maze. Today Gary is working in his chosen field as a geneticist.

Moving Ahead

Ask the following key questions of yourself as you begin to develop your personal support team:

- What information do I still need before I can make a choice?

- Who in my community can help me find the information I need?

- Will I need a formal assessment to help me sort through my choices, meet my needs, and provide documentation to a funder?

- Do I simply need an opportunity to try out and evaluate a range of equipment and software before making decisions?

- Who can help me find a place to try the equipment or software?

- Who do I know, who knows me well and whom I trust, to help me consider and evaluate my options?

- Will I be paying for my new equipment or software, or will I need assistance from a funding source? Do I know which source? If yes, would I want to include a representative of that source on my team from the very beginning?

- Do I anticipate a challenge from my potential funding source? If yes, would it be helpful to include a trained advocate on my team?

How many people you have on your personal support team is entirely up to you. It is important for you to feel comfortable and confident, so choose people who will enhance those feelings. Most of all, choose people who will support the idea that you are the person who ultimately must make the decisions, based upon the best information available.

Once you have chosen your team, you will need to consider how it will function. Some people find that informal consultation with individual team members is all that is needed, but others use their team members more extensively.

Alicia is an 18-year-old in a regular high school. She has been using tech-

92

—

Computer
and Web
Resources
for People
with
Disabilities

nology since she was six years old, and her current and primary educational goals focus on developing her skills to communicate appropriately with peers and adults and learning to write fluently. Alicia's family has put together a team that includes Alicia, a speech pathologist expert in augmentative and alternative communication, a rehabilitation engineer, two special educators, her English teacher, the special education director, and a technology specialist from the local Alliance Center. They use the outside consulting services of an occupational therapist and a physical therapist when appropriate.

Their goal is to put together a communication system that can be mounted on Alicia's wheelchair and that she can access using a switch with her chin. The family is at the center of the process, which has been long and involved. Together they are brainstorming ideas, testing proposed solutions, preparing computer setups with Alicia's choices of words and phrases, and troubleshooting technical problems that arise. They are currently using a program called Speaking Dynamically (Mayer-Johnson) to design the communication boards on the computer screen.

In addition to providing technical assistance, one of the key roles team members can play is to help you financially plan for computer acquisition. Knowing funding sources is one support role; helping you budget is another. As you come closer to knowing what products you will need, you can begin to develop a budget that includes the conventional and assistive technologies and reflects a knowledge of the cost of things. You will revise your budget many times, but it is good to have a plan in mind, especially as you prepare to approach funders. Your team can help you make sure that you are accounting for such things as software, future upgrades, and training in addition to your equipment needs.

Teams may not be as elaborate as some of those mentioned here, but they should be as collaborative. Think about what you will need in terms of expertise and creativity. What are the key access issues that are emerging for you, and who can best help you address them? If you don't already know who can help you, who should you contact for a referral? As you begin to locate your personal resources, be prepared for the enthusiasm you will very likely encounter.

Chapter 8

Developing Your Funding Strategy

By now you may have a clear plan for identifying and working with the resources you need. Inevitably, though, your ability to implement your choices and achieve your goals with assistive technology depends upon the availability of financial resources.

Just as you need to formulate a plan for choosing and using technology, so must you develop a strategy for funding it. You must begin to plan the financing when you start your selection process.

Few established funding sources exist for assistive technology. For the most part, funds still need to be taken from sources designated for other purposes. This can mean hard work, but it rewards persistence, assertiveness, and imagination in extraordinary ways. Remember, the vast growth in technology devices, awareness, and use over the past decade has occurred largely as the result of grassroots efforts by people like you—people who wanted the equipment and found ways to get it.

You may encounter physical or attitudinal barriers in your search. A third kind, a systemic barrier, is more treacherous and difficult to understand. Systemic barriers usually relate to administrative and bureaucratic obstacles. They are exemplified by agencies that provide access to technology, but only for certain people, or agencies with the potential to fund the acquisition of assistive technology, but only for specific or limited activities. The funding landscape is filled with systemic barriers; working to remove them is an important effort for advocates and consumers of assistive technology.

Approaches

The best starting point for developing your funding strategy is to answer this series of questions.

- What do you mean by funding? Do you need all or some of the cost in the form of a grant?

- If you need only part of the cost in the form of a grant, will the grant be a down payment, funds for subsequent installment payments, or resources for specific components of your computer system?

94

Computer
and Web
Resources
for People
with
Disabilities

- Are you eligible for services from a program that has the authority to provide technology but must be persuaded to provide it?

- Would a loan for some or all of the cost meet your needs? Would the technology be used to facilitate repayment?

- Do you need your entire system—hardware and software—at once, or can acquisition be spread over a period of time?

- Can you modify your component selection if substitutes are cheaper or more readily fundable?

Other considerations concern what we call comfort levels. For instance, if you have a fear of debt or if you are doubtful of your ability to make payments, a loan may not be the right strategy for you, even if one is available. The issue of comfort level, and even of integrity, comes up in a number of settings. For some funding sources, one's desperation or perceived crisis is unfortunately an important criterion for support. In other settings, capabilities and potential are the keys. Your chances of getting people or organizations to do what you want increase with your ability to meet their criteria, to follow their procedures, and to use their language. Research it. Find out what they need to know.

Revisit your budget throughout your search, and review and adjust it according to the information you are gathering. Having a clear idea of what kind of computer system you would ideally like and how much it would cost—along with what it will take financially to get a system that will at least get you started—is very important.

Your goals for technology will determine your selection and prioritizing of potential funding sources. As early as possible, you will find it useful to begin collecting information on all potential sources. Generally speaking, funding sources can be organized according to their criteria, which may include:

- Your purpose for using the technology (such as vocational, educational, communication, quality of life or independent living issues, or medical care)

- The nature of the equipment

- Your age

- Location requirements

- Financial circumstances requirements

In reviewing eligibility criteria, don't dismiss a potential source until you are certain it will not work for you. For instance, many programs use means testing (a way of determining eligibility for a program or service based upon income, resources, or other measures of individual or family economic status), but certain resources or income items may be exempted in making the eligibility determination. Until you know exactly what goes into a particular agency's calculations for the means test (such as family size and amount paid for rent, food, or health care), you should not assume you are ineligible.

The language you use with different sources should reflect their orientations. In medical settings, stress the therapeutic nature and "medical necessity" of the equipment. In vocational settings, the goal and potential for self-sufficiency are crucial elements. Again, it is important to research and understand the language the potential funder prefers. Sometimes vendors (those who supply the goods and services you want) can help you understand what is needed to obtain authorization from an agency or insurance company.

In many instances, particularly when several components are involved—including the computer itself, peripherals (such as printers and modems), and assistive devices and software—your funding will probably not come entirely from one source or all at one time. For this reason, your funding plan must prioritize, as well as identify, potential resources so that you will approach them in the best order. Prioritizing and order of approach are also important because a number of sources consider themselves "payers of last resort," meaning, they won't pay until all other sources have either paid up or refused to pay anything. Sometimes it seems there are so many contenders for this status that one wonders who is left to ask first. It is critical to find out what prior rejections, by what other sources and within what time frames, will be required for you to meet their particular definition of "last resort."

Major National Programs

People throughout the country have used an enormous range of funding resources to meet their assistive technology needs. We will focus on sources that are relevant to the largest number of people. Because many adults and children with disabilities qualify for services under federal entitlement programs of nationwide scope, we will start with the technology funding potential of vocational rehabilitation, special education, and Medicaid.

These three programs are called *entitlement programs* because anyone who meets their eligibility requirements automatically has the right to receive their assistance. But saying someone is *entitled* to services is not saying what those services will be. Services vary according to decisions the state has made concerning the implementation of the program, to the availability of funds in relation to demand, and to individualized assessments of need and potential. For example, an individual might be receiving Medicaid but not be entitled to a particular medical procedure unless the state provided it and it was deemed "medically necessary" for the individual.

96

———

Computer
and Web
Resources
for People
with
Disabilities

Vocational rehabilitation

Operating through state agencies under the auspices of the Federal Rehabilitation Act (U.S. code, title 29, sections 701 and following), the vocational rehabilitation program (called by a variety of names, such as VR, DVR, OVR, or DR, depending on the state) provides assessment, training, placement, and other services to people with physical or cognitive disabilities who could benefit in employability or other identified goals. Services are planned and provided according to a kind of annual contract between the agency and the recipient, called the Individualized Written Rehabilitation Program (IWRP). Assistive technology can be written into the IWRP in two ways: first, rehabilitation technology may be designated as one of the services that must be provided; second, technology may be deemed to be an element of another service, such as job placement.

> *Tony,* whom you may recall from Chapter 1, is an example of someone who benefited from this program, to a point. Tony was contacted by his rehabilitation counselor about a training position at a technology service center that might be appropriate for him. It seemed like a good fit, and Tony went to work as the intake counselor for a technology service program. His job required a lot of interviewing and record keeping. Because of Tony's limited vision, he needed a computer system to accomplish the required tasks. The Department of Rehabilitation agreed to purchase a computer system equipped with a speech synthesizer, large-print program, screen reading program, and a scanner. The system allowed Tony to take printed forms, scan them into the computer, read them, fill them out, and print them.
>
> The technology was very effective. However, adequate training in how to use the system was not given, and Tony had to learn through trial and error along with some help from his coworkers. And, because the system was purchased by and belonged to the Department of Rehabilitation, it had to stay behind when Tony relocated out of the state.

Although an IWRP is required by law, many adults dealing with the rehabilitation system are unaware of this requirement or of the fact that one of the documents they may have signed represents their acceptance of a proposed IWRP.

In the VR process, you have three technology-related goals:

1. To ensure that all eligibility determinations take full account of technology's potential to help achieve program goals

2. To ensure that provision for technology is incorporated into the IWRP in sufficient time to be available when it is needed for employment or other life events

3. To identify and resolve any problems that might prevent the VR agency from acquiring the technology you need (for example, one particular model of a device may be approved for state purchase, but the version you need may not be)

Special education and related services

Administered under the Individuals with Disabilities Education Act (IDEA), the special education program lists a variety of assessments and services that school systems must provide so students with disabilities may receive a "free and appropriate public education." Using a model similar to the IWRP, school placement decisions, goods, and services to be provided are outlined in the Individualized Education Program (IEP) according to the annual determinations of a student's IEP team.

Assistive technology devices and services must be specifically considered for each student and must be provided when appropriate, but once again, the determination of when this is and exactly what technology to use is highly individualized and far from simple. A person is on strongest ground when able to argue that, based on the school system's own assessment of student needs, technology represents the best or the only effective means for dealing with the barriers that have been identified. Schools have often effectively limited access to general classrooms for students with disabilities based upon an inability to speak or to use a pencil when, in fact, technology can easily provide an effective alternative. Parents have important rights in the process, including the right of participation, the right to have experts of their own choosing at the IEP conference, the right to administrative appeal, and even the right to court appeal if dissatisfied with the administration's decision.

Judith and her family knew the importance a computer could make in Judith's life but were worried they would not be able to convince the IEP team. Although a strong team of educators and support staff was in place, none of the team members were particularly well versed in technology, let alone assistive technology. And, given the workloads they all faced, they were not likely to find time to adequately research assistive technology.

So Judith and her family began the search on their own. They made calls, asked questions, and even tested some equipment borrowed from another school. When they finally had a good sense of what they needed, they borrowed a video camera and recorded Judith operating the computer to accomplish a simple but important task. They realized that a good picture of Judith effectively using the technology would be worth a million IEP words.

98

Computer
and Web
Resources
for People
with
Disabilities

They were right. A largely inexperienced team could easily see the potential and added the necessary assistive technology to Judith's IEP for purchase by the school district.

Medicaid

Established under Title 19 of the Social Security Act and administered by state agencies, Medicaid is a national program of medical assistance for the poor, including people with disabilities. When assistive technology comes within the arena of Medicaid, it must, with a few exceptions, do so under one of two headings: it must qualify as Durable Medical Equipment (DME), an optional service offered by some states; or, in the case of children, it must arise under the Early Periodic Screening, Diagnosis, and Treatment (EPSDT) program. Durable medical equipment tends to be narrowly defined, and EPSDT, while it has resulted in the availability of important medical treatment for children who might otherwise go without health care, has been of limited value in facilitating access to computers or related technology.

Many procedural and technical barriers continue to make Medicaid an extremely limited source of assistive technology support. To date, augmentative and assistive communication devices probably constitute the computer technology that has made the greatest progress under Medicaid because they have a better capacity to be described as a medical necessity and because they are dedicated systems for the primary purpose of communication. In the long run, a national health insurance program is likely to affect the availability of technology in the health care sphere far more than changes to Medicaid itself.

Though all these programs have appeals processes, both from up-front ineligibility determinations and from decisions relating to the scope of services, the systems often move slowly. When the appeals process is taken into account, eventual success may be delayed far too long to be meaningful for time-sensitive equipment needs, such as accepting a job offer or taking a school course.

Other National Programs

Several other national entitlement programs deserve brief mention. The program of early intervention for preschool children of ages three to five and the program for infants and toddlers from birth to age two can include technology in appropriate cases, as can programs for older Americans. Developmental disabilities programs, also operated through designated state agencies, now include provisions for assistive devices.

In fact, over the past decade, references to assistive technology have been added to most of the major federal disability-oriented programs as they have come up for renewal. Within any benefit program, consumers should be aware of the possibility for the inclusion of assistive technology among the goods and services authorized. If the program includes any flexibility in the nature of the goods and services it provides, you have a plausible case for arguing—unless something in the governing statute or regulation excludes the technology you need—that it should be provided.

Social Security work incentives

People with disabilities who receive Social Security Disability Insurance (SSDI) or Supplemental Security Income (SSI) are ever mindful of the risk that small amounts of work or tiny increments in income will jeopardize their benefits. Although many people perceive that employment is not feasible while receiving SSDI benefits, work incentives are available to bridge the gap. The ability to work determines eligibility for benefits, and income is a major factor in assessing that ability. SSI, by contrast, is strictly means-tested, with payments reduced proportionally as income or resources rise above specified levels.

Among work incentives, several relate directly to the ability to obtain assistive technology. An SSDI recipient's income will be considered to have demonstrated the ability of the recipient to work or perform substantial gainful activity (SGA) if it exceeds certain monthly levels. But to the extent that this income is used to meet impairment-related work expenses (IRWEs), it will not count for purposes of the SGA determination. Assistive technology devices, services, and training needed for work are a prime illustration of IRWEs. Another example would be a sign-language interpreter's services.

The same holds for SSI. Although income above the individual's benefit level will result in reduction or eventual elimination of the monthly payment, the IRWE concept (and in the case of recipients who are blind, the blind work-expenses provision) will serve to exclude income from being counted. For SSI recipients, the Plan for Achieving Self-Support (PASS) can be used to shelter income and resources for use in obtaining education or training, as well as for the purchase of technology that will contribute to or be necessary for work. PASS benefits are subject to approval requirements and must be something that furthers the self-sufficiency goal. Good examples would be assistive technology for use in training or work, tuition costs in some program leading directly to self-sufficiency, and the costs of a van-lift for a vehicle to get to work or job training. All efforts to use Social Security work incentives require fairly detailed record keeping. However, provisions such as these can be used to leverage a fair amount of work- or training-related technology for people who could not otherwise put together the sums necessary to provide it without relinquishing their benefits.

100

Computer
and Web
Resources
for People
with
Disabilities

It is vitally important to fully understand these work incentives and how benefits are affected by them. The Social Security Administration has resources publications that provide more detailed descriptions concerning incentives and their potential impact on benefits and opportunities. One such publication is *The Red Book on Work Incentives*. The Social Security Administration's website (www.ssa.gov) also contains the most current information and changes related to work incentives. Finally, remember that knowledge is power and that you have the right to appeal any work incentive plan that is denied.

Rights and accommodations

The Americans with Disabilities Act (ADA) is described as the greatest legal landmark in the history of civil rights and equality of opportunities for America's estimated 54 million people with disabilities. Its impact upon the availability of assistive technology will be substantial. The ADA requires employers, governmental and nonprofit service providers, and businesses providing public accommodations to take reasonable steps to accommodate persons with disabilities. In the provision of "reasonable accommodations" or of the "auxiliary aids and services" sometimes required in public accommodations settings, equipment is clearly included among the strategies for meeting the law's requirements. While no business or organization can be made to provide accommodations that would create an undue financial burden or hardship, in many cases assistive technology represents the most appropriate and cost-effective method for meeting the need.

> *Kendall* had been researching the sex lives of fish for the Department of Environmental Conservation for 12 years when he sustained a traumatic brain injury in an automobile accident. Kendall became legally blind and developed problems with balance and significant memory difficulties. He had a strong desire to return to work and an employer eager to have him back. His job involved fieldwork, data collection, and statistical analysis, and it seems Kendall was the only one able to manipulate the appropriate files.
>
> Kendall began working with people at his local independent living center who helped him develop strategies to compensate for some of his memory and sequencing issues. Working with the staff of his local Alliance Center, he found he was able to read print at 8x magnification as well as work with speech output on a computer. Working in collaboration with the Commission for the Blind and Visually Handicapped, he was able to test several projection and large-screen devices. One system was rejected because the office modifications needed would be too great, but they succeeded with a screen enlargement program working with

the spreadsheet on a 37-inch monitor. The system was integrated into his workplace with the support of the employer, and Kendall returned to work with the aid of a job coach. He is currently working almost independently in all of his former duties, and any necessary job description modifications were negotiated by his employer with the civil service bureau.

Where an accommodation or auxiliary aid or service is needed to meet the requirements of the law and no other defense applies—such as the cost constituting an undue hardship—the organization or business must provide it. This means that the business is obligated to pay for the technology, although the technology user may not become the owner of the equipment. One example of such an accommodation is the assistive listening devices used at public meetings. There are many applications in employment where accommodations will be required or where what is needed is the appropriate assistive device to access an existing system.

The tax system

A number of provisions in the tax laws can translate directly into financial assistance for individuals or small businesses trying to acquire assistive technology. For example, the tax law gives important subsidies to small businesses in meeting their ADA compliance goals, whether in the employment or public accommodations spheres.

Among a number of pertinent Internal Revenue Code provisions, the Disabled Access Credit (IRC section 44) gives small businesses a tax credit for 50 percent of their first $10,000 of ADA compliance expenses per year, above the first $250 spent. This means that an eligible small firm (one with 30 or fewer full-time employees or with gross revenues under $1 million per year) that spent $10,250 to accommodate persons with disabilities could claim a tax credit of $5,000, dramatically reducing the real cost of its efforts.

Favorable tax laws can lower the net cost of technology for individuals, families, and businesses. In fact, with attention to the details of justification, documentation, and expenditure timing, much of the cost of assistive technology—and virtually all of the cost of items designed or modified for use in the context of a disability—can qualify for tax deductibility either as medical expenses, impairment-related work expenses, or architectural or transportation barrier-removal expenses. Consult with a tax specialist about what your specific rights may be. *Tax Options and Strategies for People with Disabilities* contains valuable information on this topic (see Part III, Books, for reference).

102

———

Computer
and Web
Resources
for People
with
Disabilities

State telecommunications equipment programs

Earlier in this chapter, we mentioned situations in which the nature of the equipment sought will determine the best source. No better example can be found than telecommunications access equipment programs that provide the devices needed by people with hearing, vocal communications, motion, visual, or other disabilities so that they may use the telephone network. Examples of the kind of equipment available include speaker phones, text telephones (TTYs), phones with large buttons, and amplified phones.

Funded by fees of a few cents a month, charged to all telephone users, these programs vary from state to state in what disabilities and what types of equipment they cover, in their use of means tests, and in other respects. So far, these programs have been largely limited to basic telephone access. Whether, as our definition of basic and universal telephone service evolves, these programs will be extended to technology that permits use of the expanded capabilities of the telephone system, only time and advocacy will tell.

The simplest way to find out if your state has such a program is to check a phone bill for a few cents charged for something that sounds relevant. In California, for example, it is called Communication Devices Funds for Deaf and Disabled. Contact your local phone company to inquire about its programs.

Grants

If you need a grant to purchase technology, you may wish to look to the private sector. In many communities, service, religious, or fraternal organizations (such as the Elks and the Lions) provide equipment to individuals under particular circumstances. Small, case-by-case grants of this sort are hard to categorize, but tend to hinge on the community ties of the applicant and do not necessarily reflect established giving patterns or long-term funding priorities.

> *Paula* was eight years old when her family, knowing that the school district would be difficult to convince, decided to try to put together a system at home to give Paula the chance to become proficient in its use and, ultimately, her own advocate. They knew it would be difficult to find financial resources, so they explored other avenues.
>
> Because of Paula's visual impairment, they approached their local Lion's Club, knowing of the club's interest in visual impairments. They discussed their needs with the Lion's Club, and they even borrowed the equipment they had identified long enough to demonstrate it to some key members. The members were captivated by Paula, and by her tech-

nology, and worked with the family to help them purchase the initial equipment Paula needed. As a thank-you, Paula demonstrated her new computer system to a packed crowd at the next Lion's Club meeting.

Related resources

Foundations and corporate grant programs exist that concern themselves with disability-related needs on an ongoing basis. A number of directories of foundations and corporate donors, such as the *Foundation Directory* by the Foundation Center, can be found in many public libraries.

A number of barriers must be addressed when pursuing foundation funding. Foundations are far more likely to give grants, and sometimes loans, to organizations than to individuals. When their work does extend to individual recipients, higher education, followed by medical care and the relief of destitution, are their predominant reasons for giving. Think of these restrictions as creating opportunities. For example, by working with a consumer-directed organization, donors can create an environment in which more than one person can use and benefit from a particular equipment setup. When access to technology rather than its possession will meet the need, this can represent a good strategy.

A network of libraries connected with the Foundation Center maintains collections of books, articles, and reports related to foundation and corporate giving. For information about the Foundation Center library nearest you, call the headquarters in New York at (800) 424-9836.

When applying for scholarships or other educational aid, remember to include assistive technology when you compile your needs. It is significant that the National Service Program, which is reminiscent of the old VISTA volunteer program, will provide educational funding to its participants and includes provisions for accommodating individuals with disabilities.

See the section on Books in Part III for a list of several directories of funding for individuals and organizations.

Loans

Commercial credit, the source of so much of the capital for business and personal purchases in our consumer society, has not been widely available for the purchase of assistive technology. For the many people who would eagerly accept the opportunity to pay for their own equipment, this situation has proved especially frustrating and harmful.

A few strategies will improve the odds in dealing with commercial lenders:

1. Research what loans are available through your local lending institution and be sure to apply for the right kind.

104

Computer
and Web
Resources
for People
with
Disabilities

2. Deficiencies in credit-history reports—sometimes arising from minterruption of earning power due to the onset of disability, or from other, nonwillful causes—must be pointed out and explained to senior officials of the lender.

3. When the acquisition of equipment is directly linked to income enhancement, as in the case of a job offer or a return to work, this fact should be emphasized.

Sometimes even these strategies may not make a difference, so a number of nonprofit loan programs have been established in the disability community. These include programs set up by consumer and membership groups, efforts conducted by major nonprofit organizations, and joint efforts between device vendors and banks. If a loan is a viable funding strategy for you, make it a point, through networking and inquiry, to investigate the existence and applicability of any loan programs of this sort. Some state rehabilitation agencies and state Tech Act projects have loan programs or loan guarantee programs. Check them out. Your state Tech Act program, local independent living center, or Alliance Center should be a good starting point for your inquiries.

Cutting costs

Naturally, every penny you can save on the cost of technology is important. For that reason, opportunities to cut costs should be sought. You will want to evaluate product features in relation to cost and to the willingness of the vendor to extend credit if needed or to cooperate by providing timely information and documentation to third-party funders.

Another important cost-saving strategy is the purchase of used equipment. Particularly in the computer field, fast-changing technology and user obsession to upgrade often result in the availability of good-quality used equipment at attractive prices. Several state Tech Act programs have established recycling programs.

The Tech Act

The Technology-Related Assistance for Individuals with Disabilities Act (discussed in Chapter 4 and now entitled The Assistive Technology Act) is the first major federal legislation addressing assistive technology devices and services as worthy of federal attention and as public policy deserving of federal support. Funded through the National Institute on Disability and Rehabilitation Research (NIDRR), the Tech Act programs now operating in every state under Title I of the act show diversity in program design and use of funds. States are granted some discretion under the Tech Act as to which of a number of programs they adopt.

As part of their information-dissemination activities, several state programs have compiled statewide funding resource directories that should provide you with valuable suggestions (see Part III for the location of the Tech Act program in your state).

Community organizations

As a source of resource information and expertise in navigating the bureaucratic maze, independent living centers can offer insight, guidance, and advocacy and technical assistance. Though not primarily direct funders, independent living centers are a vital link in the funding chain, particularly as a source of networking—which is so essential to learning what is out there and how it works. Local and national nonprofit organizations, such as the Alliance for Technology Access, can also be a source of valuable resource information. United Cerebral Palsy Associations, Inc. operates the Assistive Technology Funding and Systems Change Project which provides information to individuals with disabilities, family members, community-based organizations, and others. For project information contact them at (202) 776-0406. You can email them (atproject@ucpa.org) or visit their website (www.ucpa.org/html/innovative/atfsc/index.html).

Organizing Your Search for Funding

As important as the funding sources are, the imagination and energy you bring to your search is even more important. While recognizing that it may not be easy and that there are no simple answers, you must believe you can find a way to fund your technology dreams.

We recommend that you document your contacts and progress as you proceed. Your records will be very useful, especially if you are working with more than one potential funder.

Chapter 9

Selecting Your Equipment

Computer technology is constantly changing, which can create a little anxiety about deciding when is the best time to buy. There are a number of steps to take and ways to think about technology acquisitions that will make the selection process manageable.

Start by asking yourself very specific questions about what kinds of access to technology you need. What pieces of information are you missing that would help you make your decision, and how can you get the information you still need? In this chapter we will focus on the selection process.

Hands-on Consultations

When starting your search in earnest, there's no substitute for hands-on demonstration and testing. Hands-on consultations to explore technology will also be important further down the road and at any point when you need new ideas, strategies, or equipment. The process is most effective when it involves the people who will be a part of the implementation of any plan.

Julia was going to begin first grade. Her mother, grandmother, first-grade teacher, and special education teacher were almost as excited as Julia, yet concerned about how to make inclusion work for her. A Macintosh computer and a switch had been purchased for Julia, but she was not motivated to use the system. Julia's computer would be available to her in the classroom, as well as a Light Talker communication device (Prentke Romich Company).

Julia's mother and teachers visited the local Alliance Center to explore computer technology as it might relate to Julia and to see how technology had been used in other classrooms to enhance the inclusion of students with issues like Julia's. They came seeking ways to motivate Julia to use technology; they left with many ideas about how to customize the first-grade environment for her.

While visiting the Center, Julia and her team explored Kid Pix (Brøderbund), The Writing Center (The Learning Company), I Can Play

Too! (Mayer-Johnson), and Gateway Stories (Don Johnston, Inc.), all excellent software to help her begin to read and become motivated to use her switch. With these programs, she could electronically turn pages and leaf through whatever content her teachers entered to interest her. Using a Jelly Bean Switch (AbleNet)—a large, round, flat, colorful switch—and Ke:nx (Don Johnston, Inc.) as an interface, she could get her hands on the technology. She tested various switches and software programs, giving feedback to those on her team through her gestures and expressions.

Julia's teachers participated in the exploration and acquired ideas about how to use the software in class to promote Julia's participation. One challenge was to find ways to work on early math concepts; Kid Pix and the picture stamps it can produce turned out to be a fine medium. Another challenge was to find a way Julia could practice matching sight words. A talking scan was devised that read words using Ke:nx Create; when the computer voiced the word Julia wanted, she pressed the switch.

Julia's outlook improved because of a better switch, Ke:nx as an access tool, and exciting software. She was motivated to use her switch to show what she had learned, and the system gave her access to all other software programs, not just to those written specifically for a switch.

Photo courtesy of Carolina Computer Access Center

*Through a guided exploration process,
many people find their technology
solutions at a local Alliance Center.*

108

Computer
and Web
Resources
for People
with
Disabilities

The experience had given the teachers ideas about how to use software to enhance curriculum. Julia's mother was integrally involved, right from the initial contact, and the team came away with a plan. Julia's mother would buy the new switch, and the teachers would find more software. Julia left so excited about the switch that she didn't want to stop playing with it. Her chances for successful inclusion were certainly boosted.

When it is time for you to visit a place where you can test out your options, the best places to start are your closest Alliance Center (see Part III) and other resource centers in your community. Contact your state's Tech Act office (see Part III) to find the nearest centers. Other options include a variety of federally funded programs, such as Rehabilitation Engineering Centers. Schedule an appointment to try out some of the options you are considering. Find out if there is a cost associated with the visit, and be sure to allow yourself plenty of time for exploration.

Another place to have contact with products is at one of the many national and regional conferences that focus on assistive technology and feature exhibits where vendors display their products. Three national annual conferences on disability and technology are: the Assistive Technology Industry Association (ATIA) conference; Closing The Gap, held each October in Minneapolis; and the International Technology and Persons with Disabilities Conference, presented each March in Los Angeles by the Center on Disabilities at California State University, Northridge. These events provide an opportunity to compare different products (see Part III for a list of conferences).

Should these options not be feasible, vendors of the devices of interest to you might provide you with demonstrations or product loans. If equipment loans are not possible, try to find another option for testing the device—perhaps visiting a nearby customer of the vendor (for help with finding vendors, see Part III for a list of the key vendors in the field of assistive technology).

Retailers of conventional technologies may allow you to try out products in their stores. Depending on the nature of the device and the setup required, it may even be possible to have a retailer cooperate with you in trying out a bit of conventional technology with your loaned access devices.

Focusing on Software

Software falls roughly into two categories: open-ended and close-ended. Open-ended programs, such as word processors, have infinite numbers of uses and possibilities and allow the user to define the parameters. Close-ended programs, such as math drill programs, have a predefined purpose and set contents. Both types should be considered, depending on the tasks at hand.

Word processors, databases, spreadsheets, graphics or drawing programs, music programs, and address book or scheduling programs are all software programs that have an infinite number of uses. These kinds of open-ended software come with a basic framework or design, but you, the user, add the contents. You can remove, delete, or change the contents whenever you wish. There is a wide range of features to choose from among software programs of the same type. Word processors, for example, come with or without a dictionary or thesaurus and with or without speech, among many other features. Open-ended programs offer teachers greater options for integrating technology into existing curricula. If you want a program for writing letters or for managing your coin collection with a database, you want to be able to control the contents and would need an open-ended program.

With the more structured, close-ended programs, the contents have been defined. Many programs designed for young children fall into this category. Some programs—such as drill and practice programs for spelling, and math or writing programs—have some predetermined content, but allow the user to add to it within parameters set by the developer. If your goals include helping your children to improve their math skills, become more automatic, or have faster recall, a drill and practice program might be appropriate.

A few software programs fall in between these two types. For example, some programs help users learn the process of writing—from simple sentences to complex paragraphs—by modeling the writing process and providing the student with prompts along the way.

You need to decide where on the continuum your goals lie and select software accordingly. You will probably want a variety of software programs for your different goals.

With the above in mind, return to your prioritized list of goals. What patterns of tasks emerge? What kinds of software tools are commercially available to perform those tasks? For review, return to the list of software categories in Chapter 4. As you examine the list, within what software category or categories do your goals lie? Most adults will have goals that require, to varying degrees, access to word processing, database management, graphics, spreadsheets, and telecommunications. You might want to consider integrated programs, which include as part of a single package a word processor, a spreadsheet, a database, and sometimes drawing and presentation programs, email, and telecommunications components.

Once you have decided on the categories your interests fall under, there are a number of features to look for when selecting software that provide greater access for people with disabilities.

110

Computer
and Web
Resources
for People
with
Disabilities

One example is built-in access methods. Some programs are more friendly in their design to a variety of needs. Millie's Math House (Edmark) can accept input from a single switch, as well as from the standard keyboard and mouse. Part II contains a detailed description of these features and may help you decide whether some features would be important for you. For example, would you benefit from an uncluttered screen, where there is limited information and the choices are easy to identify and interpret? Would it help if certain things always appeared on the screen in the same place? Do you want to be able to control the difficulty level, speed, or other features of instructional programs for your student or child? Do you need the option of using the keyboard and key commands, rather than the mouse, to control computer functions?

Make sure the software you are considering will run on your computer with any needed additional devices and that it will comfortably address your goals.

A number of sources—most notably, technology magazines—offer comparisons of software features, and you can get excellent suggestions from them. (A list of publications is included in Part III.)

You can't always tell by reading a software package what features are included in the program. Before you purchase software, ask to try it. If that isn't possible, take a look at the instruction book (the documentation) that comes with the software. If it is readable and easily understood, you have a better chance of being able to load your software, learn what it will and won't do, and find out how to troubleshoot problems on your own. Some manuals are available on tape for users who would benefit from listening, rather than reading, the instructions. Nothing is more frustrating than new software that promises to write, draw, paint, and do spreadsheets, databases, and slide shows—but you can't figure out how to use it.

Compatibility issues

Programs are written to run on specific types of computer systems. Be sure the software you are considering will run on the computer and other devices you are thinking of getting or already have. Many companies are reluctant to take back software after it has been purchased and the box has been opened. If you have a PC/Windows computer and the software box says Macintosh version, you have a problem. Very often a program will come in a variety of versions to run on these and other systems, but you must be sure you buy the right version. Sometimes, if the program comes on a CD, it will be compatible with both PC and Macintosh computers, but be sure to read the label carefully to know for sure.

You can learn many things from reading software boxes and catalogs. The box will often tell you what the system requirements are—how much memory you need to run the program and what type of monitor and operating system you need—as well as the age range of the audience for which the program is intended. Look for other small words, such as disk size. If you have only a 3.5-inch disk drive, for example, make sure the package holds 3.5-inch disks, not compact disks. Ask a salesperson for assistance.

Considering Hardware

When it comes to computers, memory size, storage capacity, speed, and the quality of sounds and images are constantly being improved. An individual who spent $3,000 a number of years ago to acquire an Apple II with 64 K of memory, a 5.25-inch disk drive, and a monitor that put green text on the screen, today owns a notebook-size computer with more than 1,000 times the memory, 10,000 times the storage space on a hard disk drive, and a color monitor, all weighing one-tenth of the original computer and costing less!

Given the one dependable constant that everything changes, here are five guidelines to consider in your planning process:

1. Buy the most memory (RAM) and the largest hard disk you can afford.

2. Look for the greatest expansion capability so you have the option of adding memory and peripheral devices later on.

3. Expect to upgrade, at least partially, either hardware or software in two to four years.

4. Don't delay entering the world of technology because something more powerful may be available six months from now—something more powerful is usually always on the horizon.

5. Understand that pushing the limits of your potential with assistive technology will be rewarding and that you may outgrow your first system as you attain your initial goals and set new ones.

Above all, it is important to get a system that works best for you. The fact that something new is on the market does not necessarily mean that you need to purchase it. Your decisions need to be based on whether the system you are considering or are already using is working well for you and will continue to meet your needs. In determining your memory (RAM) and storage capacity needs, look at your list of software prospects. How much RAM does the box say they require? If you are thinking of running more than one program simultaneously—for example, having your word processor and spreadsheet program open at the same time so you can transport figures from one to the other—you will need enough RAM for both, so plan accordingly. Likewise, be generous with hard disk storage space, because pro-

Photo courtesy of Arkenstone, Inc.

Mickey Quenzer, Technical Support Specialist at Arkenstone, uses a braille display, notetaker, and scanner to read and write business correspondence.

grams are requiring more and more storage all the time, especially those with sophisticated graphics and sound.

Jose, a man in his mid-20s, sustained a severe head injury in an accident that left him with memory, attention, planning, and organizing problems. Jose's first priority was to get a computer equipped with software that would help him keep track of appointments, addresses, and phone numbers. His second priority was to have a system that would enable him to check the spelling of the letters and other communication he wanted to write, since he had difficulty remembering how to spell. His third goal was to start drawing again, since he had designed and built houses before his accident. He also wanted to be able to go from his computer directly to a telephone and to a dictionary, encyclopedia, the Internet, and other sources of information.

Fortunately, Jose had an opportunity to test various options and soon realized that his immediate need was for a computer with a modem, color monitor, and small printer. An important decision he made was to spend an extra $300 to double his hard disk space, since graphics take a lot of storage space. Jose also learned that with a flatbed scanner he could scan in drawings and print information that had already been created. He knew that at some point in his future it would be beneficial to add this to his computer system. Other future needs he identified were a more sophisticated drawing and graphing program and a higher-quality printer. His important first decision, however, was to select a computer system that would enable him to add components in the future, with enough memory for the drawings he wanted to do, and equipped with software that would give him the support he needed to write, communicate, and create.

The important tools of access

Once you clarify the types of access you need to conventional technology, your choice of computer system will become clearer.

Thousands of devices on the market fall under the umbrella of assistive or adaptive devices, ranging from tiny keyboards to speech-input or voice-activated computer systems. Take another look at the list of common assistive technologies on pages 54 and 55. Look up in Part II the ones you think may be relevant to you. Which categories of assistive devices may provide access to the conventional types of software and hardware you need to meet your goals?

Making Choices

It's time to focus on making some preliminary choices so you know what products to investigate in depth. You may want to refer to the charts at the beginning of Part II, which pose a series of questions that provide one way to think about access. The charts will guide you to descriptions of products you may then choose to explore.

First, ask yourself: *what is it I really need assistive technology for?* Consider your strengths and weaknesses. Think about all of the component parts of a conventional computer system. Think about how you might interact with them. What are your needs? Then, consider again the components of input, processing, and output.

In terms of input, do you need

- an alternative to a regular keyboard?
- a smaller, larger, or changeable keyboard?
- an alternative to using a mouse?
- a machine that talks?
- a hands-free operating mode?
- a way to operate the system by voice?

114

Computer
and Web
Resources
for People
with
Disabilities

In terms of processing, do you need

- to use as few keystrokes as possible?

- to increase the rate at which you can input information?

- help with skills development, either writing or reading?

- to find a way around some standard computer features—such as repeating keys or commands that require more than one key to be pressed simultaneously?

In terms of output, do you need

- braille output?

- large-print output?

- auditory output?

- a larger monitor?

Make a list of all the things that would help you use a computer system, and review it with your supporters. Figure out which needs are the most critical and start there. Look at the product description pages in Part II (organized by input, processing, and output) for products that address the needs you have identified. The product descriptions include information on what kinds of things people use the product for and some of the features available. If you are looking for a feature that is not listed, it does not necessarily mean there aren't products with that feature. Ask the vendor. It could be that the feature is available or will be soon.

Getting to specifics

Once you have identified the general technologies of interest to you, you can begin to research specific products. Use your team of supporters as a source for information. Refer to Part III for the names and phone numbers of product vendors, as well as their fax numbers, email addresses, and website addresses. Contact them and have them send you their brochures. Take that information to your team members to review, and compile a new list of questions based on what you now know. As you research, ask yourself:

- Which products are most likely to help you do what you want to do?

- What features are most important?

Once you have located the products you are interested in and located the vendors in Part III or in other resource guides, ask the vendors about compatibility and device requirements. Here are a few good questions to ask vendors:

- On which computer system does your product operate?

- What version of the operating system does it require?

- How much memory (RAM) is needed?

- Are there specific monitor requirements?

- Does the device need a computer card that provides the interface between the computer and the device? Does the computer I am considering (or own) have the capacity for such an interface card?

- Does the device need an external port on the computer to which it would connect by a cable? If so, what kind of port does it require?

- Are all of the components I am considering compatible? For example, will the screen reader I am considering work with the speech synthesizer I have in mind?

- What are the key features of the product?

- How is this product different from other similar products on the market?

- Do you have a distributor in my area, or do you handle your own distribution? (Keep in mind that for the most part, assistive technology vendors do business through the mail or via the Internet rather than through retail stores.)

Conventional Hardware Selection with an Eye on Access

Many of the questions we posed earlier for vendors of assistive technologies are also relevant for vendors of conventional technologies. Ask the dealer from whom you are planning to purchase your computer whether the company plans to continue the particular model or brand you are considering. The answer to this question might be very important in deciding what to purchase, including software. The general rule is that you can put old software in new machines most of the time, but you usually can't put new software in old machines. Ask the dealer about the version of the operating system the machine uses, and make sure that the software you want will run under this system. Be sure to check with your support people to confirm that all of the hardware and software you are considering, both conventional and assistive, will operate together.

Returning again to your prioritized list of goals, what types of hardware considerations emerge? One thing to consider if you are buying a machine for home use is whether you will want to have equipment that is compati-

116

Computer
and Web
Resources
for People
with
Disabilities

ble with what you use at school or at work. In many families, adults are using PCs at work, children are using Apple Macintosh computers at school, and families are looking for a machine that bridges the gap between school, home, and work. Many manufacturers are making versions of their software for the two major operating systems, Windows and Macintosh.

The field is rapidly moving toward a single standard. New equipment is regularly coming onto the market that is blending the differences between the different computer types. However, most computers still require their own software versions and, there is usually a time gap between the onset of new computer models and the availability of compatible assistive devices.

Reviewing your prioritized list of needs will also help you think about conventional equipment purchases. Here are some things to consider that can increase the usability of your equipment:

Hard disk drives. A hard disk is a good way to store programs and files to eliminate the need to constantly manipulate individual disks. Given the size of most computer programs, a hard disk is an essential part of any computer system, and most people purchase the largest capacity hard disk drive they can afford. As competition increases, most computers will have large amounts of preinstalled software on the hard disk drive. Preloaded software is a good value to the user and should provide you with many useful applications.

Other disk drives. Three other popular types of disk drives—3.5-inch drives, SuperDrives, and CD drives—will be useful when you want to add to or use new software with your system or transfer material out of your computer. A 3.5-inch disk holds 1.4 megabytes of information, SuperDrive disks can hold about 10 times that much, and CDs (compact disks) contain even more information. Nearly all software programs and electronic reference materials are now being put out on CDs. This format provides easy access to encyclopedias, atlases, dictionaries, and other major reference works. The capacity of each disk is enormous and can accommodate graphics, sounds, and video, which are being incorporated into many interesting and highly motivating programs. Because so much software is now on CD, your computer should have a CD drive and either a 3.5-inch drive or Super-Drive depending on the sizes and types of work you want to export from your computer to take to another location.

There are other types of drives you may also want to consider: DVD drives allow you to view commercial movies on your computer, Zip drives allow you to back up your hard disk drive with a minimum of effort, and removable hard disk drives allow you insert different drives according to your needs or to take all your programs and information to another location.

Printers. You can eliminate the need to continually handle paper by using a printer with a paper cassette. Also, some printers—such as those made by Lexmark—come with software that uses speech output to alert you to paper jams, expended print cartridges, job completion, etc.

Monitors. Large-screen monitors are commonly available. Standard screens today are 14 to 15 inches. However, screens can range up to 21 inches, making it possible to view a full page or two pages side by side or to use large text and graphics.

On/off switches. The placement of the on/off switch might seem a trivial matter, but if you have limited mobility, you may want the switch obvious and accessible. With young children or infants around, you may want the switch out of sight. Some computers have separate switches for the computer and the monitor, although many machines—such as portables and laptops—have monitors that automatically come on when the computer is turned on. You can also connect the system to a power strip and turn all the connected devices on with a single motion. Persons who will be using the computer independently or persons with arthritis or mobility difficulties might want to select a computer and monitor with on/off switches on the front or top. Most new computers turn themselves off automatically—or go into "sleep" mode—when not used for some predetermined amount of time and are turned back on by simply touching a key.

Operating system software. Another important consideration for hardware is the access features that are part of the operating system software, often called *utilities.* One such utility, CloseView (Apple Computer, Inc.), enlarges all the images on a Macintosh screen and lets you change from black characters on a white background to white on black. Windows 2000 contains an on-screen keyboard utility that the user can engage if desired.

Other utilities that are included in Windows and Macintosh operating systems and that are available for older Windows and MS-DOS systems allow you to adjust your computer in various ways. For example, you can delay the key-repeat function or turn it off completely. A key-latching utility will notify the computer that keys will be struck sequentially rather than simultaneously, a useful feature for people with arthritis, muscular dystrophy, poor coordination, or weak hands who aren't able to use the three fingers required by many software programs to execute a command. Another utility lets someone who has difficulty using a mouse to control the cursor on the screen use the keyboard instead. You can replace audio cues with visual ones, like a flashing menu bar or other signal. Another utility slows down the reaction of the keys so that when a key is pressed, it won't be entered as

118

———

Computer
and Web
Resources
for People
with
Disabilities

data unless it is pressed for a certain length of time. If a key is pressed twice quickly, you can eliminate the entry of the unwanted keystroke. Many new computers that come with preinstalled software may contain these helpful utilities, but you may have to read the owner's manual or contact customer support in order to install or partially install the utilities of interest to you (see Keyboard Additions and Access Utilities in Part II for more).

A few final questions to ask yourself include the following:

- According to your priorities, what hardware must you have to get started?

- Can you rank these individual items according to their priority?

- How are you doing in terms of your budget? Do you need to acquire your system in stages and, if so, do you have a plan for how that can work?

Personalizing a system of technology and access that is right for you and your goals can be complex. Identifying your human resources and gathering information should simplify the selection process. You need to take your place among them as an expert in your own right and as the one who drives the process of technology access. After all, who knows better about your circumstances and ability than you? When you engage in dialogue about technology products and disability, you already know more about the important considerations than you may realize.

Tips on Buying Your Equipment

Your range of options for software, hardware, and access technology is probably broad, perhaps even overwhelming, but now you and your support team can begin to make informed choices and narrow your options to specific components according to your priorities. As you focus on specifics, you can further test your plans by questioning and examining the components in greater detail.

Finalizing Your Purchase Decisions

After having reviewed vendors' catalogs and product information, you are ready to ask the next round of questions—questions related to previewing products and trial periods, technical support, and upgrade policies. You will also want to consider accessories and the possibility of purchasing used equipment.

Previewing products

Businesses may be willing to place their products with you for a short period of time on either a rental or short-term loan basis. You may be expected to pay for shipping or to provide the supplier with product information related to your use. These are some of the questions to ask vendors:

- How do the various types of these products differ?

- With what features am I most concerned?

- What are my options for previewing this product to learn more about it?

- Is it possible to obtain a short-term rental or loan of your product so that I can explore it further before deciding if it is right for me?

- If not, is there some other way I can try out the equipment?

The technology industry is very competitive, so expect to find sources willing to respond to your questions positively. Some vendors will fall short

120

Computer
and Web
Resources
for People
with
Disabilities

of actually placing the device in your possession, but a good supplier should be able to direct you to a setting where you can explore your questions in greater detail, such as device loan libraries, ATA Centers, or other resource centers. Many software suppliers offer demonstration or preview copies of their products (which often only work for a short period of time or perform all essential functions but won't let you print or save your work).

Technical support

For most users, technical assistance is crucial. Product manuals offer a great deal of information, but you will occasionally encounter a difficulty or want to perform a task you cannot find described in the manual. Fortunately, most software and hardware companies have technical support people on staff who work every day to make sure customers are getting the most from their purchase. Vendors in the technology field offer support ranging from little to phenomenal. It is important to know what to expect in terms of service after the sale. There are a number of important questions to ask vendors:

- What kind of technical assistance is available to users of your product or service?

- What kind of support do you offer after the sale?

- Do you offer telephone support—a toll-free or other number a user can call during regular business hours?

- Is there a charge for technical assistance?

- Do you have a product newsletter?

- What are your policies on refunds, exchanges, repairs, and replacements?

- Is training needed to use the product and is it available?

Vendors that provide a full range of support may charge a little more for their products. You may encounter a situation in which one vendor offers a better price, while another provides better service. Ongoing vendor support can be crucial, and we recommend dealing with vendors that provide good support even if they charge more than a competitor that offers little or no support.

Upgrade policies

Another important question to ask vendors is:

- How do you handle upgrades of your product for users of earlier versions?

Most developers periodically release improved versions of their technology, and you will want to take advantage of the advances. It's important to know what costs and ordering procedures are involved when upgrades are released. Registered users of a product or service will often be able to receive upgrades with little effort or cost. However, dramatically improved software products may require an upgrade fee of $50 to $100 or more.

Accessories

Be sure to examine accessories—such as blank diskettes, disk storage boxes, power strips, spare batteries, battery chargers, security devices, an additional telephone jack, and carrying cases—and include those you want in your planning and budget. You will find accessories in computer stores, department stores, catalogs, and magazines.

The table or desk you will use is also an important consideration. You don't need a fancy computer desk, but the ability to adjust the height, for example, might be important to you. Since computer use can occupy much of your time on a daily basis, human factors and ergonomics and positioning of furniture are important considerations and are discussed in more detail later in this chapter.

You will also want to explore products that can protect your system from a variety of ills. Power strips, for example, give you the flexibility to move the on/off switch to a location that improves access. Surge protectors, often part of a standard power strip, can eliminate the threat of surges or spikes in the flow of the electrical current to your equipment, such as those that can occur during thunderstorms and brownouts. You may want to contact your insurance agent to determine whether your homeowner's or renter's policy will cover the computer. If your general insurance does not cover computer equipment, check the phone book for companies that specialize in insuring personal computer equipment. Also, if you are purchasing a laptop or portable computer, make sure your insurance carrier will cover it in all situations. We encourage you to consider this protection.

Used equipment

Should you consider used equipment? The answer to this question depends on your circumstances. If a warranty and support are important to you, you may not want to buy from an individual but might consider a used-computer store. As with all manufactured goods, every once in a while you find a lemon—which is why computer warranties are important. Some manufacturers offer a warranty on new computers. It is commonly believed, however, that if you are going to have electronic difficulties, you will probably have them within the first three months. Most stores that sell used equip-

122

Computer
and Web
Resources
for People
with
Disabilities

ment will include warranties. Make sure you are getting the warranty protection and level of support you require.

If you are buying a used computer from an individual, plug it in and make sure it is working properly before you close the deal. Try to find out why the owner is selling. Good news—the seller is upgrading to a faster system. Bad news—a cup of coffee was accidentally dumped on the keyboard, and it's never been the same since.

If you are not sure whether the computer will work for you and think there is a possibility you will return it, don't buy used equipment, or make sure you can return it. If you have done your homework, have checked prices in your local stores or discount catalogs, and hear about a used computer for sale that is very close to what you have in mind, it might be a real cost saver for you. Computers are electronic rather than mechanical devices and usually become outdated before they wear out. If the circuitry goes bad—which it can, particularly when not protected with a surge protector or if it gets wet or dirty—it can be replaced at a cost (with the warning that you might lose information you have stored on your hard drive).

Approach buying a used computer in much the same way you would approach buying a used car. If it all works except for the transmission, price a new transmission and determine if it is still a good deal. If parts of the computer system need to be replaced, find out what they will cost before you make your decision.

Photo courtesy of Edmark Corporation

*Millie's Math House, a fun and educational learning program,
comes from a company that incorporates access into their
software programs. (Edmark Corporation)*

Computer user groups are often a good source for used equipment because their members tend to upgrade frequently. You can find ads for used equipment in the back of many computer magazines. Stores selling used computer equipment can often be found in the yellow pages of your phone directory.

If you decide to buy a used system, use the following checklist of standard components to make sure you have everything you will need in terms of conventional equipment. The checklist will also be handy if you are inheriting a system from someone else.

- CPU or central processing unit (the main computer box)

- CPU power cord

- Disk drives (may be internal or external to the CPU)

- Modem (may be internal or external to the CPU)

- Monitor (in some systems, the monitor and CPU are one unit)

- Monitor cable (connects monitor to the CPU)

- Monitor power cord (this cord may be permanently attached to the monitor)

- Keyboard

- Keyboard cable (connects the keyboard to the CPU)

- Mouse (most computers come with a mouse)

- Printer

- Printer cable (connects the printer to the CPU)

- Printer cartridge, toner, ink, or ribbon

- Printer power cord

- Manuals for CPU, monitor, and printer

When you have gathered enough information to satisfy all of your questions, you are finally ready to purchase. Do it! Order what you need from the sources you have identified as appropriate for you.

Setting Up Your Equipment

When you get all the components together and are ready to set up your system, consider the following suggestions.

Computer
and Web
Resources
for People
with
Disabilities

First things first

Fill out the warranty and/or registration cards and send them in. These register you as a customer and set a purchase date. Most warranties cover products for one year from the date of purchase. Registering your product may put you on the manufacturer's mailing list to receive information regarding updates or recalls. Some warranty cards register you for technical support services. Keep a copy of the cards in case you encounter problems later. It's also a good idea to keep the original packaging in case you need to return products or have them serviced.

Virtually every piece of equipment and the more-expensive software programs contain serial numbers. Record your serial numbers and store them in a safe place. Also, keep a copy posted near your computer in case you need to contact technical support about a particular product.

Read the installation information

Read the manual, especially if it says "Read Me First" in large red letters. If you have some knowledge of computers, you may want to go to the "quick start" portion of the manual to get your basic computer system up and running. Have the manual available in case you run into something you don't understand or have questions during the setup. If you are a beginner, do yourself a favor and read through the manual step-by-step. Despite reputations to the contrary, most manuals are now fairly easy to follow, jargon-free, and do help people start using their equipment quickly.

Read the manuals for your assistive devices thoroughly. You will be better off spending a little more time making sure everything is set up correctly, and it could save having to go back and troubleshoot later.

Hook up your equipment

The manuals that came with your computer and assistive devices will have diagrams that show how to hook up everything. Many systems have matching icons on the cables and hardware to make connections easier. Most equipment cables now have connectors that can be tightened by hand, although some require an ordinary screwdriver.

Get the computer running with its basic component parts first. Once that system works, add your assistive technology pieces one at a time. This will help you in troubleshooting a problem should there be one.

Environmental considerations

A few environmental considerations should be kept in mind as you establish a home for your equipment. Some environments are unfriendly to computers, particularly those that are too hot or cold, too dusty, or have the potential to be moist. Placement too close to a window will not only create temperature-control problems, but might interfere with the visibility of the monitor because of glare.

A computer system needs air to stay cool, and you will need space to connect cables easily. Make sure there is plenty of space for the CPU; do not push it against a wall or tightly enclose it. Email and Internet access will require you to locate your equipment near a telephone outlet or to use a long telephone cord extension. Here are other general cautions to consider when you are working with computers and assistive devices:

- Keep your system away from moisture—such as drinks and high humidity—that can affect the tiny circuits of the computer. Moisture guards are thin, plastic keyboard covers that provide extra protection if necessary (for more information on moisture guards, see Keyboard Additions in Part II).

- Magnetic fields create problems. Keep all magnets away from the computer. Some common sources of magnetic fields are speakers, telephones, radios, and paper clips that have become magnetized by a paper clip dispenser.

- Static electricity may be annoying to you, but it is dangerous for your computer. If you have problems with static electricity, purchase a grounding strip, which is available in most hardware stores and allows static electricity to be harmlessly eliminated.

- Smoke can be damaging to the disk drives and circuits in the computer.

- To avoid damage to any of the components, turn your computer off before hooking up or unhooking any devices.

- Store individual disks with caution. Magnetic fields can erase disk information. Storing disks in a box, away from extreme temperatures, will help ensure their safety. Don't bend diskettes or place heavy objects on them. The metal clip on 3.5-inch disks can become bent or jammed if not handled carefully. You can buy inexpensive disk holders in any computer store.

Positioning the elements of your system

The science of ergonomics focuses on the effects of computer use on the human body.

It is important to take preventative measures to avoid problems down

Computer
and Web
Resources
for People
with
Disabilities

the road. For example, take frequent breaks from the computer. It's good for the body, eyes, and mind.

Make your computer setup as comfortable as possible. Easy access and comfort are the top priorities. The table surface on which you put the computer should be low enough so that when you sit you are looking down slightly at the monitor. If you are using a standard keyboard and mouse, your hands should rest comfortably on the desk and keyboard. Wrist rests and arm supports can help make your computing environment more healthful and comfortable (see Arm Supports in Part II for more information).

If the computer must accommodate several different users or must be moved around from home, school, and work, use tables with adjustable height and tables on wheels. For very young users, consider a table close to the ground, where children can stand to work on the computer or sit on small chairs. Office furniture stores and catalogs are sources for these types of tables and other computer furniture. Furniture does not have to be expensive, but it is something you need to think about carefully. Computers and assistive devices can take a fair amount of space on a tabletop or desk.

Monitors can be placed on top of or alongside the CPU. We have even seen monitors placed on the floor to provide access to young children. If more than one person or someone with a physical disability will be using the computer, consider a floating monitor arm. This is a mechanical arm that connects to a table and allows the monitor to move up, down, in, and out with ease, thus allowing people to change positions during the day and move the monitor into a position for best access (see Monitor Additions in Part II for more information on mounting devices).

Keyboard placement is also flexible; place the keyboard and other input devices where they can be used comfortably.

Be creative. It is not necessary to set up your computer to look like an ad in the Sunday paper. Some—but not all—CPUs can be turned on their sides. You can put the CPU on the floor or another place to provide easier access to the disk drive. Keyboards can be mounted on trays, angled, or padded to fit the user.

Positioning can be a complex issue for some people. You may choose to consult with an occupational or physical therapist who could help determine the best arrangement for you. If you need a customized setup—such as a way to mount a laptop computer on a wheelchair and use the chair's battery to run the computer—you might want to consult with an engineer or someone with the expertise to work with you. Many things can be fabricated to meet your needs. One resource for this type of expertise is the federally funded Rehabilitation Engineering Centers. Contact RESNA at (703) 524-6686 or on the Internet at www.resna.org for more information on these centers.

Powering up

Rather than plugging your computer directly into the wall, we recommend using a power strip, which comes in many styles and prices. Some have filters, and some provide protection against power surges or significant current fluctuations. Unless you have a special requirement or a power problem in your area, a simple power strip with a surge protector should meet your needs inexpensively.

If you cannot activate the small toggle on the power strip, there are a number of alternative ways to get electricity to the power strip. There are power modules that can be activated by a switch and mounted anywhere. A tread switch is an on/off switch that can be activated by rolling a wheelchair across it. Many solutions can be individualized to meet your needs.

If, when you press the switch on the power strip, it whirs and beeps and you get a DOS prompt, a Windows menu, or a "happy Mac" icon, you may want to let out a cheer. You have successfully powered up!

Troubleshooting

If, however, you press the switch and nothing happens, you need to investigate or troubleshoot the problem. Your problem could be something simple such as a loose plug or cable, or something technical such as a conflict among special utility programs within your system. If you suspect the latter to be the case, it's time to make some calls. Before you call, however, always check all your cable connections!

If you bought the equipment at a local computer store, call there first. You can call the vendor of your assistive technology. You can also try the toll-free support number that came with your computer. All major companies have support staff who answer questions and troubleshoot problems. But don't expect them to know anything about your assistive technology. When making these calls, have the model numbers of your equipment, the version of the operating system you are running, and, if possible, your computer turned on and near the telephone so you can test the suggestions offered. If you can't resolve the problem, call on your support team. Remember, they are there to help.

Once you get started, we recommend you use your computer as much as possible during the warranty period. If anything is going to go wrong with the machinery, it will most likely happen during this period. You will become comfortable with your new tools more quickly if you spend time with them right from the beginning.

128

———

Computer
and Web
Resources
for People
with
Disabilities

Alternative resources

What if you cannot physically handle your computer or if you feel uncomfortable setting it up and connecting the assistive devices? Some computer stores offer to set up the computer in your home for a nominal fee if you purchased the machine from them. If you bought your computer by mail order, however, you will need to find another source of help. Computer clubs and user groups can be excellent resources, as they are filled with people who enjoy setting up computer systems and may be happy to show off their skills. For the most part they will know conventional technology, but may or may not be able to help you figure out the assistive technology. You might contact the assistive technology vendor about setup support. The vendor may have other customers who would be interested in providing some assistance to you.

Once you have your system up and running, it's time to develop proficiency with your technology.

Chapter 11

As You Become More Expert...

Throughout this book we have been asking, "What are your dreams?" Now it's time to make those cables, boxes, chips, and disks fulfill them. With your first steps, aim for projects that will give you a lot of positive reinforcement and success.

Your supporters have had an important role to play in helping you get up and running. You may want to bring in some new players to help you develop skills and strategies for using your assistive devices, learning new software programs, and getting connected to the vast world of online and Internet services.

Learning and training

The disks are spinning, the lights are blinking, the beeps are beeping, and now you need to make something productive happen. What you need to learn can be divided into four categories: 1) the computer, 2) the conventional software, 3) the adaptive software and hardware, and 4) online information resources or the Internet. You only need to know as much as it takes to run them appropriately; you don't have to know how to build or program a computer. It is easy to get overwhelmed by all there is to learn. Keep your focus clear and start with the minimum. Operate, at least initially, on a need-to-know basis, learning what you need when you need it.

Learning on your own

Personal computing is getting more intuitive all the time. You can learn a great deal on your own or with the help of a friend or two.

Begin by going through what you received with the computer. Many computer companies include good step-by-step tutorials on disk, which cover using the mouse, opening and closing files, saving data, printing, and other basic skills.

When it comes to learning software, do not underestimate your ability to train yourself. Many technology users are self-trained and enjoyed every minute of the process. Everything you buy will come with instructions, and many software programs have on-disk tutorials. If you purchased a com-

130

Computer
and Web
Resources
for People
with
Disabilities

puter with some software already installed, get to know those programs first. There is nothing like learning to use the mouse with a few hundred games of solitaire. Install one program at a time, learn how to use it, then move to the next program on your priority list. This way, installing your software doesn't become a huge tedious task, and as your confidence builds, you will look forward to experimenting with the next piece of software.

A number of training videotapes and audiotapes with disk activities for popular software titles are available, as is a growing assortment of introductory books on the major computer systems. All are available in local book and computer stores, as well as through Internet booksellers. Check with your sources for their favorite titles.

Whenever you are experimenting or troubleshooting a problem, do one thing at a time and keep track of what you did. Make one change at a time, especially when you are testing assistive devices. If you make a mistake, it will be easier to fix—and if you get it right, you'll be able to do it again.

Don't be afraid to try things. Many new computer users believe they can bring about disaster by pressing the wrong key or making the wrong choice at the wrong time. You really can't blow up a computer by pressing the wrong key. Disasters can be avoided fairly easily. Here are a few suggestions to help eliminate both the fears and the disasters:

Save your work. Learn how to save your work before you learn how to do anything else. Get in the habit of saving your work on a hard disk or on a diskette. If the project you are working on is important, save it! Save often. Save compulsively. In the case of a power failure or a system error, you will lose anything you haven't saved to disk. A system error—also known as a crash—happens to everyone at one time or another. A crash indicates that there was a temporary problem with your operating system. The treatment for a crash is to turn off your computer and restart—or reboot—your computer. If the problem persists, seek advice.

Back up your work. Keep copies of your work and your applications (your software programs) on disks, and store them in a safe place. Making a copy of your data can save you a great deal of time and frustration if anything happens to the hard disk or an individual disk.

Experiment. Once you are in a program and your work is saved, look around. Make choices, push buttons, pull down the menus. You usually can't do much harm if you have saved your data. And you can always reload the program if something really goes wrong.

Learning more about conventional technologies

There are times and situations that call for a more structured approach to learning computing. Everyone has his or her own learning style, and awareness of your own style should guide you in selecting a teaching method or instructor to meet your needs. Private teachers can tailor their approach to match your style and preferred pace. Check your community resources and contacts for referrals.

Should you want to explore them, quite a few options for learning how to use conventional technologies exist. Community colleges, computer user groups, adult education programs of local school districts, computer stores, and even copying service centers offer beginning, intermediate, and advanced classes. Classes usually focus on a particular type of computer or on a particular software application, such as Microsoft Word, a word processing program, and Excel (also from Microsoft), a spreadsheet program. Many classes are available to help you get started on the Internet or to learn how to design Web pages. Enrollment fees are usually modest.

Question the suppliers of training as you would vendors of equipment and software. Ask if you can preview sessions or visit the location, and learn what you can about follow-up or ongoing support. Accessibility of the training site and the equipment might be concerns for you. If you need assistive devices to access their computer systems, you will probably need to bring your own to participate in the class. Be aware that the instructor will be teaching the class how to use a keyboard and a mouse and will probably know little about how to assist you with your adaptive devices.

Learning more about assistive technologies

Finding training in how to use assistive technologies is more complex. As we mentioned in the budgeting discussion, it is important in your planning to set money aside for training. When comparing prices, ask vendors if they provide training. This may explain why one vendor charges more money than a competitor. Factor in what it would take to get training elsewhere if it's not included. Vendors that don't offer training may be able to point you toward an individual or organization that has purchased the same device in your area. Many people who have mastered a device themselves are happy to share their expertise. Private tutors and consultants can help people learn how to use adaptive equipment.

Today only a few community colleges and other community-based programs offer classes using assistive technology. Some community colleges—in California, for example—do have such courses and provide accessible computer labs. However, you may need to enroll as a student in order to take advantage of community college classes.

If your community does not offer these opportunities, ask for them. Talk to people who offer educational programs about what it would take to make the existing program accessible and how you can assist them in mak-

132

Computer
and Web
Resources
for People
with
Disabilities

ing it work. The ultimate goal should be not to set up separate learning environments, but to make existing ones accessible.

Professional development

Taking advantage of continuing education opportunities in your community can be one of the most beneficial moves you will make to learn new skills and to network with others in your community. Many universities and teachers' colleges offer courses in the use of technology for students with disabilities. In some cases, these courses are required for degree candidates in special education. University extension programs and community-based organizations also offer opportunities for teachers to learn about assistive technology and to receive continuing education units (CEUs) in the process.

Computer conferences are conducted around the country. In addition to opportunities to see and test new products, they often offer training sessions on strategies for using products, especially in classroom and clinical settings (see Part III for a list of conferences).

Pushing the Limits of Technology

Technology does not replace humans; it challenges them to do better. Its effectiveness depends solely on how it is used. In a classroom, technology is not the teacher. But, when used creatively by a teacher, it can transform a mediocre lesson into an exciting, attention-grabbing learning experience.

Innovations in education

When used in conjunction with cooperative learning strategies, technology can be a powerful tool to promote the inclusion of students with disabilities in regular education classrooms.

Mrs. Rodriguez's sixth-grade social studies class was studying ancient Egypt. In her room were 11-year-olds of every description, some excited about exploring the wonders of the ancient world, and others quite reluctant, because they had experienced failure so often. Mrs. Rodriguez, using the principles of cooperative learning, had organized her class into heterogeneous learning groups of four students each.

Each group worked as a unit in the school library, exploring one aspect of ancient Egypt using books and the multimedia information available on CD-ROM. Mrs. Rodriguez, working with a local technology resource center and another halfway across the country via the Internet, had accumulated many scanned images—called clip art—with an Egyptian theme: pharaohs, a sphinx, pottery, and pyramids, all available in electronic form.

Fresh from their library experience, each group worked as a team to produce a presentation for the class. Groups took turns planning, typing, organizing synthesized-speech examples, and choosing clipart illustrations and sound clips. Everyone, regardless of ability level, contributed, and everyone's imagination worked overtime. Finally, the day came for the groups to demonstrate their collaborative efforts. They projected the images on a large screen using a computer specially connected to an overhead projector projection plate and amplified the sound through a speaker. Every student will remember something about ancient Egypt because everyone contributed.

Children often discover unanticipated ways to use technology. We can learn a great deal from them.

Kendra is 11 years old and in a regular fifth-grade class. She has cerebral palsy and operates the computer using just one finger with the help of Sticky Keys and Mouse Keys (for information on these programs, see Keyboard Additions in Part II). She is very creative and loves to add graphics to her work. She also likes to paint and color with her friends. Using Kid Pix and Kid Pix Companion (Brøderbund), she has been able to paint and create for hours on end.

Kendra learned the names of the continents and their locations using these tools. Starting with a map of the world from Kid Art (Brøderbund), she listed the names of the continents around the perimeter of the screen. Using the Moving Truck tool, she selected the name of the continent and "drove" it to the proper location on the map. She colored the continents to distinguish them, then labeled them. She repeated this process until she had the names of all the continents down. Her peers had to use paper and pencils and only had a couple sheets of paper to practice on. Because she was using the computer, Kendra was able to play and learn until she had mastered the subject. She thoroughly enjoyed the independence and sense of accomplishment it gave her.

Stretching technology to work for you

We all are stretching technology to do what we need, regardless of what it was originally designed to do. In this field, you just can't settle for "because that's just the way it is." If the way it is doesn't work for you, there is often someone who can help figure out how to change it. Question things; don't take them for granted. You may not be the only person who has wanted to do what you want to do.

If you want your computer to do more than it is currently doing and you haven't found a way to make it work, check around. Refer to the manual. Ask other people you know who use the program, consult with mem-

134

Computer
and Web
Resources
for People
with
Disabilities

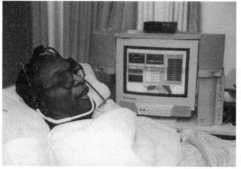

Photo courtesy of Carolina Computer Access Center

Assistive technology gives people greater control over their environment by translating actions such as head movement into computer commands.

bers of your support team, call the vendor, or learn to get online and put your interest out, literally, into a world of resources. You just might discover that it can easily be made to do what you want.

Assuming that the program cannot do what you need, try combining it with another program. There are lots of little programs, some of them shareware, that may or may not have been designed to work with adaptive technology but that can increase the functionality of your system. For example, a program that writes macros (keyboard shortcuts) can decrease the time it takes to accomplish a complicated task. No matter what input device you are using, you can probably benefit from a program that allows you to do more than one thing with a single keystroke (see Abbreviation Expansion and Macros and Access Utilities in Part II).

What would you like to see? Why do you want it? What will it help you accomplish? If you have an idea on how a product can be improved, consider talking to the people who designed it. Vendors are usually interested in users' insights. Those of us in the trenches often have ideas that designers are eager to hear.

Achieving Comfort

Once you are using your computer to fulfill your original goals, you will be surprised how comfortable you feel with your new tools. Let us say that you purchased your computer to help your child write reports for school. The largest percentage of your time at first was spent on getting familiar with the equipment. Later, you were focused on your tasks. Preparing the first report took a long time and caused quite a bit of tension; the second report was somewhat stressful; the third report was a lot easier; and by the time your child was working on the fourth report, you found yourself comfortable enough to experiment with some of the software's special features. Your original mission was accomplished. Now what?

Mollie is 11 years old. A combination of learning disabilities and fine-motor problems make learning and writing very difficult for her. Her mother explains that Mollie needs to "overlearn everything." When she was six years old, her parents purchased a few drill and practice programs for an older computer that had been given to them and used the early software programs to provide Mollie with the repetitious practice she needed to learn short and long vowel sounds and basic math facts. They found that the computer practice was much more enjoyable and effective than flash cards. As Mollie got older, her parents wanted to address her writing difficulties, so they purchased a more powerful computer. To learn about new software, her mother began volunteering at her local Alliance Center, organizing the Center's software collection.

Mollie now uses the computer as her primary writing tool at home. Her handwriting is poor—barely legible to Mollie herself—and writing takes her a long time, so she completes most of her written homework on the computer. For science homework she writes definitions and answers questions using a word processing program. This has the added advantage of providing her with a copy of the homework from which to study (she cannot study from notes written in her own hand). She writes her compositions on the computer, taking full advantage of the computer's ability to assist with spell checking, editing, and rewriting. Freed from the mechanics of writing, she is able to focus on thinking and expressing her thoughts. Her mother is also pleased that she is getting enrichment from playing such educational programs as Oregon Trail (The Learning Company) and Millie's Math House (Edmark).

Mollie's story is a good example of a family getting involved with computers for a specific purpose and then moving on to other beneficial uses. We think you will find this part of your journey to be the most fun. Once you have acquired the right computer system for you, much of the pressure is off. You can pursue the fulfillment of your original goals and be free to experiment, improvise, and discover other uses of your system.

Trying new software for new uses

Your first new use will probably entail trying a different software program or becoming immersed in the Internet. Mollie progressed from relatively simple drill and practice programs to word processing and problem solving programs for entertainment and education. Many adults begin with a word processing program as a writing tool, then move on to a paint or draw program (they're so much fun, they're irresistible) or to a spreadsheet program for working with finances and budgets. As a parent, you may surprise yourself and find the next use of your child's computer system will be to make your work easier—perhaps to print labels for all those holiday greeting cards or to produce the PTA's annual directory (which you volunteered to do even though last year it took hours of tedious typing).

Adding options: the upgrade phenomenon

You may have noticed the upgrade phenomenon already. It is occurring on two levels: the technology is advancing, and so are you. You may have started out in awe of what technology could do, but now, as a more sophisticated user, you have higher expectations and want the technology to do more. Look at what has happened with copy machines. Not too long ago, copy machines were a marvel of modern science: no more retyping an entire page, no more carbons. After a while, we got tired of feeding papers one by one and of only printing on one side of the page; we wanted to use different sizes of paper and different colors of ink. The evolution of copy machines and their users pales in comparison to computer technology and its users. Whereas copy machines have one basic function, computers are tremendously versatile and every aspect is being constantly revised. Take it for granted that technology will improve. This is the good news: change means you will have new options that might be important to you. However, just because there are new products on the market doesn't mean you need them, but it does give you an opportunity to review your situation in light of new developments.

No matter which computer system and adaptations you purchase, within a couple of years you will probably want to add hardware or peripherals. Your first add-on might be an item you had originally considered but rejected in an effort to keep your costs down, such as a scanner, backup system, or a super fast modem. If you enjoy programs with music, you may decide to purchase a pair of heavy-duty external speakers to improve the quality of sound coming from your computer. If your computer did not have one built-in, you may choose to add a CD-ROM drive to take advantage of the exciting new programs being released in CD-ROM format.

Probably the most common addition to personal computer systems is more memory. As your interests in software expand, you will eventually find a program you feel you must have but that requires more memory to operate than your computer has. Or, you might find that you are rapidly filling your hard disk and need a larger one or some other storage device. You may also want to invest in a larger monitor.

We cannot foresee what changes the next few years will bring, but you can be sure that the computers of five years from now will be able to do things we can't even imagine now. By then, as an experienced computer user, you will be eager to move on. Rest assured that deciding on your next computer will not take half as long as purchasing your first.

Connecting to the world

One of the things we can foresee is that computers will be easier to use. Current and future generations of technology are constantly being designed to seamlessly connect us to a universe of information and knowledgeable people. A response to a survey on how to improve special education included this comment: "Stop buying computers; children need to connect with human beings." Clearly the writer had not spent much time around children working with computers. Everyone needs to connect with other human beings, especially youngsters with disabilities. Technology has the power to bring people together by providing them with the ability to interact and communicate in new ways.

> *Andy* and *Jonathan* are two boys in a school in Australia for children who are deaf. Through a commercial online service connected to the Internet, the boys posted a message asking for pen pals. Joshua and Caleb are brothers, ages 12 and 10, who have no disabilities and who live in Kentucky. Their father, an Internet user, saw the message and had them write Andy and Jonathan. Now the four boys exchange electronic pen-pal letters. They write about Nintendo games, basketball, school, their homes, their friends, and the weather, which is especially interesting

Photo courtesy of IntelliTools, Inc.

Computers can help to foster social interaction as children enjoy the learning process.

138

———

Computer
and Web
Resources
for People
with
Disabilities

because it's winter in Australia when it's summer in Kentucky. It was a month before Joshua and Caleb knew that Andy and Jonathan were completely deaf. The boys think it's great that they can't tell anything about race, size, age, appearance, or disability by sending and reading email, but they can share the secrets of Nintendo and have a lot of fun getting to know each other. Andy and Jonathan hope to come to the United States one day, and Joshua and Caleb are finding someone to teach them sign language.

The new frontier of the Internet, sometimes called the World Wide Web (www), allows you to use your phone to access databases of information stored on another computer and, in most cases, to transfer (or download) information to your own computer. The number of people using the Internet is increasing at a phenomenal rate. How could someone with a disability take advantage of this technology? First of all, in the same ways that anybody would:

- Telecommuting in order to work from home

- Operating a home-based business

- Accessing vast databases of information beyond their geographic limits

- Tapping online educational programs

- Sending and receiving electronic mail to share interests with others

- Having live, real-time dialogues in "chat rooms" with people who have similar interests

- Engaging in video teleconferences where participants can see and hear each other by way of small video cameras mounted on each computer

Some aspects of telecommunications and the Internet are particularly well suited to people with disabilities because of the access they provide. You can bring information right into your home and use your computer and assistive technology to read or edit it. You can write a message with any sort of input device and take as much time as necessary. After you have composed the message, you can send it to one individual or to many by posting it to a bulletin board (an electronic information center) or by addressing the message to multiple recipients. A person's functional limitations or disability are not apparent or relevant to the process.

Through the Internet, you can take advantage of a wide range of services without leaving your home. You can get up-to-date information on the stock market, make airline reservations, and order clothes. You can access libraries that are otherwise inaccessible to you because of transportation and architectural barriers or because of a difficulty with manipulating books or reading print. You can also use your computer to fax documents or to receive them from others, provided your system has faxing software installed. You can develop and maintain friendships via email. Says *Vanessa*,

> For the first time in my life, I am totally independent. I am doing what every other teenager is doing—talking on the phone. The great thing is there's no one looking over my shoulder! Being online is exciting. I love to hear the voice of America Online say, "You've got mail!"
>
> I talk to all kinds of people on the Internet. I talk to my uncle at Oracle. Now, I can write my feelings down and email them to my best friend, who just got online. This is important because she just started college and I don't see her as often as I would like, especially when I'm used to seeing her every day and chatting with her every day. Email helps ease the pain.
>
> There's a lot of stuff waiting to be explored online. I almost ordered flowers for my sister, but Mom caught me in the act! Sometimes I use chat rooms to talk to people online. You can download all kinds of research. You can even download games.
>
> Recently, I discovered how to use my modem to access the telephone relay service (TTY) for deaf and disabled people. I can call people who don't have email without the help of anyone. Here's how it works: I use my modem to dial the relay service. When I've made a connection, I type the number I want them to call. They read what I write on the computer to the person I'm calling. The agent writes back to me what the person says and I read it on my computer monitor. It is neat having "private" conversations. For the first time in my life I've had secrets.

There are ways you can experiment with online services for free or nearly free to make sure they would be of value to you. Ask the services if they have demonstration packages or trial subscriptions. Find out if any of your friends are connected and willing to show you around. Your local library or school may have access to online services or the Internet, which connects thousands of universities, schools, businesses, and government offices across the nation and around the world and provides for the free flow of electronic mail and information.

Gaining access to commercial services using assistive technology might require some effort or customization, depending on the system you are using. For example, using a voice recognition system to access bulletin boards might be a problem because of telephone-line noise. If these problems arise for you, call an Alliance for Technology Access Center to help work through them.

Computer
and Web
Resources
for People
with
Disabilities

Many services have forums where you can exchange messages with people who have similar interests. You can develop friendships with people you may never physically meet. You may want to check out the areas that focus on people with disabilities. People share their experiences, frustrations, and triumphs. You will find letters from people who are experiencing life-changing adjustments and others who have gone down similar roads and are able to commiserate and guide.

Internet Accessibility Considerations

How can you try the Internet? You will need a computer, an external or built-in modem, a phone line, a decision about your accessibility requirements, and telecommunications software, if it was not included when you purchased your computer system (see Part III for a list of selected online services and bulletin boards, then call and get brochures).

The Internet can be thought of as a huge body of data and programs, all contained on thousands of computers, linked together in a vast network. The World Wide Web, or just Web, is a subset of the Internet, consisting of all the data on the interconnected computers, stored primarily in HTML form (hypertext markup language), although other computer languages are being used, too. Data stored in HTML can be presented in a graphically interesting manner, and, more importantly, can be linked to data in other documents on other computers. By activating these links between documents, the user can go from one bit of information to another as though it is all stored sequentially on the same computer, instead of being scattered on different machines around the world.

Information on the Web is accessed by means of software called browsers. These programs interpret the codes embedded in the HTML documents (or Web pages) and display the documents graphically. They also manage the process of following the links contained in the documents to information on other computers.

A tremendous amount of valuable information is available on the Web. Because this information can be located and accessed entirely through a computer—rather than by, for example, a trip to the library—it is especially valuable for people with disabilities. However, the Web poses some unique access problems.

While a person's home computer can be modified for access, the data on the Web is not under the user's control and may not be presented in an accessible manner. For example, some Web pages contain text information, while others display a picture of text—one can be read by a blind user's screen reader, the other cannot. Similarly, some links are designated by underlined text, whereas others may activated by clicking on an area of a graphic image. There is no consistency to the placement of links; they can appear anywhere on a page. These problems can be addressed by good, consistent design of Web pages, but the user can't rely on this. He or she must take whatever is out there and not much of it is designed with access in mind.

Here we will examine ways to make Web browsers accessible, and, through them, gain access to the information on the Web.

Which browsers?

The two major commercial browsers are Netscape Navigator (in the newest version, a part of Netscape Communicator), and Microsoft's Internet Explorer. These programs are available for both Macintosh and PCs using Windows 95 or later. There are also several special-purpose browsers, such as PwWebSpeak (The Productivity Works) and Home Page Reader (IBM), both designed for people with vision impairments.

The nation's largest Internet provider, America Online (AOL), uses a browser that is a version of Internet Explorer but that is much more difficult to access due to a lack of menu bar features and a heavy reliance on graphics. Some of the concepts we'll be looking at apply to AOL, but this software is generally not a good choice for people with moderate-to-severe disabilities if you are trying to adapt a computer for access to the Web.

We will be focusing on Web browsers and not on alternative means of obtaining information from the Internet. As usual, the access issues break down into those affecting the user's ability to *input* information into the computer, *processing* aids to simplify or accelerate the operation of the computer, and issues affecting *output* of information from the computer.

Input

Mouse access

Most aspects of Web browsing can be easily accomplished without a keyboard. Because links can appear anywhere on a Web page, they are most conveniently accessed by clicking with a mouse or alternative pointing device. Additionally, most browsers have toolbar icons and buttons, or at least menu options, to allow everything to be controlled by mouse. As a consequence, people who can use the mouse or an alternative pointing device can operate Web browsers fairly easily.

You will rarely need to enter text when browsing the Web. One text item you may need to enter is the unique Internet address for the page you want to go to, called the Uniform Resource Locator or URL. This is not a lot of text, however, and once you get to the page you can bookmark it so you never have to type in the URL again. Most of the time, you get to a page by following links, not by entering an address. You may want to enter text in a search engine, a piece of software—accessed with a browser—that searches

142

Computer
and Web
Resources
for People
with
Disabilities

the Web for pages containing certain words or phrases. However, you will generally only enter a few words. You may also need to enter text into a form, such as your name and address to download a program. But that's about it. Occasional use of an on-screen keyboard would provide fairly complete access to a browser for someone who could use a mouse or mouse emulator.

Of course, other online tasks do require text input, such as email and chat rooms, but these do not pose unique access problems beyond what would be encountered in using a word processor.

Keyboard access

A trickier problem is keyboard access. As you may be guessing by now, the challenge with a lot of software is figuring how to operate it without the mouse. If we can operate it with keyboard commands, we can make an IntelliKeys or Discover Board overlay or make a custom switch scanning matrix, use Morse code, or conveniently make speech macros for a voice input system. So a crucial physical access issue is keyboard accessibility of Web browsers and how we can then make them accessible to switch and alternate keyboard users.

Voice input

Most voice input systems are not yet very good at controlling the mouse; the process tends to be pretty cumbersome ("mouse up," "stop," "mouse left"). Therefore, keyboard-based Web access methods will be helpful in using voice input as well. If you know the keyboard command to control a browser, you can make a speech macro to do this by voice.

Processing

Processing aids for browsers fall into three categories: word-prediction and abbreviation-expansion programs, spell checkers, and text-to-speech software. Word-prediction and abbreviation-expansion programs work with Web browsers the same way they work with other software. They are primarily important for email and online chat rooms, where large amounts of text must be entered. The same is true for spell checkers; the text that must be entered while actually browsing the Web is usually limited to one or two word search terms.

Text-to-speech programs that speak highlighted text can be helpful to people with learning disabilities or low vision in accessing text on Web pages. The primary difficulty is when words on a page are presented as graphics, rather than actual text; the text-to-speech programs cannot read this, nor can the screen readers be relied upon by users who are blind.

Output

Adapting the output of a computer—which is primarily comprised of the information displayed on the monitor screen—can take the form of modifying this visual output or supplementing or replacing it with auditory output.

Modifying the visual output usually means enlarging the text, the cursor, or the entire displayed image. Enlarging the text can be accomplished within the preferences controls of the browser itself. Preferences can be set by individual users by using the program's pull-down menus. For example, Internet Explorer has under the "View" menu an item called "Internet Options" where users can select the color contrast and fonts they prefer.

Several utility programs enlarge the cursor for better visibility: Biggy (R. J. Cooper) and Fat Cursor (shareware) for the Macintosh; MetaMouse (shareware) for Windows 3.1; and ToggleMouse (shareware) and Biggy (R. J. Cooper) for Windows 95 and later versions.

Enlargement of the entire displayed image can be accomplished with a screen magnification program like inLarge for the Macintosh (ALVA Access Group), ZoomText (AI Squared), or Easy Access, which is built into the Macintosh Operating System and is accessed from the Control Panel settings. Programs for Windows include LPWindows (Optelec) and Magic (Henter-Joyce). Screen magnification programs can be difficult to use, however, since only a part of the enlarged image can be displayed on the monitor at a time—it can be very hard to keep track of your place.

The visual image can also be modified by altering the color of the text and background for better contrast. Most Web browsers allow the user to control this feature, most screen magnification programs also incorporate color control, and Windows 95 and later versions have a high-contrast display option available (see Part II for more information).

Supplementing the visual output means having the computer read aloud text that is visually identified and selected. This can be accomplished with several text-to-speech programs, described above in the Processing section.

Replacing the visual output with auditory output means using a screen reading program to interpret the graphical information audibly. A number of these programs are available, each of which deals somewhat differently with the problem of presenting the unpredictable graphic data produced by the Web browsers in audible form (for more information see Parts II and III).

A constantly growing number of online resources focus on issues of interest to people with disabilities, including discussions about access to technology. They appear in many different formats such as websites, discussion lists, newsgroups, and bulletin boards. Through these routes you

144

Computer
and Web
Resources
for People
with
Disabilities

can find out virtually everything you'd like to know and keep updated on the issues (for specific ideas on where to start, see Part III, Internet Resources).

There are a great many resources to explore in developing strategies for computer use at home, at school, and on the job. Part III contains references for books and periodicals that can be of use in this process.

The tools of technology are fabulously flexible. The possibilities are limited only by our imaginations. The challenge is to use our powers of creativity to maximize their potential now and in the years ahead, as our needs change and as technology transforms the ways in which we connect with our environment and the people in it.

Chapter 12

Sharing What You Learn

Interest in the field of assistive technology is exploding on every level. And the demand for knowledge about how to make it work in real life is likewise increasing. Throughout your search for technological solutions, you will encounter individuals who are at different points in their search and are as determined as you are. The potential of technology energizes people in a way that is both creative and contagious. Most people are only too happy to share what they have discovered and how it works for them.

You may want to find ways to share your knowledge and experience with people who are starting on the journey, answering their questions the way someone answered yours. You may be thinking, "I hardly know how to turn my computer on; how in the world could I help anyone?" But you will be surprised. You may be able to recommend a piece of software your child loves or a good place to purchase educational software.

Mara, the mother of a son with cerebral palsy and visual impairments, helped her son become involved with computers. Other parents said to her, "That's interesting, but my child can't use a regular keyboard." Although Mara's knowledge of assistive technology was limited, she found herself telling parent after parent that "you don't have to be able to use a keyboard; there are lots of other ways to use a computer." She succeeded in communicating to them that many possibilities exist.

Whatever small piece of the technology puzzle you have had experience with, someone else may be seeking the same piece, and you can help.

Phyllis considers herself a newcomer to the world of assistive technology. She does not yet realize that other people can learn from her experience of getting her state office of vocational rehabilitation to pay for her laptop computer.

Phyllis is in her mid-30s and a recovering alcoholic. Recently she discovered that the problems she had had all her life with reading, memorizing, and numbers were not due to a lack of intelligence but to learning disabilities. For the first 10 years of her adult life, she worked

146

Computer
and Web
Resources
for People
with
Disabilities

as a horse trainer, but couldn't move up in the world of horse training because she could not reliably read a stopwatch or racing forms. She finally decided she wanted to get away from the tough racetrack environment and find a job with security. She was fearful but enrolled in a community college.

At the same time, Phyllis was referred to the county office of vocational rehabilitation. She took its required tests and was told that she was not college material and that they would not provide support for her to attend college. However, when she finished her first semester with a 4.0 grade point average, the decision was reversed. While at the community college, Phyllis taught herself to type in the college's computer lab and began to complete assignments on a computer. She transferred to a four-year college and continued to rely on the college computer lab for doing her written assignments.

When laptop computers became affordable, Phyllis saw a more efficient solution to her problems. She could carry a laptop to class and the library for note taking, and she could work on papers at home. She completed all the paperwork to apply for assistance from the vocational rehabilitation office, including a formal letter with a clear rationale for the laptop, several cost estimates, and a letter from one of her professors. The rehabilitation office approved the purchase. One of her fellow students, who also has learning disabilities, approached her and asked how the laptop helped her and how she acquired it. Before she had even mastered her computer, Phyllis found herself sharing her beginning experiences and advising others.

One of the exciting things about the field of assistive technology is how supportive people have been to each other. The name of the game is problem solving. Instead of, "It can't be done," you are more likely to hear, "There must be a way; how can we find it?" This commitment to finding solutions is coupled with a willingness to help. Everyone is new to some degree, and no one person knows everything, so most people are willing to share their experiences with others who are interested. The guiding belief is, "If I answer your question today, maybe someone will answer my question tomorrow."

Becoming a Leader

As you gain more experience and answer more and more questions about your computer system, you may decide to take an active role in a number of efforts: organizing an assistive technology user group, participating in a bulletin board on a telecommunications network, working with your PTA to promote creative computer use in your school district, lobbying political bodies to support technology integration in vocational or educational programs, or, like many of the writers of this book, organizing a technology access center in your area. These activities are natural extensions of informal networking and well within the realm of possibility. In fact, it has been grassroots efforts such as these that have resulted in assistive technology having the impact it has had on the lives of people with disabilities. The initiative, creativity, and persistence of people like you have turned possibilities into realities.

Chris is the mother of *Franklin,* who has physical disabilities as a result of anoxic brain damage from near-drowning. When Franklin was two and a half, Chris discovered that computers could do interesting things, and she sent away for a slew of brochures, hoping to find the right equipment for her son. When that approach did not work, she enrolled in a special education technology program at a local university. She bought Franklin his first computer when he was four years old. At Franklin's preschool, other parents and therapists asked Chris all kinds of questions about computers, and before long she started tutoring other parents in her dining room. Because of Franklin's needs, the aspects of technology she knew best were switches, scanning, and software to teach cause-and-effect and choice-making to young children. She was not comfortable answering other technical questions, such as which word processing program is best for children with learning disabilities. But she enthusiastically answered questions in her area of experience.

Then Chris read an article in *Exceptional Parent* magazine about computer resource centers in other areas of the country that had joined together to form the Alliance for Technology Access, and she realized that a resource center was what her city needed—and what *she* needed to keep up with new developments in technology. She contacted the professor at the university who coordinated the special education technology program, her local office of The Arc, and fellow parents and led a collaborative effort that resulted in the establishment of an Alliance for Technology Access Center. Now Chris is Director of Education at the Center and a self-described "technology junkie." In addition to her knowledge about computers and augmentative communication systems, she probably knows more about adapting video games than anyone.

People can become leaders in this field in many ways, bringing others together over a variety of issues and topics. Collaborating on the development of an Alliance for Technology Access Center is just one of many avenues open to people (for information on starting a Center, contact the ATA directly).

148

Computer
and Web
Resources
for People
with
Disabilities

Sue helped establish an Alliance Center and, in addition, has shared her skills and enthusiasm for computers with children living in poverty in a New Jersey inner city.

Before Sue raised five children, she taught high school math and science and worked at AT&T, managing a group that helped set up office computers. At that time computers were large machines that required their own climate-controlled rooms. Several years later, when Sue was a full-time homemaker, microcomputers came on the market, and Sue bought an inexpensive computer "just to keep up." She volunteered at her children's school as a computer tutor, then got the PTA interested in organizing a Computers in Education program. The PTA purchased a few computers and some early educational software, and small groups of children started coming in for the simple computer classes Sue taught. The program grew to 12 computers, with every class participating. Eventually, the school hired a math teacher to take over the program and make computers an integral part of the curriculum.

Around this time, a pastor from a grassroots community corporation spoke at Sue's church, and in describing his organization's needs, mentioned that old computers had been donated to their school by local corporations but nobody knew what to do with them. Sue saw a new volunteer opportunity. She took her computer skills to the school, recruited a few volunteers, and now devotes two days a week to designing and running its Computers in Education program. With the program having demonstrated its viability, the community foundation has been able to procure funds for new equipment, and now all children enrolled at the school—those with and without disabilities—receive weekly instruction in computer use.

One person can accomplish astounding things if she or he has a vision, a desire, and the willingness and perseverance to work toward translating that vision into reality and sharing it with others. We all started with our own technology needs, but eventually we connected with others and became part of the community of people who believe in the vast potential of technology to change the lives of children and adults with disabilities. And, in helping others, we definitely help ourselves.

Chapter 13

More Thoughts about the Future

John Scully, when serving as the CEO of Apple Computer, once remarked, "The best way to predict the future is to invent it." That way of thinking and that attitude speak to the real power of technology. Seymour Papert, in his book *Mindstorms: Children, Computers and Powerful Ideas,* says that computers, because they help people form new relationships and allow us to question standard assumptions, can be carriers of powerful ideas and of the seeds of cultural change.

These two attitudes are reflected in this book, and it will have accomplished its purpose if it convinces you that assistive technologies can empower you to invent your own future and to change cultural notions and assumptions about the abilities and potential of people with disabilities.

When you consider the bold language contained in recent pieces of legislation like the Americans with Disabilities Act, the Reauthorization of the Rehabilitation Act, the Assistive Technology Act, and the Telecommunications Act, it becomes clear that all across the nation a spirit of empowerment and high expectation is seizing people's hearts and imaginations. Every day, people using assistive technologies are eliminating barriers and expanding the concept of what is or isn't an accessible activity. And who better to decide what is or isn't—what will or will not be—an accessible activity for an individual with a disability than that individual? In every sense of the word, *empowerment* is an attitude available to everyone with a disability. The law provides the legal rights and sanctions, but technology and imagination provide the real capacity and ability to choose, to act, and to invent your future.

Every achievement should give rise to new and expanded expectations. And, in pursuing the tools to realize those expectations, let no one ever say, "It can't be done." Instead, let the response be, "I don't know of that having been done before, but let's find out," or, better yet, "Let's see who and what we need to bring together to make it happen."

New Dimensions in Computer Technology

Two trends in technology—integration and miniaturization—are resulting in portable, personalizable, versatile equipment. This means that individu-

150

Computer
and Web
Resources
for People
with
Disabilities

als like Victor, the young man you may remember from Chapter 2, can have more functionality and far better quality of speech in a computer they can transport to different environments. It also means they can use the same computer and system of access for word processing, creating spreadsheets, drawing, controlling their environments, and using the phone. They might also choose to access printed text by placing it in a scanner and letting optical character-recognition software decode and transfer it into a standard computer text file, which can then be read aloud by a computer with a speech synthesizer. And, if or when the needs of these individuals change, they can add other features that will let them control their computers and their environments or communicate using eye gaze, brain waves, or thoughts.

A whole new wave of miniature and very powerful technologies (personal digital assistants, or PDAs) are even more portable, have interfaces that can be personalized to individual abilities, and are developing cellular, fax, message, satellite locator, and speech capabilities. An older person or someone with a cognitive disability, for example, could carry a PDA in a pocket and be reminded of everything from taking medication to showing up on time for a job interview or catching a bus. Such a system was put into place in the Chicago area, where a group employed a personal computer to call and send messages to up to 50 people with traumatic brain injury as many times as needed during the day to help them stay on track. With the new generation of PDAs, capabilities will be even more extensive. For example, the locator capability could alert someone with Alzheimer's disease that he or she is more than a certain number of blocks from home and, if requested, give them printed or verbal instructions as to how to return.

By way of another emerging technology, a man in Atlanta who is now speechless and immobile from a stroke and tracheotomy is controlling a computer with his thoughts. He can move the cursor around the screen solely by brain power by using technology that translates electrical nerve cell signals in the brain to signals a computer can understand.

For more than a decade, Honda Motors has been developing a robot that is bipedal, meaning it can walk on two legs like a human, pivot, and climb stairs. It uses binocular vision, giving it depth perception. Although the robot is being developed with commercial and industrial uses in mind, we who work in the field of assistive technology can easily envision the practical applications it could have for people living with severe disabilities.

These are just a few examples of what is available for us today, what is under development, and what we can dream about for the future. Think back to June's new millennium scenario in the first chapter, and try to imagine what is coming, what is in the works in labs around the country, or what will be developed in the next five years.

Much of what is being done focuses on what the government is calling *technology transfer*—finding new uses for technologies originally developed for other reasons, often military. A great deal of technology originally developed for military purposes has had extremely important implications in the peacetime realm of assistive technologies. For example, pilots flying in multinational forces or within foreign territories already have a foreign language translation system that automatically translates what a pilot is saying into any one of several languages and that translates whatever language other pilots or service people are using into the language of the first pilot. It's easy to imagine how this technology could be adapted to recognize the speech of individuals with disabilities in articulation and to put an individual's speech into an articulated form in either his native language or any of several foreign languages. In another area, virtual realities are already being employed to train pilots in flying over territories thousands of miles away without ever leaving the safety of the training room. At a university in Washington state, a group of rehabilitation engineers employs virtual reality to allow wheelchair users to try a full range of chairs, terrains, and control devices before the final design is produced. There is a vast educational potential in the ability to simulate realistic experiences for people who have not had the opportunity to access such experiences before.

Speech recognition technology (the ability of the computer to understand the human voice) is taking quantum leaps and will be a mainstream tool that we will soon use for everything from word processing to environmental control. We will also have virtual reality options (the ability to provide realistic, interactive, multisensory experiences) for everything from educational experiences and vocational simulation to social decision-making simulations and recreational experiences.

Looking toward the Future

Seymour Papert said something else significant in his query about the role technology has in our collective future. He said that sometimes the important thing is not so much what we do with what is in the future, but what we do with what we have now.

When we dream about the future, about new forms of technology, we must also dream about a world where funding is available to purchase devices people need and want, where computers and other forms of information technology are universally accessible and affordable, and where people who use assistive technology are valued as contributors to our society.

What is available now is merely a shadow compared to what is coming. And, while none of us can anticipate exactly what the next technology will be or how it might be used, we need to be aware of apparent and accelerating trends and to see these developments as more conclusive evidence that

151

More
Thoughts
about
the
Future

152

Computer
and Web
Resources
for People
with
Disabilities

we should never limit our expectations or be completely content with today's solutions.

Tomorrow we will have fast, accurate, and reliable speech recognition systems that will allow any of us to talk to all computers and to many things we won't recognize as computers such as our home temperature controls and kitchen appliances. We will have vastly improved eye interface capabilities that will allow us to control many types of technology or indicate where we want our wheelchair to go with a glance. We will have countless practical applications of virtual reality to provide educational, vocational, and recreational experiences for a wide range of persons with disabilities, and these applications will be available in multisensory format, with each individual choosing how he or she wants to receive the information.

We now have almost instantaneous access to electronic mail communications and to information in most libraries worldwide. In the future we will each be able to customize the way we interact with that wealth of information. We will have interactive access to information, education, employment, medical attention, government services, and recreational opportunities in whatever form we choose.

David, a man with a disability who lives independently in Massachusetts, says that for him the Internet is a form of natural support because with it he can order groceries, get the latest news, or find out which state parks are accessible and how he can get there.

The Right to Achieve Unrealistic Expectations

There has never been a better time for an individual with a disability to challenge all of the stereotypes and notions of "unrealistic" expectations existing in our culture. Not only do we have the right to envision and develop unrealistic expectations, we also have the right to achieve them. Numerous legislative mandates have affirmed the right of people with disabilities to access assistive technology and services which help support its use to increase independence and participation at home, school, work, recreation, and community environments. This includes off-the-shelf technologies, as well as technology that is customized or specifically developed for an individual's abilities and needs.

We have only scratched the surface of what we can do with the technology that exists right now, today. Technology will continue to develop at exponential rates, and people with disabilities have the right to access it and integrate it into all aspects of their lives, the right to realize their own expectations, and the right to develop new expectations. Technology is redefining human potential—and that means the potential of all of us, according to our individual hopes and dreams.

Your action is required

153

More
Thoughts
about
the
Future

There is much work to be done if we are to ensure that new technologies are being designed with access in mind. Perhaps you thought that buying this book was going to make your life easier. Hopefully it has, in many respects. We hope it has also inspired you to take on a whole new set of challenges that may cancel out some of that ease. Access now—and access in the future—cannot occur without your diligent, active involvement in every area of your life. From education, employment, recreation, and communication to living self-sufficiently in the community, individuals and organizations can make universal access a reality for all of us, one neighborhood at a time—and starting in *your* neighborhood.

Part II

The Technology Toolbox

Contents

Using the Technology Toolbox

Many people start their search for technology by asking questions—questions that often follow a similar pattern. The Technology Toolbox was created with a knowledge of these common questions, and it can help you develop your own route for navigating the technology solutions you will find. Rather than approaching the subject from a problem or disability perspective, the Technology Toolbox approaches it from the viewpoint of the significant task to be done and a person's ability to perform that task. This approach reflects our philosophy that it is not the person with the disability that has the problem, but the environment that is deficient for not appropriately accommodating the individual's needs.

The Technology Toolbox was designed to provide you with information and ideas so you can be a good consumer of technology and make well-informed decisions. We provide information but do not suggest that any one approach or tool is right for you. Only you can make that determination.

Charts

To use the charts, start by finding the **question** that most closely fits the key questions you are asking about the access you, your child, your student, or your client needs in order to use technology. If you have a number of issues to address, you will probably choose to employ more than one chart.

Next, locate the ability on the continuum, which runs from top to bottom, that most aptly describes your situation. When there are multiple choices in a column, each is keyed to a symbol (●■▲◆☆○). In the next column, identify the difficulty or difficulties you feel you might encounter in attempting to use computer technology. Then read through the approaches to consider and the tools to explore that are marked with the same symbols in the next two columns.

For difficulties marked with ●, read the approaches marked with ● and the tools marked with ●. For difficulties marked with ■, read the approaches marked with ■ and the tools marked with ■. And so on.

Once you hit on a tool that bears further investigation, turn to the product description for that item to learn more (page numbers are in parentheses).

Product Descriptions

The product descriptions are intended to provide you with enough information to get a good feeling for the assistive technology product without going into complex technical details. You will get a sense of the range of available features and an understanding of why there may be a wide variation in cost—for example, because of differences in sound quality, speed, capacity, or user flexibility and friendliness.

Each product description lists related products that may also be useful. For more comprehensive information about specific assistive technology products, the following resources will be helpful (see Part III for phone numbers and addresses):

- Closing the Gap Annual Resource Directory.

- Trace Resource Book: Assistive Technologies for Communication, Control and Computer Access, 1998-99 Edition.

- Adaptive Device Locator System (ADLS), a database on CD-ROM containing the full range of adaptive and assistive technology products. This product is available from Academic Software, Inc., and Internet users can browse its contents at www.acsw.com.

- CO-NET, a CD-ROM containing the Cooperative Electronic Library on Disability. This CD, available from the Trace R&D Center, contains several databases on assistive technology products and vendors, service providers, and publications. It also contains copies of legislation and other relevant documents.

- ABLEDATA, a database containing information on the full range of assistive technology products. This database is included on the Trace CO-NET CD. You can also call the Trace R&D Center at (608) 263-1156 and they will search the database for specific information for you. Additionally, you can contact the National Rehabilitation Information Center (NARIC) at (800) 346-2742.

All the products in the Technology Toolbox meet the following criteria: they have been used successfully by people with disabilities, the manufacturer or the vendor generally offers customer support, and they run on either a Macintosh or PC. The inclusion of a product is not an endorsement of its suitability for any one individual or situation. It is simply one product to consider in your search for solutions.

It is true that specific information on technology is often out-of-date before it is printed—an inevitability in a field that is changing so rapidly. Companies expand, reduce, and merge, often changing addresses, phone numbers, and sometimes even names. Although we can't include tomor-

Using the
Technology
Toolbox

TECHNOLOGY TOOLBOX

160

Computer
and Web
Resources
for People
with
Disabilities

row's products, we have listed today's key vendors. Part III includes an alphabetical listing of all the vendors mentioned in the Technology Toolbox, along with the most current information about them. Stay in touch with them; they will be putting new products on the market soon. In addition, more and more people around the country are specializing in keeping track of what is happening in the field. Find and befriend them. And, happy exploring!

★ Ability	🔒 Difficulty	🔑 Approach	🔧 Tool
See the screen well	● Small text ▲ Small cursor ■ Screen glare	● Increase text size ▲ Increase cursor size ■ Reduce glare	● Software features: easy-to-read screens (168) ▲ Software features: optional cursors (171) ■ Monitor additions (243)
See the screen close up	● Monitor not close enough ■ ▲ Small monitor	● Modify position of monitor ■ Use large monitor ▲ Magnify screen	● ▲ Monitor additions (243) ■ Monitors ▲ Screen enlargement programs (240)
See large text and graphics	Small text and graphics	● Magnify screen ■ Large-print program ☆ Use speech output	● Screen enlargement programs (240) ● Monitor additions (243) ■ Software features: easy-to-read screens (168) ☆ ■ Talking and large-print word processors (228) ☆ Screen readers (238) ☆ Speech synthesizers (235)
Use senses other than vision	Information is visual	◆ Use speech output ● Tactile output	◆ Screen readers (238) ◆ Speech synthesizers (235) ● Refreshable braille displays (233) ● Braille embossers and translators (230)

TECHNOLOGY TOOLBOX

Ask Yourself...How Effectively Can I Use the Keyboard?

★ Ability	🔒 Difficulty	🔑 Approach	🔧 Tool
Use two hands	● Task is tiring ■ Typing goes slowly ☆ Keys too close together ▲ Keys too far apart	◆ Use physical supports ● Accelerate input ☆ Isolate keys ▲ Use small or programmable keyboard	◆ Arm and wrist supports (208) ● Word prediction (214) ● ▲ Alternate keyboards (173) ● ■ Abbreviation expansion and macros (212) ● Voice recognition (192) ☆ Keyboard additions (181)
Use one hand	◆ ● Must hit two keys at a time ■ ▲ Typing goes slowly ○ Keys too close together	◆ Latching keys ● ▲ Alternate keyboard layouts ■ Accelerate input ○ Isolate keys	◆ Access utilities (179) ● ▲ Alternate keyboards (173) ■ Abbreviation expansion and macros (212) ■ Word prediction (214) ■ Voice recognition (192) ○ Keyboard additions (181)
Point	■ ☆ Limited use of hands ▲ Keys too close together ○ Typing goes slowly	● Larger keys ■ Point and type ○ Accelerate input ☆ Use on-screen keyboard with mouse alternative ▲ Isolate keys	○ ☆ ● Alternate keyboards (173) ☆ Trackballs (206) ■ ■ Pointing and typing aids (200) ○ Voice recognition (192) ☆ Touch screens (202) ○ Abbreviation expansion and macros (212) ☆ Electronic pointing devices (198) ○ Word prediction (214) ▲ Keyboard additions (181)
One or more controllable movements	Physically accessing keyboard	◆ Use speech input ● Use switch input	◆ Voice recognition (192) ● Switches and switch software (184) ● Interface devices (188)

★ Ability	🔒 Difficulty	🔑 Approach	🔧 Tool
Make hand movements	Relating the mouse to the screen	● Use direct selection ▲ Use mouse replacements	●▲ Touch screens (202) ▲ Joysticks (204) ▲ Alternate keyboards (173)
Make some hand movements	◆ Fine motor dexterity ■ Gross motor dexterity	◆ Use gross movements ■ Use fine movements	◆ Alternate keyboards (173) ■ Trackballs (206) ■ Joysticks (204) ■ Access utilities (179)
Use other controllable movements	Manipulating mouse	☆ Use mouse replacements	☆ Pointing and typing aids (200) ☆ Electronic pointing devices (198) ☆ Switches and switch software (184) ☆ Interface devices (188) ☆ Joysticks (204)

Ask Yourself...How Effectively Can I Interact with Information?

★ Ability	🔒 Difficulty	🗝 Approach	🔧 Tool
Interact with auditory support	Written instructions, directions, or prompts	● Use programs with verbal instructions, directions, and prompts	● Speech synthesizers (235) ● Software features: auditory cues (170) ● Talking and large-print word processors (228)
Interact with written support	Verbal instructions, directions, or prompts	◆ Use programs with written instructions, directions, and prompts	◆ Software features: visual cues (170) ◆ Operating system
Understand information	▲● Maintaining attention ■ Inaccessible format	● Use motivating and interesting approaches ▲ Simplify methods of input ■ Create accessible format	▲● Talking and large-print word processors (228) ● Speech synthesizers (235) ▲ Joysticks (204) ▲ Touch screens (202) ● Software features: interactive ▲ Software features: easy-to-read screens, instructional choices (168, 169) ▲ Alternate keyboards (173) ■ Optical character recognition, scanners (196)
Interact with limited information	Excessive or overwhelming information	◆ Limit information presented ● Use graphics ■ Provide fewer keys	◆ Software features: instructional choices (169) ● Software features: graphics (169) ■ Alternate keyboards (173)
Interact with some of the environment	Understanding cause and effect	▲ Train in cause/effect skills	▲ Switches and switch software (184) ▲ Touch screens (202) ▲ Alternate keyboards (173)

Ask Yourself...How Effectively Can I Read (Comprehend)?

★ Ability	🔒 Difficulty	🔑 Approach	🔧 Tool
Read at a lower than expected level	Reading at expected level	● Have computer speak text ■ Isolate text into manageable chunks ☆ Transfer print materials to computer ◆ Train in reading comprehension	● Speech synthesizers (235) ● Talking and large-print word processors (228) ■ Software features: easy-to-read screens (168) ☆ Optical character recognition and scanners (196) ◆ Reading comprehension programs (216)
Comprehend single sentences	Too many words at a time	● Have computer speak text ■ Isolate text into manageable chunks ☆ Transfer print materials to computer ▲ Train in reading comprehension ◆ Support reading with graphics	● Speech synthesizers (235) ● Talking and large-print word processors (228) ■ Software features: easy-to-read screens (168) ☆ Optical character recognition and scanners (196) ▲ Reading comprehension programs (216) ◆ Software features: graphics (169)
Comprehend single words	Decoding	■ Practice letter recognition ☆ Practice letter-sound recognition	■ Reading comprehension programs (216) ☆ Alternate keyboards (173) ☆ Speech synthesizers (235)
Comprehend the meaning of symbols	Understanding words	◆ Use graphic symbols ● Have computer speak text	◆ Reading comprehension programs (216) ◆ Software features: graphics (169) ◆ Alternate keyboards (173) ● Speech synthesizers (235) ● Talking and large-print word processors (228) ● Software features: auditory cues (170)

TECHNOLOGY TOOLBOX

Ask Yourself...How Effectively Can I Write (Compose)?

★ Ability	🔒 Difficulty	🗝 Approach	🔧 Tool
Write at a lower than expected level	◆ Organizational skills ■ Writing ideas	■ Train in composition	◆ ■ Writing composition programs (221)
Compose single sentences	◆ Vocabulary ● Grammar/syntax ▲ Spelling ■ Writing ideas	◆ Support vocabulary ● Support grammar ▲ Support spelling ■ Train in composition	◆ Electronic reference tools (224) ◆▲ Word prediction (214) ●▲ Software features: built-in utilities (171) ■ Writing composition programs (221)
Combine words and phrases	● Communicating meaning	● Train in composition ■ Enter whole words and phrases	● Writing composition programs (221) ■ Alternate keyboards (173)
Use alternative to writing	● Communicating meaning	◆ Use graphics with voice output ● Speak sentences to computer	◆ Software features: custom programs, graphics (171, 169) ◆ Alternate keyboards (173) ◆ Speech synthesizers (235) ● Voice recognition (192)

★ Ability	🔒 Difficulty	🔑 Approach	🔧 Tool
Can understand how to handle equipment	● ■ ◆ Physical manipulation ▲ ○ Reading print materials and manuals	● Create access to disks ■ Create access to system ◆ Create access to printer ▲ Request accessible format ○ Create accessible format	● Hard disk drives ■ Environmental control units (252) ◆ Printers ○ Braille embossers, translators (230) ▲ Software features: friendly documentation (169) ○ Screen readers (238) ○ Speech synthesizers (235) ○ Reading machines (256) ○ Optical character recognition and scanners (196)
Can physically handle equipment	Comprehending task	◆ Simplify entry to programs and files ● Simplify disk operation ■ Simplify on/off	◆ Operating system ● Hard disk drives ■ Menu management and security programs (225)

168

Computer
and Web
Resources
for People
with
Disabilities

Software Features

The following features, incorporated into many software programs, may be helpful to someone who needs support to access a computer. You may want to keep these features in mind when you explore and compare software.

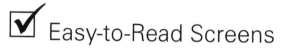 ## Easy-to-Read Screens

Screens that are easy to read and understand can make a critical difference for many users. Clear, uncluttered screens may reduce distraction. Features to consider are simple and legible text and menu items that are represented with both graphics and text, with options for large characters. It is important for some users that the style, font, or spacing of text can be altered. Many programs allow for these types of adjustments.

If voice synthesis software will be used, programs that place text in one column, rather than in multiple columns, can be read more easily. Multiple columns or boxes of text are very difficult for screen reading software to interpret. Similarly, asterisks or other nonalphabetical characters used for decoration make it more difficult to use a screen reader. For example, the user might hear "asterisk, asterisk, asterisk" or "dash, dash, dash."

 ## Consistency

Consistent placement of menus and objects on the screen makes using a program much more intuitive and predictable. A consistent layout provides easier navigation for users of screen enlargement programs, because they know where to look for things. Consistency supports the use of devices that employ "markers," which identify fixed locations on the screen where particular menus or objects are found. These locations are "marked," and the cursor jumps to the mark when a switch or key is pressed. Also important for consistency are objects and menus that respond dependably throughout the program.

 ## Intuitive Characteristics

An intuitive program makes users feel that they already know how to navigate its features. Clear and obvious options, presented as they are needed, can make a user feel comfortable right from the beginning.

Some programs alter the material presented based on the progress of the user. An example of this is an educational drill or game that automatically advances to the next level of difficulty after a certain number of correct answers. Another example is a grammar checking program that reacts to particular aspects of word usage, such as frequency and word length, by giving feedback to the user. An intuitive program will let the user make a choice and make the consequences clear and simple.

 # Logical Labels

Programs generally present the user with a series of choices, either in a list or a menu. These choices should be labeled with logical, understandable names that give the user a reasonable sense of what will happen when a specific choice is made. This is particularly important when the user—such as someone using a screen reading program—is dependent on auditory cues.

 # Instructional Choices

Instructional software programs generally allow parents or teachers to control content and lesson presentation. The difficulty level, vocabulary, sound, timing, speed, and amount of graphics and text presented can often be adjusted. Some programs of this type keep track of the student's record or progress. Some instructional programs allow parents or teachers to personalize content, such as spelling lists, vocabulary lists, and math problems.

 # Graphics

Graphics can be used to encourage interaction or to convey information in interesting and motivating ways. Graphics or icons may be used as alternatives to words or commands, providing access to nonreaders. Some programs use cues that involve color (for example, "find the red sock"). Other programs allow you to import or scan in graphics—such as a picture of your dog—to add personal content. Graphics can play a role in supporting reading. Graphics without text, however, may limit access to those with visual disabilities.

 # Friendly Documentation

Easy-to-understand software manuals can be important. Many include easy-to-follow diagrams and illustrations of what should be on the screen.

170

—

Computer
and Web
Resources
for People
with
Disabilities

Some manuals are available in large print, in braille, on audiocassette, on computer disk, or in a print layout that is easy to use with a scanner or reading machine. Remember that well-written software is often intuitive and the documentation is needed only for occasional reference.

On-Screen Instructions

Some programs provide on-screen instructions—in the form of help lines, help balloons, or help windows—and instructional prompts to guide the user through the program. It is best if the user has control over how long these instructions remain on the screen.

Auditory Cues

The form of prompts and instructions—verbal, written, or animated—is often critical to making a program accessible and, for some people, easier to understand. Some programs are written to offer verbal prompts or instructions that use synthetic (computer-generated) speech and might require a speech synthesizer. Others use digitized (recorded) speech, sounds, or music and might require a sound card. At times, both sound and visual indicators are used simultaneously and are noticeable even when one's full attention is not on the screen. Some programs use auditory prompts or signals to get the user's attention, which can be helpful for users whose attention can wander quickly from the computer program.

Visual Cues

Some programs use visual prompts at different times during program operation to assist the user in understanding the task. When visual cues accompany auditory cues, more complete access to the program is provided. This can be important to people who do not benefit from auditory cues.

Prompted writing is a feature that allows a facilitator to guide the writer in creating sentences or stories by providing step-by-step written instructions that appear in a box on the screen. These directions usually don't print out as part of the written assignment and are invisible to the person who reads the final product.

Built-in Access Methods

Some programs have built-in alternative access methods and allow you to select the option you want. You can choose to have the program accept input from alternative devices—such as a single switch, alternate keyboard, joystick, touch screen, or game controller—in lieu of the standard keyboard and mouse. Some programs change the presentation of the program to match the requirements of the device. For example, if "single switch" were selected, the program might change from a point-and-click selection method to one that scans the available choices.

Built-in Utilities

Many conventional software programs, such as word processors, spreadsheets, and databases come with utilities as part of their package. These utilities may include spell checkers, dictionaries that allow for modifications, a thesaurus, macros, abbreviation expansion capabilities, and grammar checkers. Some programs also come with text-to-speech options in the menu. Having these utilities built into the software program eliminates the need to run multiple programs simultaneously. This helps to reduce system conflicts and makes it easier to navigate between features.

Alternatives to a Mouse

Some programs are designed to be used primarily with a mouse or joystick. Some software packages allow the user to navigate and operate the program through the keyboard and avoid the use of a mouse. This is accomplished by using the arrow (or cursor) keys and by making menu choices by pressing a specific combination of keys (keyboard equivalents) that activate the desired function. These options can be modified in some operating systems. Accessing items in tool palettes—commonly found in draw programs and paint programs—can also be done through the keyboard. Be aware that some programs provide a way to operate only certain parts of the program by keyboard and require a mouse to do the rest.

Optional Cursors

A cursor is the pointer or marker—typically a small flashing square, two crosshairs, an I-beam, or an arrow—that indicates where you are on the screen. Cursors take a variety of forms. Many computer operating systems and a number of software programs allow the user to adjust what the cursor looks like. The options might include a larger arrow, a thicker I-beam, a hand, a pointed finger, a pencil, thick crosshairs, or even a snake!

☑ Creation of Custom Programs

Computer
and Web
Resources
for People
with
Disabilities

Authoring programs—for example, HyperCard (Apple Computer) for the Macintosh, HyperStudio (Knowledge Adventures) for both the Macintosh and PC, and Authorware (Macromedia), also available on both platforms— allow users to build their own tutorials, drill and practice software, communication boards, instructional aids, informational resources, animations, and other styles of software. A wide range of users—from students to business professionals—can create programs of their own using authoring software. Most authoring programs allow you to work with graphics, text, sounds, and often video. The more customized and sophisticated you want your program to be, the more knowledge you will need of the program language and tools. Custom authoring programs are also available for several augmentative communication devices, such as Speaking Dynamically (Mayer-Johnson), DynaVox, and Talking Screen (Words+, Inc.).

Product Descriptions: Alternate Input

Alternate Keyboards

Alternate keyboards offer a variety of ways to provide input to a computer through various options in size, layout, and complexity.

Programmable keyboards are versatile and often can be programmed so letters, numbers, words, or phrases can be entered by pressing custom keys. They can be larger in size than a standard keyboard, allowing for a larger target area. Smaller keys can also be set up so less range of motion is required. Overlays are used to define the customized keyboard layout.

Miniature keyboards are designed with keys spaced close together to allow someone with a small range of motion to access all the keys. They are typically lightweight and small in size.

Alternate keyboards, such as IntelliKeys, can be customized to match the needs of any software program. (IntelliTools)

174

Computer
and Web
Resources
for People
with
Disabilities

Chording keyboards generally have a limited number of keys. Text is entered by pressing combinations of keys. The keys are sometimes programmable so certain combinations will enter custom words or phrases.

On-screen keyboards are software images of a standard or modified keyboard placed on the computer screen by software. The keys are selected by a mouse, touch screen, trackball, joystick, switch, or electronic pointing device.

 Use this tool to...

Simplify the method of entering information

Create keyboards using pictures instead of words or letters

Create keyboards using tactile materials instead of words or letters

Type with words and phrases instead of letters

Access communication boards

Communicate meaning through graphics, photographs, or objects

Practice letter-sound recognition

Learn the meaning of words through graphics, photographs, or objects

Limit the number of keys to the specific ones required to do the task

Enter information using a switch with an on-screen keyboard

Replace the mouse

Enter information by head movement or eye gaze with an electronic pointing device and an on-screen keyboard

Enter information using a mouse or mouse alternative with an on-screen keyboard

Provide easy-to-use, motivating activities

 Potential users...

Interact with limited information and benefit from structured choices

Use two hands but the task is tiring

Use two hands but the keys are too far apart

Use one hand but type slowly

Combine words and phrases rather than letters to communicate meaning

Use alternative methods of writing, through symbols and speech

*ScreenDoors 2000 replaces your physical keyboard
with one that is on-screen. (Madentec Limited)*

Have limited fine motor skills

Point, but the task is designed for full use of hands

Need to operate a computer without the use of hands

Comprehend single words but require help with decoding

Communicate through language-based symbols or graphics

Comprehend the meaning of graphic symbols rather than letters

Have limited gross motor skills

See keys that have higher visual contrast

Have visual impairments that limit the ability to discriminate keys

 Features to consider

Some can be customized for different key sizes and arrangements

Some need software that translates the keyboard functions to the computer

Some have an internal computer interface; others require an external one

Some allow the standard keyboard and the alternate keyboard to be used at the same time

Some require less pressure to activate a key

Some on-screen keyboards come with dictionaries or word prediction programs

176

Computer
and Web
Resources
for People
with
Disabilities

Some replace mouse and keyboard

Some replace keyboard only

Some can customize the color contrast between the keys and the background

Some can be used to create a series of keyboard layouts by making overlays

 Cost

Programmable keyboards

Range: $250–1,700
Common: $300–500

Miniature keyboards

Range: $400–800
Common: $450

Chording keyboards

Range: $250–650
Common: $300

On-screen keyboards

Range: $100–1,200
Common: $350–800

 Common vendors

Programmable keyboards

Don Johnston, Inc.

EKEG Electronics Company, Ltd.

Exceptional Computing, Inc.

Hach Associates

Handykey Corporation

IntelliTools

Sunburst Communications

TASH International, Inc.

Zygo Industries, Inc.

Miniature keyboards

EKEG Electronics Company

In Touch Systems

TASH International, Inc.

Chording keyboards

Infogrip, Inc.

TASH International, Inc.

On-screen keyboards

Don Johnston, Inc.

Gus Communications

Innovation Management Group, Inc.

Madentec, Ltd.

Mayer-Johnson Company

Microsoft Corporation

Prentke Romich Company

R. J. Cooper and Associates

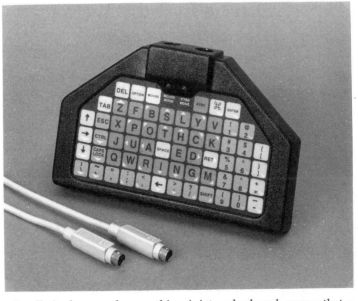

Photo courtesy of TASH, Inc.

*Small-size keys, such as on this miniature keyboard, ensure that a
small range of motion allows full access to the keyboard.
(TASH International, Inc.)*

ALTERNATE INPUT

178

Computer
and Web
Resources
for People
with
Disabilities

Words+, Inc.

World Communications

 Additional information

The layout and key size of the standard keyboard is not always the best choice for access. Alternate keyboards provide different means of accessing a computer. Some alternate keyboards can be modified and the layouts customized for individual use. Paper or plastic overlays fit on top of the keyboard and are used to designate where to press on the keyboard for a desired keystroke or customized response. The areas to be pressed can be defined by letters, numbers, punctuation, words, pictures, tactile materials, or objects. Many innovative teaching strategies can be implemented using an alternate keyboard.

Chording keyboards often come with a tutorial for learning chord combinations and a quick reference chart of chord combinations. The hand size the device accommodates may be limited (for example, some are sized for an adult, male hand only). The number of keys varies among devices (12 finger keys and 6 thumb keys, 10 finger and 4 thumb, etc.). Software may allow reconfiguration of the chords. Additional software utilities—such as abbreviation expansion programs—can be used with a chording keyboard to increase typing speed by reducing keystrokes. Braille notetakers are another chording device.

On-screen keyboards may have built-in scanning options to be used with a single switch.

 Related products

Arm and wrist supports

Joysticks

Keyboard additions

Electronic pointing devices

Pointing and typing aids

Speech synthesizers

Talking and large-print word processors

Touch screens

Trackballs

Switches and switch software

Access Utilities

Access utilities are software programs that modify various aspects of the standard keyboard to simplify operation of the keyboard, replace the mouse, substitute visual cues for sound signals, or add sound cues to keystrokes.

 Use this tool to...

Increase speed when using a pointing aid or typing device

Change the layout of the keyboard

Limit the entering of unwanted keys

Provide other indicators (visual or auditory) when some key functions are on or off

Eliminate the need to press more than one key at a time

Enhance visibility of system cursors for pointing and editing

 Potential users...

Use one finger or a pointing aid and need to increase speed or reduce the number of keystrokes required

Have better gross motor dexterity than fine motor dexterity

Use one hand but the task requires pressing two keys at a time

Strike keys by mistake because of tremors

Require visual notification of computer alert sounds

 Features to consider

Some allow access to menus through function keys or combinations of keystrokes

Some eliminate the need to press two keys at a time

Some can adjust the key repeat rate

Some can adjust the time required to hold a key down before it is entered

Some prevent the keyboard from accepting two quick presses of the same key (repeat defeat)

180

Computer
and Web
Resources
for People
with
Disabilities

Some let the user replace the mouse and use the number pad on the keyboard to control cursor movements

Some indicate if keys such as Num Lock, Scroll Lock, and Caps Lock are on or off

Some replace computer sounds with visual indicators

Some allow the user to redefine the keyboard to create other layouts

 Cost

Range: free–$1,200

Common: $150

 Common vendors

Apple Computer, Inc.

Gus Communications

IBM Independence Series Information Center

IntelliTools

The Matias Corporation

Microsoft Corporation

Microsystems Software, Inc.

R. J. Cooper and Associates

Words+, Inc.

World Communications

 Additional information

Macintosh: The system software for Macintosh computers comes with two "Universal Access"control panels—called Easy Access and CloseView—that have many customization features. They offer a variety of keyboard and output adjustments, depending on the version of the system software that you are using. Check your Macintosh user's manual for more information. Depending on the source of the computer, these control panels are not always preinstalled but are included in a Universal Access folder on the system installation CD.

PCs: Basic keyboard modification programs are available for both MS-DOS (AccessDOS) and Windows (Access Pack for Windows).

Windows 95 and later versions offer a number of accessibility options that are built into the software itself. For more information about these features and Access Pack you can visit the "Accessibility Support" page at Microsoft's World Wide Web site (www.microsoft.com/enable). In Windows 98, the user can install the Accessibility Options program, which includes the Accessibility Wizard and the Magnifier. The Accessibility Wizard customizes options for vision, hearing, and mobility. The Magnifier displays an enlarged section of the screen in a separate window. Windows 2000 adds a Narrator for limited text to speech and an On-Screen Keyboard.

AccessDOS is available free from IBM by calling (800) 426-7282 and ordering Part #83G7828. Access Pack for Windows 3.0 and 3.1 is available from Microsoft and can be ordered by calling (800) 426-9400. AccessDOS and Access Pack for Windows 3.0 and 3.1 can also be ordered directly from the Trace Center by calling (608) 262-6966 (voice) and (608) 263-5408 (TTY).

AccessDOS can be downloaded from the Trace Center website (www.trace.wisc.edu). Access Pack for Windows can also be downloaded from Trace (www.trace.wisc.edu), as well as other online bulletin boards and services.

 Related products

Abbreviation expansion and macro programs

Keyboard additions

Joysticks

Pointing and typing aids

Trackballs

Word prediction programs

Keyboard Additions

A variety of accessories have been designed to make keyboards more accessible.

Keyguards are hard plastic covers with holes for each key. Using a keyguard, someone with an unsteady finger or with a pointing device can avoid striking unwanted keys.

Moisture guards are thin sheets of plastic that protect keyboards from spills and drooling.

Alternative labels add visual clarity or tactile information to the keys.

182

Computer
and Web
Resources
for People
with
Disabilities

 Use this tool to...

Keyguards

Increase accuracy

Maintain correct placement of hand while typing

Moisture guards

Protect from spills and other moisture

Alternative labels

Provide cues for frequently used keys

Increase color contrast on the tops of the keys

 Potential users...

Need more separation between the keys

Benefit from visual or tactile enhancement of the keyboard

Benefit from guarding keys from accidental pressing

 Features to consider

Keyguards must match the specific keyboard layout

Moisture guards must match the specific keyboard layout

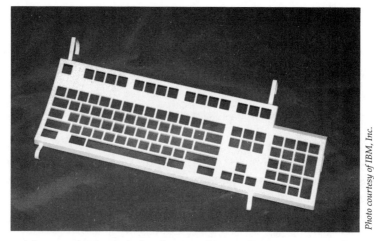

Photo courtesy of IBM, Inc.

*A keyguard helps to isolate keys, making each target
easier to find. (IBM, Inc.)*

Some labels add color to specific keys

Some labels add tactile cues to the keys

Some labels enlarge the name or include the function of specific keys

 Cost

Keyguards

Range: $50–150

Common: $80

Moisture guards

Range: $25

Common: $25

Alternative labels

Range: $5–20

Common: $10

 Common vendors

Keyguards

Enabling Devices

IBM Independence Series Information Center

IntelliTools

Prentke Romich Company

TASH International, Inc.

TechAble

Turning Point

Words+, Inc.

Moisture guards

Don Johnston, Inc.

Global Computer Supplies

Hooleon Corporation

Span-America Medical Systems, Inc.

ALTERNATE INPUT

184

Computer
and Web
Resources
for People
with
Disabilities

Alternative labels

Carolyn's Products for Enhanced Living

Data Cal Corporation

Don Johnston, Inc.

Hooleon Corporation

 Additional information

Keyguards are available for many of the alternate keyboards. Many stationery stores carry printed labels that can be put on keys to enlarge letters and numbers or to increase the color contrast.

 Related products

Access utilities

Alternate keyboards

Arm and wrist supports

Monitor additions

Pointing and typing aids

Talking and large-print word processors

Switches and Switch Software

Switches offer ways to provide input to a computer when a more direct access method, such as a standard keyboard or mouse, is not possible. Switches come in various sizes, shapes, colors, methods of activation, and placement options. An interface device and software are usually required to connect the switch to the computer and interpret the operation of the switch.

Some software programs have been developed specifically for use with a switch and can employ on-screen scanning. With on-screen scanning, the computer highlights (either by sound, visual cue, or both) options available to a user about what action he or she wants the computer to take. Using these specialized products, when a visual or auditory prompt indicates a desired keyboard or mouse function, the user activates the switch and the desired function occurs.

Other programs have built-in options to allow switch use. Many standard software programs can be accessed through a switch with the use of additional software and devices.

 Use this tool to....

Enter text or data when using the keyboard is not feasible

Interact with the computer by selecting choices as they are highlighted

Set up a series of responses using multiple switches

Train in cause and effect

Facilitate choice-making

Control the computer via Morse code

 Potential users...

Need an alternative to the keyboard

Need to operate a computer with one or two movements

Benefit from structured interaction with the environment

 Features to consider

Most can be mounted and activated by any part of the body

Photo courtesy of TASH, Inc.

Single switches come in a wide range of sizes and shapes and allow you to do anything on the computer that anyone else can do with one touch of the switch. (TASH International, Inc.)

186

Computer
and Web
Resources
for People
with
Disabilities

Some are sensitive to light touch

Some are activated by pressure (the pressure required may vary from switch to switch)

Some are activated by sound

Some are activated by interrupting a light beam

Some can be fastened to any part of the body

Some are activated by pulling

Some are activated by squeezing

Some are activated when bent

Some are available in different sizes and colors

Some are activated by the blink of an eye

Some are activated by a specific motion detected by a digital camera

 Cost

Range: $30–400

Common: $40–65

 Common vendors

Switches

Ability Research

AbleNet, Inc.

Adaptivation

Apt Technologies, Inc.

Don Johnston, Inc.

Edmark Corporation

Enabling Devices

Exceptional Computing, Inc.

Hach Associates

Innocomp

KY Enterprises/Custom Computer Solutions

Luminaud, Inc.

ORCCA Technology

Prentke Romich Company

TASH International, Inc.

Toys for Special Children, Inc.

Zygo Industries, Inc.

Switch software

Academic Software, Inc.

Assistive Technology, Inc.

Computers to Help People, Inc.

Consultants for Communication Technology

Don Johnston, Inc.

Easter Seals Colorado

Edmark Corporation

Gus Communications

IntelliTools

KidTECH

Laureate Learning Systems, Inc.

Madentec, Ltd.

MarbleSoft

Mayer-Johnson Company

Microsystems Software, Inc.

NanoPac, Inc.

Prentke Romich Company

R. J. Cooper and Associates

Simtech Publications

Soft Touch / KidTech

Switch In Time

Switch Kids

188

Computer
and Web
Resources
for People
with
Disabilities

Synergy

Technology for Language and Learning

UCLA Intervention Program for Young Handicapped Children
(UCLA/LAUSD)

Visuaide 2000, Inc.

Words+, Inc.

World Communications

 Additional information

Switches can operate environmental controls, radios, appliances, battery-operated toys, and augmentative and alternative communication devices and can control powered mobility. A switch and switch interface will operate programs designed for single-switch input. Some programs that require a single input (mouse click, space bar, return key, etc.) may also work with a switch interface. For access to the entire keyboard and most commercial programs, additional software and hardware are required.

Switches can be custom made. *Utilizing Switch Interfaces with Children Who Are Severely Physically Challenged*, by Carol Gossens and Sharon Sapp Crain, contains useful information on this topic (see Part III, Books, for reference).

 Related products

Interface devices

Joysticks

Interface Devices

Interface devices provide access to the standard alphanumeric keyboard, the keyboard functions, and sometimes the mouse controls by enabling the use of single switches, alternate keyboards, or other input devices.

Switch interfaces are used to connect the switch to the computer and are used with software written for single-switch use.

Multiple-switch interfaces are used to connect a series of switches to the computer. Each switch can be defined as a character, word, phrase, or action.

Multiple-input interfaces are used to connect switches, alternate keyboards, and other input devices to the computer. Software that interprets the information from these devices to the computer is often included. These devices can allow the user to operate software with a switch even when not originally written for switch use.

When switches are used, the choices of letters, numbers, or pictures are displayed and sequentially highlighted on the screen. When the highlight indicates the desired choice, the user activates the switch, which enters the choice into the computer. This selection process is called *scanning*.

 Use this tool to...

Enter text or data when the keyboard is not feasible

Design customized keyboards to simplify activities

Make communication boards that can be accessed by a switch or alternate keyboard.

Set up a series of responses or keyboard functions, one for each switch, using multiple switches

Enter text by sending Morse code through one or two switches

Use standard software programs through a switch-and-scanning method

Connect a switch, and use software with built-in scanning options

Photo courtesy of WesTest Corporation

Darci Too, an interface device, lets you control a wide range of computers using switches, joysticks, video-game controllers, and expanded keyboards. (WesTest Engineering Corporation)

190

Computer
and Web
Resources
for People
with
Disabilities

 Potential users...

Need to operate a computer without the use of their hands

Use switches, alternate keyboards, or directional joysticks to operate a computer

Need to operate a computer with one or two movements

 Features to consider

Most have control of the rate at which the selections are highlighted when scanning is used

Some keyboard interfaces operate with any software program

Most can work while the standard keyboard and mouse remain active

Some can use pictures or graphics, instead of text, to indicate choices

Some show the highlighted choices on the computer screen

Some show the highlighted choices through a built-in display on the interface device

Some can replace the mouse

Some allow a variety of methods for selecting the choice (for example, the choice is made when switch is pressed versus when it is released)

Some can interpret Morse code

Some can work with a speech synthesizer for auditory prompts to indicate choices

Some have built-in word prediction capabilities

 Cost

Switch interfaces

Range: $75–500

Common: $125

Multiple-switch interfaces

Range: $75–150

Common: $100

Multiple-input interfaces

Range: $400–1,000

Common: $500–800

 Common vendors

Switch interfaces

AbleNet, Inc.

Consultants for Communication Technology

Don Johnston, Inc.

Gus Communications

Hach Associates

R. J. Cooper and Associates

Multiple-switch interfaces

AbleNet, Inc.

Don Johnston, Inc.

Multiple-Input Interfaces

TASH International, Inc.

WesTest Engineering Corporation

Words+, Inc.

 Additional information

Some software programs have built-in scanning. All that is needed is a simple switch interface to connect the switch to the computer.

Some standard software programs can be operated by a switch. This requires an interface device that connects the switch to the computer and has software that creates the choices and interprets the switch activation.

Morse code can be used to enter text into the computer by using switches. One, two, or three switches may be used depending on the needs of the user. This requires an interface device that connects the switch to the computer and has software that interprets the code.

PC/Windows users must carefully select software for the on-screen display to make sure it is compatible with other programs and the operating sys-

192

Computer
and Web
Resources
for People
with
Disabilities

tem, especially when using Windows. Hardware solutions have the advantage of being independent of software compatibility problems, but may require the user to visually attend both to the computer screen and to a separate scanning device.

 Related products

Abbreviation expansion and macro programs

Alternate keyboards

Joysticks

Speech synthesizers

Switches and switch software

Word prediction programs

Voice Recognition

Different types of voice recognition systems—also called speech recognition—are available. Voice recognition allows the user to speak to the computer instead of using a keyboard or mouse to input data or control computer functions. Voice recognition systems can be used to create text documents such as letters or email, to browse the Internet, and to navigate among applications and menus by voice.

 Use this tool to...

Input text or data by voice

Navigate among files, applications, and menus by voice

Execute standard commands by voice

Control all functions of a computer hands-free

 Potential users...

Have difficulty using a standard keyboard and mouse due to motor skills issues or repetitive stress injuries

Have learning disabilities resulting in some difficulties with spelling or grammar

Use speech recognition as voice therapy to encourage clear and distinct enunciation

Use dictation as the method of typing instead of a keyboard

 Features to consider

Most must be trained to respond to a particular voice (a predetermined list of words or a passage is read into the computer microphone by the user to provide the user's unique information on pronunciation and inflection).

Most systems require the user's speech to be consistent

Discrete dictation systems require the user to pause slightly between words and are generally more forgiving of speech or articulation differences

Continuous dictation systems use more fluent and natural speech patterns and are more successful with users who have good enunciation and who use organized and sequenced speech

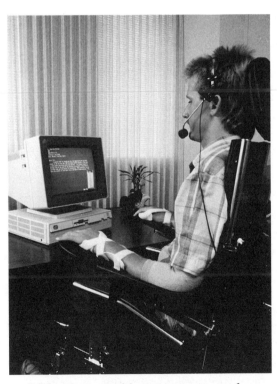

With voice recognition systems you can be a computer user by talking instead of typing.
(IBM Corporation)

194

Computer
and Web
Resources
for People
with
Disabilities

Many allow the user to navigate the computer—that is, to control the cursor and execute commands—by voice

Some have larger vocabularies and provide a wider range of navigation or dictation capabilities

Some have vocabularies (legal, medical) specific to a vocational field

Some dictation systems can recognize phrases that the user uses frequently

Some can recognize a wide range of voices and do not require training

Some computers have voice navigation built into the system

 Cost

Range: $50–400

Common: $150

 Common vendors

Apple Computer, Inc.

Dragon Systems

IBM Independence Series Information Center

Lernout & Hauspie, Kurzweil Educational Systems Group

Microsoft Corporation

NanoPac, Inc.

 Additional information

Discrete vs. continuous speech: Initially, all speech recognition programs required discrete speech, meaning at least a short pause between words. This made the analysis of the sounds and determination of the word spoken an easier computing task. It also made the system somewhat more forgiving of speech differences. Almost all systems are now moving toward a more natural, continuous speech model. This is more intuitive, especially for new users, and is made possible by more powerful processors and more sophisticated recognition models. Experience to date has shown continuous speech to be less tolerant of speech differences. Additionally, some of these newer applications are giving up some of the hands-free command and control in favor of continuous dictation.

Readiness: Readiness for use of voice recognition includes such factors as understanding the operating system and software to be used, sustaining attention, and motivating for and coping with frustration during the training process.

Environment factors: Consider the environment in which the system will be used, such as home, work, or classroom. Background noise can affect the system, which generally needs to be used in an environment consistent with the one in which training was done. Confidentiality issues must also be addressed, as all input is spoken aloud.

Support and training: Thorough training of the software is very important for success of voice recognition. Some users may require customized training and equipment along with high levels of support. Post-training support is also a key issue. Technical difficulties often arise with the voice recognition software, application software, operating system, or hardware. Proper computer setup and troubleshooting can be especially critical if voice recognition is the main computer input method for an individual with a disability.

Hardware: All hardware is not created equal. A compatible combination of software, microphone, sound card, and computer are required for successful voice recognition. The software should be chosen first and then tried on the intended computer before a final purchase is made. This is especially true of laptop applications.

Macintosh: Apple Plain Talk, a navigation program only, is an extension of System 7.1 and later versions. To do dictation, you need a product that will enable both dictation and navigation. There is not currently a viable dictation program available for the Macintosh computer, but both IBM and Dragon have announced Macintosh versions of their continuous speech products.

PCs: Windows requires a program specifically designed to allow navigation in that environment. Several voice recognition products require the appropriate sound card. Most Windows voice applications are moving rapidly toward continuous speech models. However, a discrete speech application, customizable specifically for individuals with disabilities, is anticipated.

 Related products

Environmental control units

Optical character recognition and scanners

196

Computer
and Web
Resources
for People
with
Disabilities

Optical Character Recognition and Scanners

Optical character recognition (OCR) software works with a scanner to convert images from a printed page into a standard computer file.

A scanner is a device that converts an image from a printed page to a computer file. With optical character recognition software, the resulting computer file can be edited. Pictures and photographs do not require OCR software to be manipulated.

 Use this tool to...

Transfer a printed worksheet to the computer so it can be accessed by assistive devices

Transfer printed documents so they can be read aloud by a speech synthesizer, printed in large text, or embossed in braille

Transfer printed materials to the computer to change text size, style, and layout

Scan family photographs to include in stories or create personal overlays for alternate keyboards

 Potential users...

Can handle the equipment physically but cannot read printed manuals or documents

May read at a lower level than their potential

Need materials in an accessible format to complete an activity

 Features to consider

All OCR programs translate text from print form to a text file on the computer, which can then be edited

Most OCR programs adjust for scanning single or multiple pages

Most OCR programs have light adjustment

Most OCR programs can be set for a specific adjustment for page orientation (portrait or landscape)

Some OCR programs can be set to scan a whole page or selected portions of a page

All scanners have utility programs that allow the scanner to communicate with the computer and save the scanned image as a graphic file on the computer

Most scanners store images in shades of gray (called gray-scale images)

Some scanners are capable of detecting colors

Handheld scanners can scan small portions of text at a time

Flatbed scanners can scan full-size pieces of paper at a time

Some scanners require the installation of an interface board to the computer

 Cost

OCR programs

Range: $300–700

Common: $600

Scanners

Range: $300–2,000

Common: $1,500

Common vendors

Integrated System Vendors

Arkenstone, Inc.

Lernout & Hauspie, Kurzweil Educational Systems Group

Reading Technologies

 Additional information

OCR software is invaluable in converting materials from print to electronic formats. The OCR software translates the images into text by comparing the scanned-in materials against a table of letters, numbers, and symbols and makes a best guess as to what each character is. The resulting file can then be altered like any file.

Scanners come in two varieties: flatbed and handheld. Flatbed scanners look very much like desktop copiers. Handheld scanners are easily held in

198

Computer
and Web
Resources
for People
with
Disabilities

the hand. Flatbed scanners are great for scanning full-sized images and multiple pages at high resolutions (the amount of detail that a scanner can perceive), but cost substantially more than the handheld variety. Scanners, with their accompanying software, are available to run on both Macintosh and PC platforms. Most scanner software does not distinguish between pictures and text. To the scanner, everything is just an image. To edit text that has been scanned, the user must also have OCR software.

Copyright laws must be respected when scanning printed material.

 Related products

Reading machines

Screen readers

Electronic Pointing Devices

Electronic pointing devices allow the user to control the cursor on the screen using ultrasound, an infrared beam, eye movements, nerve signals, or brains waves. When used with an on-screen keyboard, electronic pointing devices also allow the user to enter text or data.

 Use this tool to...

Enter text or data into a computer when a mouse and keyboard are not feasible

Operate a draw program or a computer-aided design program

Actuate an on-screen keyboard

Operate assistive communication systems and environmental controls

Access the Internet

 Potential users...

Need to operate a computer without the use of their hands

Have good head control, eye control, or the ability to learn control through nerve signals or brain waves

Features to consider

Some require activating a switch to make a selection

Some allow the user to pause or dwell on a key to select it

Some require an eye blink to make a selection

All work with an on-screen keyboard

Some allow the user to control the cursor by head motions

Some require the head to be held still while the computer is controlled with eye movement

Some have wires connecting them to the computer; others operate remotely

 Cost

Range: $1,000–17,500

Common: $1,500

 Common vendors

Ability Research

Brain Actuated Technologies

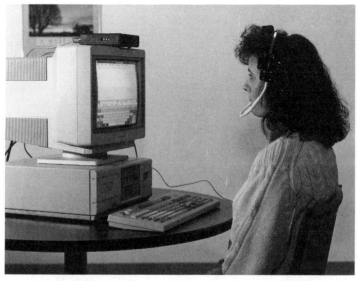

*The HeadMaster provides full mouse control for people who
are unable to use their hands but have good head control.
(Prentke Romich Company)*

200

———

Computer
and Web
Resources
for People
with
Disabilities

EyeTech Digital Systems

Madentec, Ltd.

Origin Instruments Corporation

Technos America, Ltd.

Prentke Romich Company

Words+, Inc.

 Additional information

Once the cursor has been placed in the desired location, the user can make a selection by dwelling in that location or using one of a variety of switches. The pointer will work with any on-screen keyboard compatible with the computer system. Electronic pointing devices that rely on eye movement or nerve impulses are newly emerging and rapidly becoming more sophisticated and economically viable.

 Related products

Alternate keyboards

Switches and switch software

Word prediction programs

Pointing and Typing Aids

A pointing or typing aid is typically a wand or stick used to strike keys on the keyboard. They are most commonly worn on the head, held in the mouth, strapped to the chin, or held in the hand.

 Use this tool to...

Enter text or data using a standard or alternate keyboard

Operate a trackball, touch screen, or alternate keyboard

 Potential users...

Need to operate a computer without the use of their hands

Need to point with a single digit

Features to consider

All can be used with keyguards

All can be used with standard, alternate, or modified keyboards

Most are adjustable in length and fit

Some have an adjustable head strap to be worn on the head or across the chin

Some have a bite plate to be held in the mouth

Some are used with a splint on the hand or arm

 Cost

Range: $25–600

Common: $60

 Common vendors

Adlib, Inc.

Crestwood Company

Photo courtesy of Madenta

Bill Miller shows how Tracker can be used to help him in his career as a graphic designer.

202

Computer
and Web
Resources
for People
with
Disabilities

Extensions for Independence

Fred Sammons, Inc.

Maddak, Inc.

North Coast Medical, Inc.

 Related products

Alternate keyboards

Access utilities

Touch screens

Trackballs

Touch Screens

A touch screen is a device placed on the computer monitor (or built into it) that allows direct selection or activation of the computer by a touch of the screen.

 Use this tool to...

Provide an intuitive interface for young children and those with cognitive disabilities

Build cause-and-effect skills

Motivate computer use

Enter text or data using an on-screen keyboard

Make a direct selection by pointing at the screen

 Potential users...

Need a more intuitive interface

Need a more direct method of moving the cursor on the screen

Interact well with information but need a simpler method of input

Interact well with information but require interesting and motivating approaches

Interact with environment with a closer connection between cause and effect

Features to consider

All allow direct selection of items on the screen by touching a monitor

All take the place of the mouse

Some are integrated into the monitor

Some are detachable from the monitor

Some require software specifically written to work with the touch screen

Some can be used with an on-screen keyboard

Some are available in several sizes to accommodate different sized monitors

 Cost

Range: $200–5,000

Common: $350–2,000

 Common vendors

Edmark Corporation

KEYTEC

Microtouch Systems, Inc.

Troll Touch

 Additional information

Touch sensitive screens may be used to move a cursor, imitate a mouse, or make selections. The touch screen may be used as one large single switch with some switch software. Some users point and type on an on-screen keyboard using a touch screen to provide a direct cognitive connection between the keys and the screen. The mouse and keyboard may still be used while the touch screen is active.

Touch screens are effective with young children or people whose skills are at a lower functional level when the software has simple point-and-click options. Touch screens tend to be most effective with programs where the target or active area is as large as the individual's fingertip. A stylus, with a soft point, could be used for greater accuracy.

A consideration in the purchase of a touch screen is the continued lifting of the arm to activate the window. Raising the arm could prove tiring over time for some individuals. On the other hand, the same motions could be incorporated into the individual's therapy to improve gross motor skills.

Macintosh: The detachable screen plugs into the Apple Desktop Bus (ADB) port on the back of the computer. It functions transparently as a mouse replacement with all software programs.

PCs: The detachable screen plugs into the serial port. Other types of screens may be built directly into the monitor. Most versions for PCs require special drivers (utility programs) that are supplied with the touch screen. The screen will only work with those programs that involve the use of a mouse.

Both Macintosh and PC/Windows computers are now making use of the Universal Serial Bus (USB) port and vendors will be developing USB interface touch screens.

 Related products

Alternate keyboards

Pointing and typing aids

Speech synthesizers

Switches and switch software

Joysticks

A joystick may be used as an alternate input device. Joysticks that can be plugged into the computer's mouse port can control the cursor on the screen. Other joysticks plug into game ports and depend on software that is designed to accept joystick control. Three types of control are offered by joysticks: digital, glide, and direct. Digital control allows movement in a limited number of directions such as up, down, left, and right. Glide and direct control allow movements in all directions (360 degrees). Direct-control joysticks have the added ability to respond to the distance and speed with which the user moves the stick.

 Use this tool to...

Motivate computer use

Operate a communication system or environmental control unit

Activate the computer with different parts of the body

Enter text or data using an on-screen keyboard

Practice mobility skills for operating a power wheelchair

 Potential users...

Have use of hands but the task requires relating the mouse movement to the screen

Need to operate a computer without the use of their hands

Interact well with information but need a simpler method of input

Interact well with information but require interesting and motivating approaches

Practice use of a joystick for wheelchair control

 Features to consider

Some are equipped with up to three control buttons that can be programmed to perform various functions

Some require more force to operate than others

Some are designed to be operated with the chin or head

Some work only with software written specifically for use with joysticks

Some have switch adaptation

 Cost

Range: $60–500

Common: $70

 Common vendors

Advanced Gravis Corporation

KY Enterprises

Penny and Giles Computer Products Ltd.

Prentke Romich Company

R. J. Cooper and Associates

TASH International, Inc.

206

Computer
and Web
Resources
for People
with
Disabilities

 Additional information

Joysticks come in many sizes and shapes. Available options include the capacity for audio feedback, mounting hardware, and cables allowing use with different computers. Some interface devices accept joysticks as an input method.

Macintosh: Joysticks can plug directly into the mouse port and control the cursor on the computer screen in all programs.

PCs: The joystick may plug into the mouse port or serial port and may need software for mouse emulation.

Both Macintosh and PC/Windows computers are now making use of the Universal Serial Bus (USB) port and vendors are beginning to make USB interface joysticks.

 Related products

Interface devices

On-screen keyboards

Switches and switch software

Trackballs

Trackballs

A trackball looks like an upside-down mouse, with a movable ball on top of a stationary base. The ball can be rotated with a pointing device or hand.

 Use this tool to...

Enter text or data with an on-screen keyboard

Perform mouse functions using fewer hand movements or a pointing aid

 Potential users...

Have fine motor skills but not gross motor skills

Use a pointing aid to manipulate the cursor

Control a single finger well

Need to separate the cursor position function from the clicking function

Features to consider

Some have buttons that lock in the down position for easy dragging

Some have buttons that are programmable to perform computer operations

Some have adjustable cursor speed and sensitivity

Some are designed for maximum comfort of the user

Some have balls available in a variety of diameters ranging from 1" to 4"

 ## Cost

Range: $60–170

Common: $75–130

 ## Common vendors

Fellowes

Ergo Kare

Kensington Microware Ltd.

Logitech, Inc.

Microsoft Corporation

Mouse Systems

Penny and Giles Computer Products Ltd.

 ## Additional information

A trackball is a mouse alternative used to control cursor movements and actions on a computer screen. The cursor is activated when buttons on the device are pressed, similar to a standard mouse. Trackballs are common features in laptop computer systems. The drag and click-lock feature enables the user to operate a trackball with a single digit. Trackballs added to existing computers have the same interface and compatibility issues as joysticks.

 ## Related products

Joysticks

Alternate keyboards

Touch screens

208

Computer
and Web
Resources
for People
with
Disabilities

Arm and Wrist Supports

Arm supports are devices that stabilize and support arms and wrists while the user is typing or using a mouse or trackball. Wrist rests support the wrist while using a keyboard.

 Use this tool to...

Provide physical support while typing or using a mouse or trackball

 Potential users...

Need support to avoid fatigue or pain

Benefit from having arms stabilized

 Features to consider

Most provide support at the arm or wrist

Some attach to the table in front of the computer

Some have cuffs to support the forearm

Some have adjustable heights

Some swivel in two or more directions

Some mount on the chair instead of the table

Some wrist supports are built into the keyboard

 Cost

Arm supports

Range: $100–600

Common: $100

Wrist supports

Range: $10–20

Common: $15

Common vendors

Adaptability

Ergo Kare

Keyboard Alternatives and Visions Solutions, Inc.

Less Gauss, Inc.

SaundersErgo Source

XYBIX Systems

 Additional information

One or both arms can be supported in a variety of ways, depending on individual preference. Before the release of commercial products, people used foam wedges, foam bars, and other supports.

 Related products

Alternate keyboards

Keyboard additions

Monitor additions

Product Descriptions: Processing Aids

Browsers

The Internet is the term used to describe the multitude of computers, large and small, around the world linked by cables, modems, telephone lines, and satellites. Many individuals, organizations, and companies offer websites with information or opinions in the form of text, graphics, and—increasingly—sounds and video. To access these websites on other computers, you must have a browser on your computer, a modem or other Internet line, and an Internet Service Provider (ISP). Hundreds of Internet Service Providers are available in every community. Some ISPs are free; others charge a monthly fee. If you connect with a nonlocal telephone number, you may also end up paying for the time your computer is using your phone line. Services and connection speeds vary. Part III contains a list of the more popular Internet resources you may wish to consider.

Once you have chosen an ISP and configured your computer for access to the Internet, browsers allow you to navigate your way among the millions of websites available. Analogous to dialing a telephone number, you can go directly to a particular website by typing the website address (URL)—a string of letters, punctuation, and/or numbers that often contain "www" ".com" ".net" or ".org." You can also find sites containing key words or phrases using a search engine, "surf" from one site to another by selecting the hyperlinks on screen, and "bookmark" websites of interest so you can easily return to them later.

Like all other computer programs, browsers pose considerations for users with disabilities in that your methods of providing input and perceiving output must be addressed in order to use them. Section I of this book provides a discussion of browser accessibility and the various input and output options available.

 Use this tool to...

"Surf" or browse the millions of websites and resources on the Internet

Locate information of potential interest to you using various "search engines"

Keep a record of sites you have visited during current and past Internet sessions

Download files to your computer, including software, utilities, graphics, or text files

Shop for or order items of interest to you

 Potential users...

Need quick access to news, information, and opinions on a variety of topics

Need access to information and reference material in alternative formats

Have difficulty accessing brick-and-mortar stores for shopping

 Features to consider

All vary in terms of compatibility with individual needs for alternate input, processing, and output

Many come preinstalled on newer computers

Many are provided by the Internet Service Provider along with a trial or paid subscription

Most work best on computers with faster processors and connection speeds

Most allow the user to set text size, color, and fonts for viewing Web pages

Most have options to turn graphics, sounds, or video on or off

Most allow the user to choose which website comes up each time the browser is opened

Some have built-in text-to-speech support

In many cases, accessibility depends on the design of the particular website, rather than the features of the Web browser

 Cost

Browsers

Range: free–$100

Common: free

212

Computer
and Web
Resources
for People
with
Disabilities

Internet service providers

Range: free–$50 per month for unlimited Web access, email account, and personal Web page

Common: $20 per month

 Common Vendors

America Online

IBM Independence Series Information Center

Microsoft Corporation

Netscape

The Productivity Works

SETI

 Additional Information

See Chapter 11 for a discussion of browser accessibility considerations and Internet Resources in Part III for a listing of ISPs. Website addresses for vendors and organizations are also included in Part III.

 Related products

Word prediction programs

Abbreviation expansion and macro programs

Spell checkers

Alternate keyboards

Electronic pointing devices

Screen readers

Screen enlargement programs

Abbreviation Expansion and Macro Programs

Abbreviation expansion programs allow the user to assign a series of letters, words, or sentences to one or more keystrokes. When the assigned keys (the abbreviations) are entered, the program will automatically insert the expanded text.

Macros allow users to "record" a long series of commands and assign them to a function key, combination of keys, menu item, or on-screen button. Once a macro is recorded, the user can execute the complicated task exactly as recorded simply by typing the assigned key(s), selecting from the menu, or clicking the button. For example, with one or two keys, you could open a word processor, enlarge the text, and enter your name or address. You might create another macro to save and print your document in one keystroke.

213

Product
Descriptions:
Processing
Aids

PROCESSING AIDS

 Use this tool to...

Assign simple keystrokes to frequently used words, phrases, sentences, or paragraphs

Automate a series of events such as locating a word processor, starting it up, setting the text to a large size, entering the date at the top, and setting the margins

Create a simple communication tool by storing phrases that can be entered by a keystroke into a word processor and read aloud by a speech synthesizer

Store phrases that can be entered by a switch interface, an alternate keyboard, or a communication device

 Potential users...

Benefit from using fewer keystrokes

Need to increase speed

Need to perform repetitive tasks on the computer accurately and efficiently

Need shortcuts or reminders for difficult tasks

 Features to consider

Many can be used with the operating system as well as most software programs

Some can be found as a feature of other programs, such as word processors and word prediction programs

Some come with prestored abbreviations for specific fields of study

Some can record mouse movements

214

Computer
and Web
Resources
for People
with
Disabilities

Some can use multiple characters as the abbreviation

Some can use only single characters as the abbreviation

Some require two or more keys to be typed simultaneously

Some allow the user to create on-screen buttons for each macro

Some can open Internet browsers and go to particular websites

 Cost

Range: $40–500

Common: $80–150

 Common vendors

ActiveWords, Inc.

Apple Computer

CE Software, Inc.

Gus Communications

Microsoft Corporation

Sunflower Software

TASH International, Inc.

 Additional information

Many abbreviation expansion features are combined with word prediction programs (see Word Prediction Programs for vendors to call). Some word processors and standard packages come with built-in macro features.

 Related products

Access utilities

Word prediction programs

Word Prediction Programs

Word prediction programs enable the user to select a desired word from an on-screen list located in the prediction window. This list, generated by the computer, predicts words from the first one or two letters typed by the user. The word may then be selected from the list and inserted into the text by typing a number, clicking the mouse, or scanning with a switch.

215

Product
Descriptions:
Processing
Aids

PROCESSING AIDS

 ## *Use this tool to...*

Increase written productivity and accuracy

Increase vocabulary skill through word prompting

Reduce fatigue by eliminating unnecessary keystrokes

 ## *Potential users...*

Can recall the first few letters of a word but need assistance with spelling to produce written work

Benefit from word prompts to build vocabulary skills

Need to increase speed or reduce keystrokes

Need assistance with word recall

 ## *Features to consider*

All have prediction windows that appear on the screen

Most can be used with common word processing programs

Some allow users to add their own words

Some can customize text size and position of the word list on the screen

Some can present word choices alphabetically or by frequency of use

Some predict words based on rules of grammar

Some make predictions based on the user's pattern of word usage

Some automatically capitalize the first word in a sentence

Some provide built-in scanning features that visually or auditorily high-light word choices

Some can use text-to-speech to speak the selection or the completed sentence

Some are packaged with abbreviation and expansion features

216

Computer
and Web
Resources
for People
with
Disabilities

 $ Cost

Range: $100–1,000

Common: $300–500

 Common vendors

Don Johnston, Inc.

Gus Communications

Innovative Designs

Madentec, Ltd.

Microsystems Software, Inc.

OMS Development

Prentke Romich Company

textHelp Systems, Ltd.

Words+, Inc.

World Communications

 Related products

Abbreviation expansion and macro programs

Access utilities

Reading Comprehension Programs

Reading comprehension programs focus on establishing or improving reading skills through ready-made activities, stories, exercises, or games.

 Use this tool to...

Improve reading level and comprehension skills

Practice letter sound recognition

Increase understanding of words by adding graphics, sound, and possibly animation

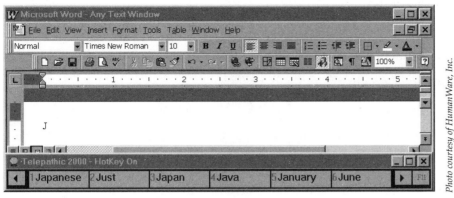

Photo courtesy of HumanWare, Inc.

217

Product
Descriptions:
Processing
Aids

PROCESSING AIDS

Begin typing a word and Telepathic 2000, a word prediction program, helps you quickly finish it by offering you a list of intelligent word choices. (Madentec Limited)

Develop decoding skills

Provide letter sequence practice for word building

Provide word sequence practice for sentence building

Improve word recognition

Improve reading comprehension

Increase vocabulary

 Potential users...

Read lower than their potential level

Comprehend single sentences

Comprehend single words

Comprehend the meaning of symbols

 Features to consider

Some allow adjustment of the vocabulary level

Some have speech output

Some have placement tests

Some do student record keeping

Some have supplementary materials for use off the computer

218

Computer
and Web
Resources
for People
with
Disabilities

Many provide graphics

Some provide animation and sound

Some highlight text as it is read aloud

Some allow adjustment of the font size

Some allow the user to record written or spoken notes

Some provide icons on menu bars or in menus

Some speak items in menus or dialog boxes

Some include built-in scanning for switches

 Cost

Range: $25–2,000

Common: $50–100

 Common vendors

Advanced Ideas, Inc.

A/V Concepts Corporation

Arkenstone, Inc.

CAST, Inc.

Compu-Teach

Continental Press, Inc.

Creative Learning, Inc.

Discis Knowledge Research, Inc.

Don Johnston, Inc.

Edmark Corporation

Educational Activities, Inc.

Great Wave Software

Hartley/Jostens Learning

Houghton Mifflin School Division

IBM Independence Series Information Center

K-12 MicroMedia Publishing

Knowledge Adventures

Laureate Learning Systems, Inc.

The Learning Company

Learning Well

Lernout & Hauspie, Kurzweil Educational Systems Group

Lexia Learning System, Inc.

Little Planet Software / A Division of Houghton Mifflin

Looking Glass Learning Products, Inc.

MarbleSoft

MECC / A Division of The Learning Company

Millenium Software

Milliken Publishing Company

Mindplay

Optimum Resources, Inc.

Scholastic Software

SVE and Churchill Media

Stone and Associates

Sunburst Communications / A Division of Houghton Mifflin

Taylor Associates Communications

Teacher Support Software

Tom Snyder Productions

William K. Bradford Publishing Company

 Additional information

The software may start at the level of letter recognition and move sequentially to the level of passage comprehension, or it may focus only on a more limited set of reading comprehension skills.

Most reading comprehension programs now come in CD-ROM versions which allow for greater voice output, graphics, and animation. The size of the text, the complexity of the graphics and text on the screen, and the level of voice output vary greatly from program to program.

220

Computer
and Web
Resources
for People
with
Disabilities

 Related products

Optical character recognition and scanners

Speech synthesizers

Talking and large-print word processors

Reading Tools and Learning Disabilities Programs

Reading tools include software designed to make text-based materials more accessible for people who struggle with reading. Options may include scanning, reformatting, navigating, or speaking text aloud.

 Use this tool to...

Change the size, style, and spacing of written text for people with low vision

Hear printed text spoken aloud

Create easy-to-navigate "electronic books" from printed or electronic text

Add or modify graphics

 Potential users...

Read at a level below their potential due to visual, learning, or physical disabilities

Comprehend better when they hear and see text highlighted simultaneously

Have difficulty seeing or manipulating conventional print materials

Have emerging literacy skills or are learning English as a foreign language

 Features to consider

Some allow scanning and viewing of the original page

Some allow adjustment of the font style, size, and spacing as needed

Some highlight text as it is spoken

Some allow insertion of written or spoken notes

Some provide a button bar with icons for reading or navigation

Some have built-in switch scanning for reading or navigating the text

 Cost

Range: $200–2,000

Common: $400

 Common vendors

Arkenstone

CAST, Inc.

Lernout & Hauspie, Kurzweil Educational Systems Group

 Additional information

These tools vary greatly in price as well as features offered, such as acquisition of text, options for reading, and user customization. As with all assistive technologies, the user is encouraged to try the various options before purchasing to make sure the tools provided meet their individual needs.

 Related products

Multimedia authoring tools

Reading comprehension programs

Screen readers

Optical character recognition and scanners

Talking and large-print word processors

Writing Composition Programs

Writing composition programs provide a structured environment that enhances an individual's ability to produce written material.

 Use this tool to...

Train in brainstorming, mapping, freewriting, journal writing, and classification

222

Computer
and Web
Resources
for People
with
Disabilities

Develop outlines and main ideas, write first drafts, and learn how to proof-read

Learn sentence completion, story completion, and proper sequencing

Facilitate communication using graphics and speech output

 Potential users...

Write at a level lower than their potential

Compose simple single sentences but require writing ideas and prompts

Combine words and phrases but need help to communicate meaning and organize content

Use an alternative to traditional writing methods

 Features to consider

Most have activities at various levels to develop writing skills

Some have prewriting activities

Some have writing development activities

Some have graphics to use in place of written words

Some have instructional choice options

Some have voice output

Some have text prompts on-screen to use as guides

Some have graphics combined with text

 Cost

Range: $40–250

Common: $50

 Common vendors

ACS Technologies

Blissymbolics Communication International

Communication Skill Builders

Creative Learning, Inc.

Don Johnston, Inc.

Edmark Corporation

Humanities Software

IBM Independence Series Information Center

Information Services, Inc.

Inspiration Software

Knowledge Adventures

The Learning Company

MECC/A Division of the Learning Company

Microsoft Corporation

Mindplay

PEAL Software

Psychological Corporation

Scholastic Software

Stone and Associates

Sunburst Communications/A Division of Houghton Mifflin

Teacher Support Software

Tom Snyder Productions

William K. Bradford Publishing Company

 Additional information

As there are a vast number of programs for Macintosh and PC computers, it is possible to match programs to individual user needs at different skill levels. Most products are standard educational programs.

PCs: Programs using voice output will need to be matched with speech synthesizers that support the particular program. Many create speech using the internal sound card (i.e., Sound Blaster or compatible).

 Related products

Software features: Built-in utilities

Abbreviation expansion and macro programs

223

Product
Descriptions:
Processing
Aids

PROCESSING AIDS

224

___

Computer
and Web
Resources
for People
with
Disabilities

Electronic reference tools

Talking and large-print word processors

Voice recognition

Electronic Reference Tools

Electronic reference tools provide the user with ways to access traditional print materials and resources via the computer. Such references include dictionaries, thesauruses, atlases, almanacs, encyclopedias, and professional journals.

 Use this tool to...

Access traditionally print-based materials via computer

Transfer information, definitions, images, or statistics into a word processing program

Electronically search for a specific name, date, word, or topic

Interact with multisensory reference materials

 Potential users...

Need access to reference materials in formats other than print

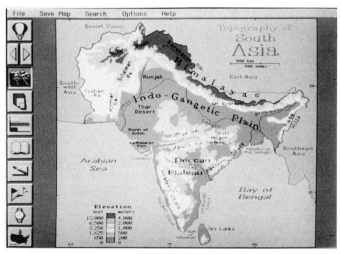

Electronic reference tools, such as this World Atlas, can make the world more accessible than ever.

Interact well with information but require interesting and motivating approaches

Need clear, direct access to information

 Features to consider

Many are available on CD-ROM disks and hold huge volumes of information

Some are available free or for a subscription rate through the Internet

Some are accompanied by photos, music, sounds, video clips, animation timelines, or tables

Most allow a variety of search options

Most provide some standard computer operations such as copy, paste, and print

 Cost

Range: free–$2,000

Common: $100

 Common vendors

Arkenstone, Inc.

Franklin Electronic Publishers, Inc.

Microsoft Corporation

SVE and Churchill Media

 Related products

Built-in utilities

Menu Management and Desktop Security Programs

Menu management programs allow users to interact with a simplified and customized computer environment while providing some protection for the contents of the hard drive.

Computer
and Web
Resources
for People
with
Disabilities

 Use this tool to...

Operate programs and utilities independently at home or at school

Set up access to different sets of files for groups of students in a classroom

Provide access to menus for a nonreader

Personalize access to programs and utilities

Protect files by limiting access by young or inexperienced computer users

 Potential users...

Benefit from a simplified access route to computer programs

Interact well with a structured environment

 Features to consider

Most allow menu selection by mouse or keyboard

Some provide easy access to selected programs from predesigned menus or button bars

Some can hide and secure menu items and files not in use

Some use icons to identify available applications

Some can be set up for scanning with a switch

Some are specifically designed for use in classrooms or by young children

Some require passwords to open, change, or delete files

Some can be set to limit Internet access

Some include various utilities such as a calculator, calendar, and time-and-date display

Some allow saving setups for different users

Some allow the user to designate where files should be saved

 Cost

Range: $45–65

Common: $55

Common vendors

Apple Computer, Inc.

Edmark Corporation

Microsoft Corporation

Smart Stuff Sortware

Symantec

 Related products

Abbreviation expansion and macro programs

227

Product
Descriptions:
Processing
Aids

PROCESSING AIDS

228

Computer
and Web
Resources
for People
with
Disabilities

Product Descriptions: Alternate Output

Talking and Large-Print Word Processors

A talking word processor is a software program that uses a speech synthesizer to provide auditory feedback of what has been typed. Large-print word processors allow the user to view everything in large text without added screen enlargement.

 Use this tool to...

Talking word processors

Have text spoken out loud by chosen parameters (letter, word, sentence, selected text)

Practice letter-name recognition

Combine graphics with speech

Provide a motivating and interesting element to the task

Provide confirmation of a keystroke without looking at the screen

Create a simple communication board using an alternate keyboard

Large-print word processors

Use large-text options without losing full view of the program

 Potential users...

Need alternatives or supplements to printed text

Need large text

Read at lower than potential level

Are assisted by auditory input

Comprehend the meaning of symbols but not words

Interact well with auditory support

Need text specifically formatted to be readable

 Features to consider

Some have speech options

Some have large-text options

Some have both speech and large-text options

Some have cursor options

Some have color text and background options

Talking word processors

All speak selected text aloud

Most allow letter, word, or sentence to be read

Some have speech editing capability to correct the pronunciation of words by the computer

Some have voice options, including male, female, child, and adult

Some have more speech control—such as start, stop, repeat—than others

Large-print word processors

Some come with built-in spell checkers

Most may be used with a word prediction program

 Cost

Range: free–$1,700

Common: $100

 Common vendors

Talking word processors

Bytes of Learning

Center for Applied Special Technology (CAST)

Don Johnston, Inc.

Hartley / Jostens Learning

230

Computer
and Web
Resources
for People
with
Disabilities

IBM Independence Series Information Center

IntelliTools

Teacher Support Software

Large-print word processors

Don Johnston, Inc.

Gus Communications

Hartley/Jostens Learning

Institute on Applied Technology

IntelliTools

Sunburst Communications/A Division of Houghton Mifflin

Teacher Support Software

 Additional information

A talking word processor does not generally have all the capabilities of a screen reader. Some programs can be both large-print and talking word processors.

Macintosh: No special sound cards or synthesizers are needed to use talking word processors with Macintosh computers. You do need software specifically designed for speech output.

PCs: You may need to have a sound card or a speech synthesizer to use a talking word processor on these computers. Check the programs to see what systems and/or synthesizers are compatible.

 Related products

Screen readers

Speech synthesizers

Braille Embossers and Translators

A braille embosser transfers computer-generated text into embossed braille output. Translation programs convert text scanned in or generated via standard word processing programs into braille that can be printed on the embosser.

Use this tool to...

Print computer-generated braille documents

Produce braille materials including books, handouts, signs, restaurant menus, and maps

 Potential users...

Require braille instead of standard print

 Features to consider

All emboss braille

Most need translation software to create Grade 2 braille

Some use speech to help users navigate through printer options menus

Some have liquid crystal displays to indicate page count

Some will print graphics

Some emboss on two sides of a page (this is called interpoint braille)

Some will do braille and standard ink print on same page

A braille printer such as Braillo can print out text files in braille format. (American Thermoform)

232

Computer
and Web
Resources
for People
with
Disabilities

 Cost

Embossers

Range: $1,700–40,000

Common: $3,000–4,500

Translators

Range: $200–1,000

Common: $400

 Common vendors

Embossers

American Thermoform Corporation

Beyond Sight, Inc.

Blazie Engineering, Inc.

Enabling Technologies Company

Index Braille Printer Company

Reading Technologies

Telesensory

Translators

Duxbury Systems, Inc. (includes the former Braille Planet and Raised Dot Computing)

GW Micro

HumanWare, Inc.

MicroTalk

 Additional information

Braille embossers are available in two categories: those designed for individual use, and those designed for high-volume production of embossed materials. Some embossers and other technologies—such as products by American Thermoform—are able to produce tactile graphics.

Related products

Refreshable braille displays

Reading machines

Screen readers

Refreshable Braille Displays

Refreshable braille displays provide tactile output of information presented on the computer screen. Unlike conventional braille, which is permanently embossed onto paper, refreshable braille displays are mechanical in nature and lift small, rounded plastic or metal pins as needed to form braille characters.

Refreshable braille displays contain 20, 40, or 80 braille cells. After the line is read, the user can "refresh" the display to read the next line.

Photo courtesy of HumanWare, Inc.

Alva, a refreshable braille display, provides tactile feedback from the computer for braille users, including those with hearing impairments. (HumanWare, Inc.)

ALTERNATIVE OUTPUT

234

Computer
and Web
Resources
for People
with
Disabilities

 Use this tool to...

Display commands, prompts, and electronic text in braille

Allow the user to get precise information about text attributes, screen formatting, and spelling on the computer display

Provide computer access to persons who are visually impaired, where speech output might not be practical or desired

 Potential users...

Require braille output from the computer

 Features to consider

All can display text from the computer screen

Some can show an 80-column screen on a single braille line

Some can indicate text attributes, such as upper case, highlighted text, and boldface

Some have a touch cursor, which enables the user to move the computer cursor to a particular character with the touch of a button located directly above it

Some have controls for reviewing screen contents with the braille display conveniently located on the front panel

Some include software that provides braille access to Microsoft Windows

 Cost

Range: $3,500–15,000

Common: $4,500–8,000

 Common vendors

American Thermoform Corporation

Blazie Engineering, Inc.

HumanWare, Inc.

Telesensory

Additional information

No refreshable braille access is currently available for Macintosh computers.

Some manufacturers of screen reading programs provide facilities for using refreshable braille displays for screen access.

Some devices connect to a parallel port, others connect to a serial port on PCs.

 Related products

Screen readers

Braille embossers and translators

Speech Synthesizers

With appropriate software, a speech synthesizer can receive information going to the screen in the form of letters, numbers, and punctuation marks, then "speak" it out loud.

 Use this tool to...

Have computer text spoken out loud

Practice letter-sound recognition

Provide a motivating and interesting element to a task

Provide confirmation of a keystroke without looking at the screen

Hear auditory prompts and feedback from a screen reading program or talking word processor

Listen to text from manuals and documents transferred to the computer using an optical character recognition program and a scanner

 Potential users...

Read lower than their potential level but benefit from text spoken aloud

Comprehend single words but require decoding skills

Comprehend the meaning of symbols but need to hear words

236

Computer
and Web
Resources
for People
with
Disabilities

Require manuals and documents read aloud

Need auditory support when screen text is too small

Need auditory feedback to navigate the screen and select commands

Need materials in an accessible format to complete activities

Benefit from auditory feedback

Understand information but need to maintain attention to the task

Use auditory feedback when information on the screen is not usable

 Features to consider

Most work together with software that can convert text to speech

Quality of synthesized speech varies from synthesizer to synthesizer

Most have adjustable volume

Most are equipped with an external jack for speakers or headphones

Some have settings for pitch or speaking voices (for example, male or female)

Some can define special pronunciation rules and add words to the synthesizer's dictionary

 Cost

Range: free (sound card bundled with computer)–$1,200

Common : $125–750

 Common vendors

American Printing House for the Blind, Inc.

Aicom Corporation

Artic Technologies

Beyond Sight, Inc.

Duxbury Systems Inc. (including former Braille Planet)

Compaq Corporation (including former Digital Equipment Corp. products)

Compusult Limited

Consultants for Communication Technology

Gus Communications

GW Micro

HumanWare, Inc.

Institute on Applied Technology

MicroTalk

Personal Data Systems, Inc.

Reading Technologies

Telesensory

 Additional information

To read text characters, speech synthesizers use special memory chips or software in which is stored the thousands of rules the synthesizer uses to translate written text into speech. The translated text is known as synthesized speech, as opposed to digitized speech, which is recorded sound. A synthesizer is either an external device that plugs into the computer (an external synthesizer) or a card that is put into a slot in the computer (an internal synthesizer). Many programs now create synthesized speech through the sound card (i.e., Sound Blaster or compatible) bundled with the computer.

Macintosh: In Macintosh computer systems, speech synthesis is built-in but still requires a screen reading program or talking word processor.

PCs: In MS-DOS computers, a separate speech synthesizer or speech card is required for text-to-speech capability. A software program, usually referred to as a screen reader, that supports that specific speech synthesizer must be used. Most new Windows-based computers come with sound cards preinstalled, while some may not. They will likely require a screen reading program even if a sound card is preinstalled. Be sure to consult with the vendor and computer salesperson to make sure your requirements are met. This is one area where it is recommended you consult with a specialist in screen reading technology, a local group for the visually impaired, or an experienced user of this technology for help with purchase decisions.

 Related products

Optical character recognition and scanners

Screen readers

Reading machines

Computer
and Web
Resources
for People
with
Disabilities

Screen Readers

A screen reader is a software program that works in conjunction with a speech synthesizer to provide verbalization of everything on the screen including control buttons, menus, text, and punctuation.

 Use this tool to...

Provide access to print materials and manuals after they have been scanned into a computer

Provide auditory prompts, menus, and commands

Provide confirmation of keystrokes without looking at the screen

Make a computer accessible to someone with limited or no vision

 Potential users...

Need auditory feedback to read text on the screen

Understand how to handle equipment but need print materials and manuals to be read aloud

Need auditory feedback to navigate the screen and select commands

 Features to consider

All can read units of text such as characters, words, lines, and paragraphs

Most new versions of the programs are designed to work with the graphic user interfaces of Windows and Macintosh operating systems

Some older versions of the programs are designed to work with MS-DOS and other text-based operating systems

Some read selected portions of the screen either automatically or through commands from the keyboard

Some control the rate, pitch, and volume of speech output

Some are compatible with a variety of internal and external speech synthesizers

Some use an external keypad or a touch tablet instead of or in addition to the regular keyboard to control screen reading functions, but most do not

Some employ artificial intelligence to make decisions about what the user wants spoken

Some include the speech synthesizer as part of the package

 Cost

Range: $75–2,100

Common: $450–600

 Common vendors

ALVA Access Group, Inc.

American Printing House for the Blind, Inc.

Artic Technologies

Beyond Sight, Inc.

Blazie Engineering, Inc.

Photo courtesy of Henter-Joyce, Inc.s

A screen reader reads printed material for people who have visual impairments.

240

Computer
and Web
Resources
for People
with
Disabilities

Dolphin Computer Access Limited

Duxbury Systems, Inc. (including former Braille Planet)

GW Micro

Henter-Joyce, Inc.

HumanWare, Inc.

Knowledge Adventures

MicroTalk

Reading Technologies

Syntha-Voice Computers, Inc.

Telesensory

 Additional information

Macintosh: A screen reader designed for the Macintosh can use the built-in speech hardware to access Macintosh applications. It does not require an additional speech synthesizer.

PCs: Speech synthesizers are available in internal and external versions. Internal versions require a suitable expansion slot to be available in the computer; external versions require a free serial or parallel port compatible with the synthesizer. Check for compatibility of screen readers and speech synthesizers or cards when using MS-DOS or Windows operating systems. Some new programs create synthesized speech using the sound card (i.e., Sound Blaster or compatible) bundled with the computer when purchased.

 Related products

Optical character recognition and scanners

Reading machines

Speech synthesizers

Talking and large-print word processors

Screen Enlargement Programs

A screen enlargement program focuses on a single portion of the screen and enlarges it.

Use this tool to...

Magnify the text and graphics on the screen

 Potential users...

Need large text

 Features to consider

Most have variable magnification levels (2x to 16x or more)

Most have a cursor that tracks the area being magnified or jumps to pop-up windows

Some have split-screen viewing of magnified and unmagnified windows to magnify by line, selected segments, horizontal or vertical screens, and other windowing options

Some include screen reading for auditory output in addition to magnification

Most are software only, while some are software/hardware combinations

 Cost

Software

Range: free–$700

Common: $500

Hardware

Range: up to $2,500

Common: $2,000

 Common vendors

Ai Squared

ALVA Access Group, Inc.

Apple Computer, Inc.

Artic Technologies

242

Computer
and Web
Resources
for People
with
Disabilities

Beyond Sight, Inc.

GW Micro

Henter-Joyce, Inc.

Hexagon Products

HumanWare, Inc.

Knowledge Adventures

Optelec USA, Inc.

Reading Technologies

Syntha-Voice Computers, Inc.

Telesensory

Visionware Software, Inc.

 Additional information

Magnification systems may be hardware, software, or a combination. Hardware magnification can be magnifying lenses placed over the monitor for low-level magnification. See Monitor Additions for more information. Other hardware screen enlarging includes cards and software installed into the computer along with peripheral controls for high-level magnification.

Screen enlargement programs work best with software programs that do not use a large portion of the screen at one time. Programs with graphic images that stretch from one side of the screen to the other (or from the top to the bottom), such as games, will not work well with screen magnifiers, because the "zoom" window leaves out too much of the image. Programs with graphics that rapidly jump to different parts of the screen will also be difficult to use with screen enlargement software. Instead, large-print word processors may be easier to use. Screen enlargement software installs a magnification program into the computer that runs at the same time that other software programs are used. In some instances, this may cause compatibility problems with the operating system and application programs.

Macintosh: CloseView, a screen magnifying utility, is included in the Macintosh System Software. This is a part of Universal Access, which is included on every Macintosh System CD. It may or may not have been pre-installed on the computer, depending on purchase source.

PCs: A basic screen magnification program is included with Windows 98 and Windows 2000 software in the Accessibility Options. It may be used for short-term magnification needs such as installing more advanced magnification software. Compatibility issues involve the type of monitor, the version of operating system, and the software programs to be used with the screen enlargement program.

 Related products

Monitor additions

Speech synthesizers

Talking and large-print word processors

Monitor Additions

A monitor addition or add-on is any device that enhances or alters the use of a standard computer monitor.

Screen magnifiers fit over the screen of a computer monitor and magnify the images that appear on the screen.

Anti-glare filters are clear screens that fit over a computer monitor screen and reduce glare and improve contrast. They also reduce ultraviolet rays and other energy emissions.

Monitor mounts come in a variety of styles and degrees of flexibility and allow adjustment of the monitor position.

 Use this tool to...

Screen magnifiers

Magnify the images of graphics or text on the monitor

Anti-glare filters

Reduce glare from overhead lights and large windows

Reduce screen flicker

Increase the contrast on the monitor

Monitor mounts

Modify the position of the monitor to increase visibility

Accommodate many users of different heights or those in a prone or other nonstandard position

Computer
and Web
Resources
for People
with
Disabilities

Accommodate users with visual field restrictions by placing the monitor in the most easily seen position

 Potential users...

Need low-level magnification to see the screen

Have sensitivity to bright light or work in areas of glare

Need increased clarity by reducing glare and/or increasing contrast

Need a monitor mount to position the screen closer or in a better viewing position

Need a monitor mount to operate the computer from a nonstandard position

 Features to consider

Screen magnifiers

Some are made to reduce distortion caused by the magnification

Some include an anti-glare polarizing filter and/or mounting hood to reduce room reflections and soften the light from the screen

Anti-glare filters

Some have protection to reduce ELF and VLF electromagnetic energy

Some block damaging UV and UVB rays to protect eyes from burning

Monitor mounts

All have a specific weight capacity

Some can move 360 degrees, tilt, or swivel

Some can be part of the table or can clamp to a table, bolt down, or attach to a wall or ceiling

 Cost

Screen magnifiers

Range: $80–250

Common: $80

Anti-glare filters

Range: $10–200

Common: $50

Monitor mounts

Range: $50–800

Common: $50

 Common vendors

Screen magnifiers

AbleTech Connection

Florida New Concepts Marketing, Inc.

Innoventions

Less Gauss

Anti-glare filters

Kensington Microware Ltd.

Power Plus: The Accessories People

Any general computer store

Monitor mounts

American Marketing Executives

Cables to Go

Curtis Computer Products, Inc.

 Additional information

The products must fit the specific monitor used.

 Related products

Screen enlargement programs

246

Computer
and Web
Resources
for People
with
Disabilities

Specialized Products

Augmentative and Alternative Communication Products (AAC)

Some individuals choose to use electronic devices to augment or replace their voices. How we choose to communicate is an important and personal decision that involves both access issues and personal preference. Some preliminary information is provided here to introduce you to this field. We recommend that individuals who are interested in assistive communication products bring together a team to explore the range of products and uses carefully.

Computer-based systems: These communication devices use specific software integrated into a standard computer. Some software allows the display on the computer screen to change in response to the communicator's input. Computer-based systems are useful for communication as well as typical computer applications such as word processing, telecommunications, and environmental control. Depending on the individual's need, additional hardware is also usually required, such as alternate keyboard, electronic pointing devices, or a single switch.

Stand-alone or dedicated communication devices: Typically, these devices use either digitized or synthesized speech and are specifically designed for the sole purpose of replacing or augmenting speech to communicate. Digitized communication devices use recorded speech for the messages that will be heard by the communicators. Synthesized communication devices use text translated into electronic speech. They are usually programmable and come in a wide variety of sizes, shapes, and means of access. A small but growing number of these devices have the capacity to use both digitized and synthesized speech. As with computer-based systems, some individuals, to meet their specific needs, may require additional hardware to operate a dedicated communication device.

 Use this tool to...

Communicate using a commercially available desktop or laptop computer

Communicate using small, portable, dedicated devices

Communicate with small, portable devices that can also be mounted as needed to wheelchairs

Communicate using short messages, phrases, and sentences

Represent symbols, pictures, and objects through recorded messages

Change content of messages on a dynamic basis

Create speech that may be age, gender, and language specific to an individual

Clarify when verbal communication is unclear

Present long messages, reports, or stories

 Potential users...

Require a method of communicating other than speech.

Require support to communicate verbally

Benefit from using symbols, pictures, and/or words when communicating

 Features to consider

Some can be connected to a computer and used to replace the mouse and keyboard as methods of providing input

Some are dedicated solely to communication

Some are easily customized by the user

Some use software with language-based symbol systems to create communication layouts

Some can be accessed through a variety of input devices including touch screens, switches, alternate keyboards, and alternative pointing devices

Many offer display options including color, black-and-white, and back-lit screens

Some screens are very difficult to see outdoors in daylight

Many units vary in the quality of speech, depending on the type of synthesizer used

Some support both digitized speech and synthesized speech

Some can integrate a variety of functions into one unit, such as operating environmental controls, aids for daily living, and computer programs

248

Computer
and Web
Resources
for People
with
Disabilities

Some can plug into a printer; some have built-in printers

Some vary in the number and size of messages that can be stored

Many are portable, but there is a significant variation in weight and size

Some have the ability to store banks of phrases or messages for easy retrieval

Some have the capacity to provide input using Morse code

 Cost

Computer-based systems

Range: $300–25,000

Common: $3,000

Stand-alone or dedicated communication devices

Range: $45–10,000

Common: $1,500

 Common vendors

AbleNet, Inc.

Adaptivation, Inc.

Assistive Technology, Inc.

Crestwood Company

Don Johnston, Inc.

DynaVox Systems (formerly Sentient Systems)

Franklin Electronic Publishers, Inc.

The Great Talking Box Company

Gus Communications

Infra-Link, Inc.

LC Technologies

Luminaud, Inc.

Mayer-Johnson Company

Microsystems Software, Inc.

Prentke Romich Company

Shea Products

Synergy

TASH International, Inc.

Words+, Inc.

World Communications

Zygo Industries, Inc.

 Additional information

When a consumer chooses a device, he or she is making a very important personal decision. In moving through the selection process, it is very important to have a strong team in place that includes the individual, the family, educators, and specialists. Devices vary in the training required and the level of independent cognitive skills needed. A trial period with several devices may help eliminate costly mistakes.

Two other sources of additional information are:

**United States Society for Augmentative and
Alternative Communication (USSAAC)**

P.O. Box 5271   (847) 869-2122
Evanston IL 60204-5271   (847) 869-2161, fax
email: aac-rerc@mc.duke.edu
website: www.aac-rerc.org/

**International Society for Augmentative and
Alternative Communication (ISAAC)**

49 The Donway West, Suite 308   (416) 385-0351
Toronto ON M3C 3M9   (416) 385-0352, fax
Canada
email: isaac_mail@mail.cepp.org
website: www.isaac-online.org

 Related products

Environmental control units

Switches and switch software

Alternate keyboards

Electronic pointing devices

250

Computer
and Web
Resources
for People
with
Disabilities

Touch screens

Speech synthesizers

Closed-Circuit Televisions

Closed-circuit televisions (CCTVs) magnify the printed page with a special television camera and display the image enlarged on a monitor.

 Use this tool to...

Read print materials with the aid of magnification

Write notes, letters, and other handwritten documents with the aid of magnification

 Potential users...

Require large text

Benefit from greater contrast

Benefit from white text on a black background

Benefit from being able to select their own text and background color combinations

 Features to consider

All provide magnification of print materials

Most magnify in adjustable increments

Most are capable of reverse polarity, i.e., a white image on a black background or a black image on a white background

Many have black-and-white screens

Some have color screens with selectable colors or full-color options

Some are handheld and portable

Some have the capability to show an image on a computer screen and on the CCTV screen at the same time

Some magnify output from a computer, typewriter, microfiche reader, chalkboard, or even a microscope

Some have motorized reading tables

Cost

Range: $1,400–3,400

Common: $2,400

 Common vendors

Beyond Sight, Inc.

Carolyn's Products for Enhanced Living

HumanWare, Inc.

LS&S Group

Okay Vision-Aide Corp.

Optelec U.S.A., Inc.

Seeing Technologies, Inc.

Telesensory

Photo courtesy of Humanware, Inc.

*A CCTV can enlarge a variety of materials,
including maps and other print resources.
(HumanWare, Inc.)*

252

Computer
and Web
Resources
for People
with
Disabilities

 Additional information

Text can be magnified up to 60 times on some units. The user normally moves, or "tracks," the item to be read under a fixed camera, either manually with a standard reading table or automatically with an optional motorized table. With some portable units a handheld camera is moved across the printed page.

 Related products

Screen enlargement programs

Monitor additions

Environmental Control Units

An environmental control unit (ECU) is used to control, from a remote location, electric appliances, telephones, and other items that typically plug into a wall outlet. Several of these devices are also capable of emulating existing remote control devices. Many people may also refer to this category of devices as aids for daily living (ADL).

 Use this tool to...

Turn on a computer system independently

Turn on lamps, fans, stereos, intercoms, and other household devices

Emulate handheld remote control devices for televisions, entertainment systems, VCRs, etc.

Activate an emergency call button wired to a remote location in the building

Lock and unlock doors

Adjust a hospital bed independently

Activate a security system

 Potential users...

Need an alternative way to handle common devices and appliances

Features to consider

Many control appliances plugged into an outlet

Some can control telephones

Some can control televisions, VCRs, stereo systems, and other devices with infrared remote control

Some can be controlled by a single switch or voice

Some are dedicated, stand-alone devices while others are computer based

 Cost

Range: $250–6,500

Common: basic functions $450; advanced functions $3,000

 Common vendors

AbleNet, Inc.

ACS Technologies

Apt Technologies/DU-IT Control Systems Group, Inc.

Consultants for Communication Technology

Gus Communications

Darryl Park uses voice commands to help him control his home through PROXI. (Madentec, Limited)

254

Computer
and Web
Resources
for People
with
Disabilities

Infra-Link, Inc.

KY Enterprises/Custom Computer Solutions

LC Technologies, Inc.

Madentec, Ltd.

Med Labs Inc.

Microsystems Software, Inc.

Prentke Romich Company

TASH International, Inc.

Teledyne Brown Engineering/Imperium Products Division

Toys for Special Children, Inc.

Words+, Inc.

X-10 (USA) Inc.

Zygo Industries, Inc.

 Additional information

An ECU can be purchased as a software package, to be used on a personal computer, or as a stand-alone device. ECU software is available for both Macintosh and PCs, but still requires additional hardware interfaces.

To use these devices with a single switch, you will need an additional interface.

 Related products

Interface devices

Switches and switch software

Voice recognition

Notetakers

Notetakers are very small, portable units that employ either a braille keyboard or a standard keyboard to allow the user to enter information. Text is stored in files that can be read and edited using the built-in speech synthesizer or braille display. Files may also be sent to a printer or braille embosser, or transferred to a computer.

Use this tool to...

Take notes in class, meetings, or conferences

Access electronic information services by connecting to a phone line

Instruct in writing and reading braille

 Potential users...

Read and write in braille

Need a way to take notes and be able to transfer them to a computer

 Features to consider

Some allow information to be entered in braille

Most have text-editing capability

Some have built-in speech synthesizers

Some can accommodate headphones to permit private listening

Some can turn auditory feedback on or off

Some include a clock and calendar

Some include an appointment book, which can sound a tone to remind the user of scheduled appointments

Most can print using conventional printers or braille embossers

Some have refreshable braille displays

Some can produce 8-dot braille

 Cost

Range: $1,000–3,400

Common: $1,300

 Common vendors

American Printing House for the Blind, Inc.

Blazie Engineering, Inc.

HumanWare, Inc.

256

Computer
and Web
Resources
for People
with
Disabilities

Intelligent Peripheral Devices

Telesensory

TFI Engineering

 Additional Information

Generally, notetakers are limited in functionality when compared to a laptop or desktop computer because of their processor design and limited memory and storage capacity. However, they do have the advantage of long battery life and portability.

 Related products

Screen readers

Speech synthesizers

Reading machines

Braille embossers and translators

Refreshable braille displays

Reading Machines

A reading machine transforms printed material into an electronic data format that is read aloud by a speech synthesizer. A standard computer can be modified to become a reading machine by adding a scanner and reading system software. A stand-alone reading machine incorporates a scanner, speech synthesizer, and other electronics in a single unit, which may be a desktop unit or as small as a writing pen.

 Use this tool to...

Read books, mail, business documents, and faxed information

Improve reading comprehension by listening to materials being read as they are displayed on the computer screen

Read isolated words that are causing difficulty

 Potential users...

Need print materials read aloud

*With VERA, a reading machine, any printed material
can be converted to an electronic format, allowing you
to read books, magazines and even junk mail.
(Arkenstone, Inc.)*

Features to consider

All have speech output

All have some type of scanner

Some have a document feeder for the scanner

Some are handheld

Some provide synonyms or definitions for scanned words

Most determine page orientation automatically

Most recognize many type styles

Most can handle multicolumn pages

Most recognize a variety of print qualities

Some are compact for greater portability

Some are specially designed to more easily accommodate books

Some support braille or large-print output

Some read faxed images

Some control scanning and reading functions with a computer keyboard, a
separate keypad, or a joystick

258

Computer
and Web
Resources
for People
with
Disabilities

 Cost

To upgrade an existing computer

Range: $1,600–4,400

Common: $1,800–3,000

Stand-alone machines

Range: $300–6,000

Common: $5,000

 Common vendors

Arkenstone, Inc.

Telesensory

Schamex Research

Seiko Instruments USA Inc., Educational Products Division

Xerox Imaging Systems, Inc.

 Additional information

Macintosh: Although there are no reading system software programs specifically for Macintosh computers and specifically for blind users, commercial OCR systems can be used with a scanner and a screen reader to give people with visual disabilities access to printed material.

PCs: The scanning hardware and reading system software for these computers have specific system requirements—such as bus architecture, processor type, and memory size—that must be taken into consideration. A reading machine is a unique combination of access products. If you are modifying a standard computer to also be used as a reading machine, you will need to be certain that all the hardware and software components are compatible.

 Related products

Notetakers

Optical character recognition and scanners

TTYs and TTY Modems

A Telecommunication Device for the Deaf (TTY or TDD) is a device with a keyboard that sends and receives typed messages over a telephone line.

A TTY modem is a Weitbrecht/Baudot-compatible modem for a personal computer. A standard modem uses ASCII code to communicate over phone lines, while TTYs use Baudot code at a fixed baud rate of 45. A standard modem generally cannot communicate with a TTY, although some TTYs allow the user to select either Baudot or ASCII code at up to 300 baud.

 Use this tool to...

Call other TTY users

Call a relay system which will read your message to a standard phone user

Connect with automated services such as a bank

 Potential users...

Require text to communicate by telephone

Communicate with someone else using a TTY for telephone communication

 Features to consider

A TTY may be portable, desktop, or personal computer based

All TTYs have a display that shows the message as it is entered or received

Some TTYs have built-in printers

Some TTYs offer options for the display such as color, text size, and direction of scrolling

Some TTYs are compatible with braille devices

Some TTYs have a large visual display for individuals with vision issues

Some TTYs have speed dialing

Some TTYs have a built-in ring flasher

260

Computer
and Web
Resources
for People
with
Disabilities

Some TTYs have voice carry over, which allows one party to speak directly to the other while the return messages are typed and appear on the screen

Some TTYs and TTY modems allow storage of conversations for later review

Some TTYs and TTY modems can answer automatically with programmable messages and record incoming messages

Some TTY modems can automatically adjust to receive from a TTY or another computer

All TTY modems require telecommunication software for communication

 Cost

TTYs

Range: $200-900

Common: $350

TTY modems

Range: $250-400

Common: $330

 Common Vendors:

TTYs

AT&T Accessible Communication Products

HARC Mercantile, Ltd.

Harris Communications, Inc.

Hear More Inc.

HITEC Group International

Phone TTY, Inc.

Potomac Technology

SSK Technology, Inc.

Telesensory

Ultratec

WCI Technology

TTY modems

Futura-TTY

Harris Communications, Inc.

Microflip, Inc.

NXI Communicators

Mobile Communication System (pagers)

AT&T Wireless Services Messaging Division

Harris Communications, Inc.

Wynd Communications

 Additional information

Wireless communications: Some newer cellular and cordless phones can connect to some model TTYs. Some pagers can send and receive TTY messages and emails and send faxes. Some can send a text-to-speech message and send a text message to any one-way alphanumeric pager.

 Related products

There are no related products at the time of this printing.

Speech-to-Speech Relay Services

Although technically not an assistive technology device, a speech-to-speech relay service certainly provides technology-related help to people with speech disabilities, taking advantage of existing telephone technology in a very valuable way.

This service, called Speech-to-Speech, provides human voices for people who have difficulty being understood by the public on the telephone. The FCC expects all states to provide Speech-to-Speech in two years. If you have a speech disability, you can dial toll free to reach a patient, trained operator who is familiar with many speech patterns and has acute hearing. This operator makes telephone calls for you and repeats your words exactly. Speech-to-Speech is currently available 24 hours a day in Arizona, California, Georgia, Maryland, South Carolina, Washington state, and Wisconsin.

Speech-to-Speech is also useful if you use a speech synthesizer. It is the only way for many people to telephone others not accustomed to their speech. Many Speech-to-Speech users have Parkinson's disease, cerebral

262

Computer
and Web
Resources
for People
with
Disabilities

palsy, multiple sclerosis, or muscular dystrophy. Other users include people who stutter, have ALS, or have had a laryngectomy. You can try out Speech-to-Speech, report problems, or get more information by calling (800) 854-7784 and asking for Dr. Bob Segalman (in the communication assistant's directory).

Here are the U.S. Speech-to-Speech access numbers as of 1999. Toll-free numbers should be available in all states by the end of 2002:

Arizona (800) 842-6520

California (800) 854-7784

Maryland (800) 785-5630

South Carolina (877) 735-7277

Wisconsin (800) 833-7637

Georgia (800) 229-5746

Washington state (877) 833-6341

Sweden is conducting a Speech-to-Speech trial now. Australia recently completed a trial. For Swedish access numbers email: Inga.Svanfeldt@ hoh.lul.se (Inga Svanfeldt), and for Australian access numbers email: Ace.Tom.McCaul@uq.net.au (Tom McCaul).

Part III:

Helpful Resources and References

Contents

This section contains a series of starter resources to point you in appropriate directions. The lists in Part III include key references and resources. In some cases the value of a given resource will be to lead you to other resources, especially if you are contacting them via the Internet and their websites. By following up on some of the national references listed here, you should be able to identify resources and contacts in your own community, which, of course, is the main goal. The references and resources are organized into eight sections:

Alliance for Technology Access Resource Centers

The Alliance for Technology Access is a growing organization with new members joining regularly. If you are interested in starting an Alliance for Technology Access Center in your community, please contact us for guidelines and an application.

Many ATA Centers currently maintain sites on the World Wide Web, and the number is increasing rapidly. Check the ATA website for the most current ATA Center Web addresses.

Alliance for Technology Access
2175 East Francisco Boulevard, Suite L
San Rafael CA 94901
email: ATAinfo@ATAccess.org
website: www.ATAccess.org

(415) 455-4575
(800) 455-7970
(415) 455-0491, TTY

Alabama

Birmingham Alliance for Technology Access Center
Birmingham Independent Living Center
206 13th Street South
Birmingham AL 35253-1317
email: dankess@mindspring.net

(205) 251-2223, voice/TTY

Technology Assistance for Special Consumers
P.O. Box 443
Huntsville AL 35804
email: tasc@traveller.com
website: http://tasc.ataccess.org

(256) 532-5996, voice/TTY

Arizona

Technology Access Center of Tucson, Inc.
P.O. Box 13178
4710 East 29th Street
Tucson AZ 85732-3178
email: tactaz@aol.com

(520) 745-5588, ext. 412

Arkansas

Technology Resource Center
c/o Arkansas Easter Seal Society

(501) 227-3602

ATA CENTERS

266

Computer
and Web
Resources
for People
with
Disabilities

3920 Woodland Heights Road   (501) 227-3686, TTY
Little Rock AR 72212-2495
email: atrce@aol.com

California

Center for Accessible Technology
2547 8th Street, 12-A   (510) 841-3224, voice/TTY
Berkeley CA 94710-2572
email: info@cforat.org
website: www.el.net/CAT

Computer Access Center
6234 West 87th Street   (310) 338-1597
Los Angeles CA 90045   (310) 338-9318, TTY
email: cac@cac.org
website: www.cac.org

iTECH Center at Parents Helping Parents
3041 Olcott Street   (408) 727-5775
Santa Clara CA 95054-3222
email: iTech@php.com
website: www.php.com

SACC* Assistive Technology
Simi Valley Hospital, North Campus   (805) 582-1881
P.O. Box 1325
Simi Valley CA 93062
email: dssacca@aol.com

San Diego Assistive Technology Center
UCP of San Diego County   (858) 571-7803
3821 Calle Fortunada, Suite C
San Diego CA 92123
email: cpsdatc@pacbell.net

Team of Advocates for Special Kids
100 W. Cerritos Avenue   (714) 533-8275
Anaheim CA 92805-6546
email: taskca@aol.com

Florida

CITE, Inc.—Center for Independence, Technology and Education
215 E. New Hampshire Street   (407) 898-2483
Orlando FL 32804
email: comcite@aol.com

Georgia

TechAble, Inc.
1112A Brett Drive   (770) 922-6768
Conyers GA 30207
email: techable@america.net

Hawaii

Aloha Special Technology Access Center
710 Green Street   (808) 523-5547
Honolulu HI 96813
email: stachi@aol.com

Idaho

United Cerebral Palsy of Idaho, Inc.
5530 West Emerald   (208) 377-8070
Boise ID 83706
email: ucpidaho@aol.com
website: http://ucpidaho.ataccess.org

Illinois

Northern Illinois Center for Adaptive Technology (NICAT)
3615 Louisiana Road   (815) 229-2163
Rockford IL 61108-6195   (815) 229-2881, TTY
email: davegrass@earthlink.net
website: nicat.ataccess.org

TAAD Center (Technical Aids & Assistance for Persons with Disabilities)
1950 West Roosevelt Road   (800) 346-2939, in state
Chicago IL 60608   (312) 421-3373
email: taad@interaccess.com
website: http://homepage.interaccess.com/~taad

Indiana

Assistive Technology Training and Information Center (ATTIC)
P.O. Box 2441   (800) 96-ATTIC (962-8842), voice/TTY
3354 Pine Hill Drive   (812) 886-0575, voice/TTY
Vincennes IN 47591
email: inattic1@aol.com
website: www.theattic.org

267

Alliance for
Technology
Access
Resource
Centers

Computer
and Web
Resources
for People
with
Disabilities

Kansas

Technology Resource Solutions for People
P.O. Box 1160   (785) 827-9383, voice/TTY
1710 West Schilling Road
Salina KS 67402-1160
email: trspks@midusa.net

Kentucky

Bluegrass Technology Center
169 N. Limestone Street   (606) 255-9951, voice/TTY
Lexington KY 40507   (800) 209-7767, in state
email: office@bluegrass-tech.org
website: www.bluegrass-tech.org

Enabling Technologies of Kentuckiana (enTECH)
301 York Street   (800) 890-1840, in state
Louisville KY 40203-2205   (502) 574-1637, voice/TTY
email: entech@iglou.com
website: www.kde.state.ky.us/oet/customer/at/

Western Kentucky Assistive Technology Consortium
Weaks Community Center   (502) 759-4233
607 Poplar, Room 211
P.O. Box 266
Murray KY 42071
email: wkatc@cablecomm-ky.net
website: www.kde.state.ky.us/oet/customer/at/

Maryland

Learning Independence Through Computers, Inc. (LINC)
1001 Eastern Avenue, 3rd Floor   (410) 659-5462
Baltimore MD 21202   (410) 659-5472, TTY
email: lincmd@aol.com
website: www.linc.org

Michigan

Michigan's Assistive Technology Resource
Physically Impaired Association of Michigan
1023 S. US 27, Suite B31   (517) 224-0333, voice/TTY
St. Johns MI 48879-2424   (800) 274-7426, voice/TTY
email: matr@match.org

Minnesota

PACER Computer Resource Center
4826 Chicago Avenue South   (612) 827-2966, voice/TTY
Minneapolis MN 55417-1055
email: jpeters@pacer.org
website: www.pacer.org/crc/crc.htm

Missouri

Technology Access Center
12110 Clayton Road   (314) 989-8404
St Louis MO 63131-2599   (314) 989-8446, TTY
email: mostltac@aol.com
website: http://stlouis.missouri.org/501c/mostltac

Montana

Parents, Let's Unite for Kids (PLUK)
516 N 32nd Street   (800) 222-7585, in state
Billings MT 59101   (406) 255-0540
email: plukinfo@pluk.org
website: www.pluk.org

New Jersey

TECH Connection—Assistive Technology Solutions
c/o Family Resource Associates, Inc.
35 Haddon Avenue   (732) 747-5310
Shrewsbury NJ 07702
email: tecconn@aol.com
website: www.techconnection.org/

The Center for Enabling Technology
622 Route 10 West, Suite 22B   (973) 428-1455
Whippany NJ 07981   (973) 428-1450, TTY
email: cetnj@aol.com

New York

Techspress
Resource Center for Independent Living   (315) 797-4642
P.O. Box 210   (315) 797-5837, TTY
401-409 Columbia Street
Utica NY 13503-0210
email: rose.roberts@rcil.com
website: www.rcil.com

269

Alliance for
Technology
Access
Resource
Centers

ATA CENTERS

270

———

Computer
and Web
Resources
for People
with
Disabilities

North Carolina

Carolina Computer Access Center
Metro School   (704) 342-3004
700 East Second Street
Charlotte NC 28202-2826
email: ccacnc@aol.com
website: www.ccac.ataccess.org

Ohio

Technology Resource Center
Job Mall   (937) 461-3305
1133 Edwin C. Moses Boulevard, Suite 370
Dayton OH 45408
email: trcdoh@aol.com

Rhode Island

TechACCESS Center of Rhode Island
110 Jefferson Boulevard   (800) 916-TECH, in state
Warwick RI 02888   (401) 463-0202
email: techaccess@techaccess-ri.org

Tennessee

East Tennessee Technology Access Center
4918 North Broadway   (423) 219-0130, voice/TTY
Knoxville TN 37918
email: etstactn@aol.com
website: www.korrnet.org/ettac/

Mid-South Access Center for Technology
University of Memphis
College of Education   (901) 678-3919
Ball Hall, Room 307A
Memphis TN 38152
email: kanderso@memphis.edu
website: www.people.memphis.edu/~coe_act/

Signal Center's Assistive Technology Center
109 North Germantown Road   (423) 698-8528, ext. 200, voice
Chattanooga TN 37411   (423) 624-1365, TTY
email: littleton@signal.chattanooga.net   (423) 698-3105, fax

Technology Access Center of Middle Tennessee
2222 Metrocenter Boulevard, Suite 126　　　　　(800) 368-4651
Nashville TN 37228　　　　　　　　　(615) 248-6733, voice/TTY
email: tac.tn@nashville.com
website: http://tac.ataccess.org

271
―――

Alliance for
Technology
Access
Resource
Centers

West Tennessee Special Technology Access Resource Center (STAR)
P.O. Box 3683　　　　　　　　　　　　　(901) 668-3888
60 Lynoak Cove　　　　　　　　　　　　(800) 464-5619
Jackson TN 38305
email: infostar@starcenter.tn.org
website: www.starcenter.tn.org

Utah

The Computer Center for Citizens with Disabilities
c/o Utah Center for Assistive Technology　　(801) 887-9500, voice/TTY
1595 West 500 South
Salt Lake City UT 84104
email: cboogaar@usor.state.ut.us

Virgin Islands

Virgin Islands Resource Center for the Disabled, Inc.
PO Box 308427　　　　　　　　　　(340) 777-2253, voice/TTY
St. Thomas USVI 00803-8427　　　　　　(340) 774-9330, fax
email: vircd@islands.vi

Virginia

Tidewater Center for Technology Access
Special Education Annex　　　　　　(757) 474-8650, voice/TTY
960 Windsor Oaks Boulevard
Virginia Beach VA 23462
email: tcta@aol.com
website: http://tcta.ataccess.org

West Virginia

Eastern Panhandle Technology Access Center, Inc.
P.O. Box 987　　　　　　　　　　　　　(304) 725-6473
300 S. Lawrence Street
Charles Town WV 25414
email: eptac@webcombo.net
website: http://eptac.ataccess.org

Computer
and Web
Resources
for People
with
Disabilities

State Tech Act Programs

The Technology-Related Assistance for Individuals with Disabilities Act provides funding to states to assist them in developing easily accessible, consumer-responsive systems of access to assistive technology, technology services, and information. State programs vary widely. Contact your state's Tech Act Project for more information. If you are unable to reach your state's project, call the RESNA Technical Assistance Project at (703) 524-6686, extension 313, for assistance.

Alabama

Alabama Statewide Technology Access and Response Project
(STAR) System for Alabamians
with Disabilities   (800) STAR656 (782-7656), in state
P.O. Box 20752   (334) 613-3480
2125 East South Boulevard   (334) 613-3485, fax
Montgomery AL 36120-0752
email: tbridges@rehab.state.al.us
website: www.rehab.state.al.us/star

Alaska

Assistive Technologies of Alaska
1016 West 6th, Suite 200   (907) 563-0138, voice/TTY
Anchorage AK 99501
email: james_beck@educ.state.ak.us
website: www.labor.state.ak.us/ata/index.htm

American Samoa

American Samoa Assistive Technology Project
Division of Vocational Rehabilitation   (684) 699-1529
Department of Human Resources   (684) 233-7874, TTY
Pago Pago AS 96799   (684) 699-1376, fax
email: EdPerei@yahoo.com

Arizona

Arizona Technology Access Program (AZTAP)
Institute for Human Development   (520) 523-8779
Northern Arizona University   (520) 523-1695, TTY

P.O. Box 5630
Flagstaff AZ 86011
email: jill.oberstein@nau.edu
website: www.nau.edu/~ihd/aztap

Arkansas

Arkansas Increasing Capabilities Access Network
2201 Brookwood, Suite 117   (800) 828-2799, in state, voice/TTY
Little Rock AR 72202   (501) 666-8868, voice/TTY
email: sogaskin@ars.state.ar.us   (501) 666-5319, fax
website: www.arkansas-ican.org

California

California Assistive Technology System
California Department of Rehabilitation   (916) 263-8687
2000 Evergreen   (916) 263-8685, TTY
Sacramento CA 95815
email: dor_dlaw@yahoo.com
website: www.catsca.org

Colorado

Colorado Assistive Technology Project
University of Colorado Health Sciences Center   (303) 864-5100
Colorado University Affiliated Program   (303) 864-5110, TTY
The Pavilion, A036/B140
1919 Ogden Street, 2nd Floor
Denver CO 80218
email: cathy.bodine@UCHSC.edu
website: www.uchsc.edu/catp

Commonwealth of the Northern Mariana Islands

Assistive Technology Project
Developmental Disabilities Planning Office   (670) 664-7005, voice/TTY
Office of the Governor   (670) 664-7010, fax
P.O. Box 2565 CK
Faipan MP 96950
email: gddc@cnmiddcouncil.org
website: www.cnmiddcouncil.org

STATE TECH ACT PROGRAMS

274

Computer
and Web
Resources
for People
with
Disabilities

Connecticut

Connecticut Assistive Technology Project
Department of Social Services, BRS
25 Sigourney Street, 11th Floor
Hartford CT 06106
email: cttap@aol.com
website: www.techact.uconn.edu

(860) 424-4881
(800) 537-2549, in state
(860) 424-4839, TTY

Delaware

Delaware Assistive Technology Initiative Applied Science and Engineering Laboratories
University of Delaware, A.I. duPont Institute
1600 Rockland Road, Room 154
P.O. Box 269
Wilmington DE 19899-0269
email: dati@asel.udel.edu
website: www.asel.udel.edu/dati/

(302) 651-6790
(302) 651-6794, TTY
(302) 651-6793, fax

District of Columbia

University Legal Services at Programs for the District of Columbia
300 I Street NE, Suite 200
Washington DC 20002
email: ajohns@ULS-DC.com
website: www.atpdc.org

(202) 547-0198
(202) 547-2657, TTY

Florida

Florida Alliance for Assistive Service and Technology
1020 E. Lafayette Street, Suite 110
Tallahassee FL 32301-4546
email: faast@faast.org
website: http://faast.org

(850) 487-3278, voice/TTY

Georgia

Georgia Tools for Life
Division of Rehabilitation Services
2 Peachtree Street NW, Suite 35-415
Atlanta GA 30303-3142
email: toolsforlife@mindspring.com
website: www.gatfl.org

(800) 497-8665, in state
(404) 657-3084
(404) 657-3085, TTY
(404) 657-3086, fax

Guam

Guam System for Assistive Technology
University Affiliated Program—
  Developmental Disabilities   (671) 735-2490
University of Guam, UOG Station   (671) 734-8378, TTY
303 University Drive   (671) 734-5709, fax
Mangilao GU 96923
email: gsat@ite.net
website: http://uog2.uog.edu/uap/gsat.html

Hawaii

Hawaii Assistive Technology Training and Service Project
414 Kuwili Street, Suite 104   (808) 532-7110, voice/TTY
Honolulu HI 96817   (808) 532-7120, fax
email: hatts@hatts.org
website: www.hatts.org

Idaho

Idaho Assistive Technology Project
129 W. Third Street   (208) 885-3630
Moscow ID 83843-4401   (208) 885-3559, voice/TTY
email: seile861@uidaho.edu   (208) 885-3628, fax
website: www.ets.uidaho.edu

Illinois

Illinois Assistive Technology Project
1 W. Old State Capitol Plaza, Suite 100   (217) 522-7985
Springfield, IL 62701   (217) 522-9966, TTY
email: gunther@midwest.net   (217) 522-8067, fax
website: www.iltech.org

Indiana

**Indiana Attain (Accessing Technology Through Awareness in Indiana)
Project**
1002 North First   (800) 528-8246, in state
Vincennes University   (317) 921-8766
Social Sciences Building, Room 312   (800) 743-3333, TTY
Vincennes IN 47591   (317) 921-8774, fax
Project Manager: Cris Fulford
email: cfulford@indian.vinu.edu
website: http://vinu.edu/attain

276

Computer
and Web
Resources
for People
with
Disabilities

Iowa

Iowa Program for Assistive Technology

Iowa University Affiliated Program
University Hospital School
Iowa City IA 52242-1011
email: mary-quigley@uiowa.edu or jane-gay@uiowa.edu
website: www.uiowa.edu/infotech

(800) 331-3027, voice/TTY
(319) 356-8284, fax

Kansas

Assistive Technology for Kansans Project

2601 Gabriel
P.O. Box 738
Parsons KS 67357
email: ssack@parsons.lsi.ukans.edu
website: www.atk.lsi.ukans.edu

(800) KAN DO IT (526-3648)
(316) 421-8367
(316) 421-0954, fax/TTY

Kentucky

Kentucky Assistive Technology Services Network

Charles McDowell Center
8412 Westport Road
Louisville KY 40242
email: katsnet@iglou.com
website: www.katsnet.org

(800) 327-5287, in state, voice/TTY
(502) 327-0022
(502) 327-9855, TTY

Louisiana

Louisiana Assistance Technology Access Network

P.O. Box 14115
Baton Rouge LA 70898-4115
email: jnesbit@latan.org
website: www.latan.org

(504) 925-9500, voice/TTY
(504) 925-9560, fax

Maine

Maine Consumer Information and Technology Training Exchange (Maine CITE)

Maine CITE Coordinating Center
Education Network of Maine
46 University Drive
Augusta ME 04330
email: kpowers@maine.caps.maine.edu
website: www.mecite.doe.k12.me.us

(207) 621-3195, voice/TTY
(207) 621-3193, fax

Maryland

Maryland Technology Assistance Program
Governor's Office for Individuals with Disabilities   (800) 832-4827
2301 Argonne Drive, RM T17   (410) 554-9230, voice/TTY
Baltimore MD 21218   (410) 554-9237, fax
email: rasinski@clark.net
website: www.mdtap.org

Massachusetts

Massachusetts Assistive Technology Partnership
MATP Center   (800) 848-8867, in state, voice/TTY
Children's Hospital   (617) 355-7153
1295 Boylston, Suite 310   (617) 355-7301, TTY
Boston MA 02115   (617) 355-6345, fax
email: matp@matp.org
website: www.matp.org

Michigan

Michigan Tech 2000
740 W. Lake Lansing Road, Suite 400   (800) 760-4600, in state
East Lansing MI 48823   (517) 333-2477, voice/TTY
email: roanne@sprynet.com
website: www.copower.org

Minnesota

Minnesota Star Program
300 Centennial Building.   (800) 657-3862, in state
658 Cedar Street   (800) 657-3895, in state, TTY
St. Paul MN 55155   (612) 282-6671, fax
email: star.program@state.mn.us
website:
www.state.mn.us/ebranch/admin/assistivetechnology/index.html

Mississippi

Mississippi Project Start
P.O. Box 1698   (800) 852-8328, in state, voice/TTY
Jackson MS 39215-1000   (601) 987-4872
email: spower@netdoor.com   (601) 364-2349, fax

278

Computer
and Web
Resources
for People
with
Disabilities

Missouri

Missouri Assistive Technology Project
4731 South Cochise, Suite 114   (800) 647-8557, in state, voice/TTY
Independence MO 64055-6975   (660) 373-5193
email: matpmo@qni.com   (660) 373-9314, fax
website: www.dolir.state.mo.us/matp/

Montana

MonTECH
MUARID, The University of Montana   (406) 243-5676
634 Eddy Avenue   (800) 732-0323, TTY
Missoula MT 59812   (406) 243-4730, fax
email: montech@selway.umt.edu
website: http://ruralinstitute.umt.edu/

Nebraska

Nebraska Assistive Technology Project
5143 South 48th Street, Suite C   (888) 806-6287, in state
Lincoln NE 68516-2204   (402) 471-0734, voice/TTY
email: mschultz@atp.state.ne.us
website: www.edneb.org

Nevada

Nevada Assistive Technology Collaborative Rehabilitation Division
Office of Community-Based Services   (775) 687-4452
711 S. Stewart Street   (775) 687-3388, TTY
Carson City NV 89710   (775) 687-3292, fax
email: pgowins@govmail.state.nv.us
website: www.state.nv.us.80

New Hampshire

New Hampshire Technology Partnership Project
Institute on Disability/UAP
#14, Ten Ferry Street   (603) 224-0630, voice/TTY
The Concord Center   (603) 226-0389, fax
Concord NH 03301
email: twillkomm@nnaat.mv.com
website: www.iod.unh.edu/projects/spd.htm

New Jersey

New Jersey Technology Assistive Resource Program
New Jersey Protection and Advocacy, Inc.   (800) 342-5832, in state
210 South Broad Street, 3rd Floor   (609) 777-0945
Trenton NJ 08608   (609) 633-7106, TTY
email: packro@njpanda.org   (609) 777-0187, fax
website: www.njpanda.org

New Mexico

New Mexico Technology Assistance Program
435 St. Michael's Drive,
Building D   (800) 866-ABLE, (866-2253), voice / TTY
Santa Fe NM 87503   (505) 827-3746, fax
email: aklaus@state.nm.us
website: www.nmtap.com

New York

New York State TRAID Project
Office of Advocate for Persons with Disabilities   (518) 474-2825
One Empire State Plaza, Suite 1001   (800) 522-4369, in state, voice / TTY
Albany NY 12223-1150   (518) 473-4231, TTY
email: traid@emi.com   (518) 473-6005, fax
website: www.state.ny.us / disabledAdvocate / technlog.htm

North Carolina

North Carolina Assistive Technology Project
Department of Human Resources   (800) 852-0042
Division of Vocational Rehabilitation Services (919) 850-2787, voice / TTY
1110 Navaho Drive, Suite 101   (919) 850-2792, fax
Raleigh NC 27609
email: rickic@mindspring.com
website: www.mindspring.com / ~ncatp

North Dakota

North Dakota Interagency Program for Assistive Technology (IPAT)
P.O. Box 743   (701) 265-4807, voice / TTY
Cavalier ND 58220   (701) 265-3150, fax
email: lee@pioneer.state.nd.us
website: www.ndipat.org

STATE TECH ACT PROGRAMS

280

———

Computer
and Web
Resources
for People
with
Disabilities

Ohio

Ohio Technology Related Information Network

1224 Kinnear Road   (800) 784-3425, in state, voice/TTY
Columbus OH 43212   (614) 292-2426, voice/TTY
email: huntt.1@osc.edu   (614) 292-5866, fax
website: www.train.state.oh.us

Oklahoma

Able Tech

Oklahoma State University   (800) 257-1705, voice/TTY
Wellness Center   (405) 744-9748
1514 W. Hall of Fame   (405) 744-7670, fax
Stillwater OK 74078-0618
email: mljwell@okway.okstate.edu
website: www.okstate.edu/wellness/at-home.htm

Oregon

Oregon Technology Access For Life Needs Project

1257 Ferry Street SE   (503) 361-1201, voice/TTY
Salem OR 97310   (503) 370-4530, fax
email: ati@orednet.org   (800) 677-7512, in state
webpage: www.taln.ncn.com

Pennsylvania

Pennsylvania's Initiative on Assistive Technology

Institute on Disability/UAP
Ritter Annex 433   (800) 204-PIAT (204-7428)
Philadelphia PA 19122   (800) 750-PIAT (750-7428), TTY
email: piat@astro.ocis.temple.edu   (215) 204-9371, fax
website: www.temple.edu/inst_disabilities

Puerto Rico

Puerto Rico Assistive Technology Project

University of Puerto Rico   (800) 496-6035, from U.S. mainland
Medical Sciences Campus   (800) 981-6033, in PR
College of Related Health Professionals   (809) 754-8034, TTY and fax
Office of Project Investigation and Development
P.O. Box 365067
San Juan PR 00936
email: pratp@coqui.net

Rhode Island

Rhode Island Assistive Technology Access Project

Office of Rehabilitation Services   (800) 752-8088, ext. 2608, in state

40 Fountain Street   (401) 421-7005

Providence RI 02903-1898   (401) 421-7016, TTY

email: solson@atap.state.ri.us   (401) 421-9259, fax

website: www.atap.state.ri.us/

South Carolina

South Carolina Assistive Technology Program

USC School of Medicine   (803) 935-5263, voice/TTY

Center for Developmental Disabilities   (803) 935-5342, fax

8301 Farrow Road

Columbia SC 29208

email: kingm@cdd.sc.edu

website: www.public.usit.net/jjendron/

South Dakota

Dakota Link

221 S. Central   (800) 224-5336, in state, voice/TTY

Pierre SD 57501   (605) 224-5336, voice/TTY

email: davev@tie.net   (605) 224-8320, fax

website: www.tie.net/dakotalink

Tennessee

Tennessee Technology Access Project

Department of MH/MR   (615) 532-9986

Andrew Johnson Tower, 10th Floor   (615) 532-1998, fax

710 James Robertson Parkway

Nashville TN 37243-0675

email: jlewis@mail.state.tn.us

website: www.state.tn.us/mental/ttap.html

Texas

Texas Assistive Technology Program

The University of Texas at Austin, UAP of Texas   (800) 828-7839

SZB252-D5100   (512) 471-7621

Austin TX 78712   (512) 471-1844, TTY

email: s.elrod@mail.utexas.edu   (512) 471-7549, fax

website: http://tatp.edb.utexas.edu

282

Computer
and Web
Resources
for People
with
Disabilities

Utah

Utah Assistive Technology Program
Center for Persons with Disabilities
6588 Old Main Hill
Logan UT 84322-6588
email: marty@cpd2.usu.edu
website: www.uatp.usu.edu

(435) 797-1981, voice/TTY
(435) 797-2355, fax

Vermont

Vermont Assistive Technology Project
103 S. Main Street, Weeks I
Waterbury VT 05671-2305
email: lynnec@dad.state.vt.us
website: www.dad.state.vt.us/atp

(802) 241-2620, voice/TTY
(802) 241-2174, fax

Virgin Islands

Virgin Islands Assistive Technology Project
University of the Virgin Islands/UAP
#2 John Brewers Bay
St. Thomas VI 00801
email: yhabtey@ uvi.edu

(809) 693-1323
(809) 693-1325, fax

Virginia

Virginia Assistive Technology System
8004 Franklin Farms Drive
P.O. Box K300
Richmond VA 23288-0300
email: vatskhk@aol.com
website: www.vats.org

(800) 435-8490
(804) 662-9990, voice/TTY
(804) 662-9478, fax

Washington

Washington Assistive Technology Alliance
DSHS/DVR
AT Resource Center
Uniersity. of Washington
Box 357920
Seattle WA 98195-7920
email: uwat@u.washington.edu
website: http://wata.org

(206) 685-4181
(206) 616-1396, TTY
(206) 543-4779, fax

West Virginia

West Virginia Assistive Technology System
University Affiliated Center for
Developmental Disabilities   (800) 841-8436, in state
Airport Research and Office Park   (304) 293-4692, voice/TTY
955 Hartman Run Road   (304) 293-7294, fax
Morgantown WV 26505
email: jstewart@wvu.edu
website: www.wvu.edu/~uacdd/wvats/wvats.htm

Wisconsin

WISTECH
Wisconsin Assistive Technology Program   (608) 266-9303
Division of Supportive Living   (608) 267-9880, TTY
P.O. Box 7851   (608) 267-3203, fax
1 W. Wilson Street, Room 450
Madison WI 53707
email: drennvi@dhfs.state.wi.us
website: www.dhfs.state.wi.us/Aging/wistech/wistech.htm

Wyoming

Wyoming's New Options in Technology
University of Wyoming   (307) 766-2095
1465 North 4th Street, Suite 111   (307) 766-2084, TTY
Laramie WY 82072   (307) 721-2084, fax
email: wynot.uw@uwyo.edu
website: http:// wind.uwyo.edu/wynot/wynot.htm

Americans with Disabilities Act

ADA technology resources

Many agencies and organizations provide support for the implementation
of the Americans with Disabilities Act. The following agencies and organizations can provide you with information and referrals.

American Printing House for the Blind
P.O. Box 6085   (800) 223-1839
Louisville KY 40206   (502) 895-2405
website: www.aph.org/

284

Computer
and Web
Resources
for People
with
Disabilities

Job Accommodation Network (JAN)

West Virginia University   (800) 526-7234, voice/TTY

P.O. Box 6080   (800) 526-2262, Canada

Morgantown WV 26506-6080

website: http://janweb.icdi.wvu.edu/

A service of the President's Committee on Employment of People with Disabilities

Office of the Americans with Disabilities Act

Civil Rights Division   (800) 514-0301

U.S. Department of Justice   (202) 514-0301

P.O. Box 66118   (800) 514-0383, TTY

Washington DC 20035-6118   (202) 514-0380, TTY

website: www.usdoj.gov/crt/ada/adahom1.htm

Equal Employment Opportunity Commission

1801 L Street NW   (800) 669-EEOC (669-3362)

Washington DC 20507   (800) 800-3002, TTY

website: www.eeoc.gov

ADA Technical Assistance Programs

The National Institute on Disability and Rehabilitation Research (NIDRR) sponsors 10 federally funded agencies, Disability and Business Technical Assistance Centers (DBTACs), one in each region of the country, to provide information and technical assistance. Call (800) 949-4232 and your call will be directed to the assistance center for your region. Spanish translation is also available at this number.

Region I: CT, ME, MA, NH, RI, VT

New England DBTAC

Adaptive Environments Center, Inc.   (617) 695-0085, voice/TTY

374 Congress Street, Suite 301   (617) 482-8099, fax

Boston MA 02210

email: adaptive@adaptenv.org

website: www.adaptenv.org

Region II: NJ, NY, PR

Northeast DBTAC

United Cerebral Palsy Associations of New Jersey   (609) 392-4004

354 South Broad Street   (609) 392-7044, TTY

Trenton NJ 08608   (609) 392-3505, fax

email: dbtac@ucpanj.org

website: www.disabilityact.com

Region III: DE, DC, MD, PA, VA, WV
Mid-Atlantic DBTAC
TransCen, Inc.   (301) 217-0124, voice/TTY
451 Hungerford Drive, Suite 607   (301) 217-0754, fax
Rockville MD 20850
email: adainfo@transcen.org
website: www.adainfo.org

Region IV: AL, FL, GA, KY, MS, NC, SC, TN
Southeast DBTAC
United Cerebral Palsy Association, Inc.   (404) 385-0636, voice/TTY
Center for Rehabilitation Technology at Georgia Tech (404) 385-0641, fax
490 Tenth Street
Atlanta GA 30318
email: se-dbtac@mindspring.com
website: www.sedbtac.org

Region V: IL, IN, MI, MN, OH, WI
Great Lakes DBTAC
University of Illinois/Chicago   (312) 413-1407, voice/TTY
Department on Disability and Human Development (312) 413-1856, fax
1640 West Roosevelt Road
Chicago IL 60608
email: gldbtac@uic.edu
website: www.gldbtac.org

Region VI: AR, LA, NM, OK, TX
Southwest DBTAC
Independent Living Research Utilization   (713) 520-0232, voice/TTY
2323 South Shepherd Boulevard, Suite 1000   (713) 520-5785, fax
Houston TX 77019
email: ilru@ilru.org
website: www.ilru.org

Region VII: IA, KS, NB, MO
Great Plains DBTAC
ADA Project   (573) 882-3600, voice/TTY
100 Corporate Lake Drive   (573) 884-4925, fax
Columbia MO 65203
email: adalh@showme.missouri.edu
website: www.adaproject.org

Region VIII: CO, MT, ND, SD, UT, WY
Rocky Mountain DBTAC
Meeting the Challenge, Inc.   (719) 444-0268, voice/TTY
3630 Sinton Road, Suite 103   (719) 444-0269, TTY

286

Computer
and Web
Resources
for People
with
Disabilities

Colorado Springs CO 80907
email: ada-infonet@mtc-inc.com
website: www.ada-infonet.org

Region IX: AZ, CA, HI, NV, PB
Pacific DBTAC
California Public Health Institute (510) 848-2980
2168 Shattuck Avenue, Suite 301 (510) 848-1840, TTY
Berkeley CA 94704-1307 (510) 848-1981, fax
email: adatech@pdbtac.com
website: www.pacdbtac.org

Region X: AK, ID, OR, WA
Northwest DBTAC
Washington State Governor's Committee on Disability Issues and Employ-
ment (360) 438-4116, voice/TTY
P.O. Box 9046, MS 6000 (360) 438-3208, fax
Olympia WA 98507-9046
email: dcolley@esd.wa.gov
website: www.wata.org/NWD

Organizations

There are thousands of organizations focused on people with disabilities.
The ones listed here represent some of the many organizations that have an
interest in technology and can provide technology-related services, information, or referrals.

Center for Best Practices in Early Childhood Education
Western Illinois University (309) 298-1634
1 University Circle (309) 298-2305, fax
27 Hooabin Hall
Macomb IL 61455-1390
website: www.mprojects.wiu.edu

Alexander Graham Bell Association for the Deaf
3417 Volta Place NW (202) 337-5220, voice/TTY
Washington DC 20007-2778
website: http://agbell.org

Alliance for Public Technology
PO Box 27146 (202) 263-2970, voice/TTY
Washington DC 20038-7146 (202) 263-2960, fax
email: apt@apt.org
website: www.apt.org

The Alliance for Technology Access
2175 East Francisco Boulevard, Suite L   (415) 455-4575
San Rafael CA 94901   (415) 455-0654, fax
email: ATAinfo@ATAccess.org
website: www.ATAccess.org

American Foundation for the Blind
National Technology Center   (800) 232-5463
11 Penn Plaza, Suite 300   (212) 502-7642
New York NY 10001   (212) 502-7773, fax
email: techctr@afb.org
website: http://afb.org

American Occupational Therapy Association (AOTA)
P.O. Box 31220   (301) 652-2682
4720 Montgomery Lane   (800) 377-8555, TTY
Bethesda MD 20824-1220   (301) 652-7711, fax
email: praota@aota.org
website: www.aota.org

American Printing House for the Blind
1839 Frankfort Avenue   (800) 223-1839
P.O. Box 6085   (502) 895-2405
Louisville KY 40206-0085   (502) 899-2274, fax
website: www.aph.org

American Speech-Language-Hearing Association (ASHA)
10801 Rockville Pike   888-321-ASHA (321-2742), voice/TTY (consumers)
Rockville MD 20852   (301) 897-5700, voice (members)
website: http://asha.org   (301) 897-0157, TTY
      (301) 571-0457, fax

The Arc (formerly Association for Retarded Citizens)
500 E. Border Street, Suite 300   (800) 433-5255
Arlington TX 76010   (817) 261-6003, voice
email: thearc@metronet.com   (817) 277-0553, TTY
website: http://thearc.org/   (817) 277-3491, fax

Autism Society of America
7910 Woodmont Avenue, Suite 300   (800) 3-AUTISM (328-8476)
Bethesda MD 20814-3015   (301) 657-0869, fax
website: www.autism-society.org

Center for Applied Special Technology (CAST)
39 Cross Street   (978) 531-8555
Peabody MA 01960   (978) 538-3110, TTY
email: cast@cast.org   (978) 531-0192, fax
website: www.cast.org

288

Computer
and Web
Resources
for People
with
Disabilities

Center for Information Technology Accommodation
GSA 18th and F Street NW, Room #1234   (202) 501-4906
MC:MWA   (202) 501-6269, fax
Washington DC 20405

Center for Rehabilitation Technology
490 10th Street   (800) 726-9119
Atlanta GA 30332-0156   (404) 894-9320, fax
email: robert.todd@arch.gatech.edu

The Council for Exceptional Children
1920 Association Drive   (888) CEC-SPED (232-7733)
Reston VA 22091-1589   (703) 264-9494, fax
email: service@cec.sped.org
website: www.cec.sped.org/

Independent Living Centers
For a directory contact: (713) 520-0232
ILRU   (713) 520-5136, TTY
2323 South Shepherd, Suite 1000   (713) 520-5785, fax
Houston TX 77019
email: ilru@ilru.org
website: www.ilru.org

Infinitec
160 N. Wacker Drive   (312) 368-0380
Chicago IL 60606   (312) 368-0179, TTY
website: www.infinitec.org   (312) 368-0018, fax

International Braille and Technology Center for the Blind
National Federation for the Blind   (410) 659-9314
1800 Johnson Street, Suite 300   (410) 685-5653, fax
Baltimore MD 21230-4998
email: epc@roudley.com
website: www.nfb.org

International Dyslexia Society (formerly the Orton Dyslexia Society)
Chester Building, Suite 382   (800) 331-0688
8600 La Salle Road   (410) 296-0232
Baltimore MD 21286-2044   (410) 321-5069, fax
email: info@interdys.org
website: www.interdys.org

International Society for Augmentative and Alternative Communication (ISAAC)
49 The Donway West, Suite 308   (416) 385-0351
Toronto ON M3C 3M9   (416) 385-0352, fax

Canada
email: isaac_mail@mail.cepp.org
website: www.isaac-online.org

International Society for Technology and Education
480 Charnelton Street   (800) 336-5191
Eugene OR 97401-2626   (541) 302-3778, fax
email: cust_svc@ccmail.uoregon.edu
website: www.iste.org

Job Accommodation Network
WVU P.O. Box 6080   (800) 526-7234
Morgantown, WV 26506   (304) 293-5407
website: http://janweb.icdi.wvu.edu/

Learning Disabilities Association of America
4156 Library Road   (412) 341-1515
Pittsburgh PA 15234   (412) 344-0224, fax
website: www.ldanatl.org

National Association of Protection and Advocacy Systems, Inc.
900 Second Street NE, Suite 211   (202) 408-9514
Washington DC 20002   (202) 408-9520, TTY/fax
email: napas@earthlink.net
website: www.protectionandadvocacy.com/

National Center for Learning Disabilities
381 Park Avenue S, Suite 1401   (212) 545-7510, voice only
New York NY 10016   (888) 575-7373
website: www.ncld.org   (212) 545-9665, fax

National Center for Youth with Disabilities
University of Minnesota
Box 721   (612) 626-2825
420 Delaware Street SE   (612) 624-2134, fax
Minneapolis MN 55455-0392
email: ncyd@gold.tc.umn.edu
website: www.cyfc.umn.edu/Youth/ncyd.html

National Easter Seal Society
230 West Monroe Street, Suite 1800   (800) 221-6827
Chicago IL 60606-4802   (312) 726-6200
email: nessinfo@seals.com   (312) 726-4258, TTY
website: www.seals.com   (312) 726-1494, fax

ORGANIZATIONS

290

Computer
and Web
Resources
for People
with
Disabilities

National Information Center for Children and Youth with Disabilities (NICHCY)

P.O. Box 1492	(202) 884-8200, voice/TTY
Washington DC 20013-1492	(800) 695-0285, voice/TTY
email: nichey@aed.org	(202) 884-8441, fax
website: www.nichcy.org	

National Information Center on Deafness

Gallaudet University	(202) 651-5051
800 Florida Avenue NE	(202) 651-5052, TTY
Washington DC 20002-3695	(202) 651-5054, fax
email: clearinghouse.infotogo@gallaudet.edu	
website: www.gallaudet.edu/~nicd/	

National Lekotek Center

2100 Ridge Avenue	(800) 366-PLAY (366-7529)
Evanston IL 60201-2796	(847) 328-0001, voice/TTY
email: lekotek@lekotek.org	(847) 328-5514, fax
website: www.lekotek.org	

National Rehabilitation Information Center (NARIC)

1010 Wayne Avenue, Suite 800	(800) 346-2742
Silver Springs MD 20910-5633	(301) 562-2401, fax
email: naricinfo@kra.com	
website: www.naric.com	

National Technical Institute for the Deaf

Rochester Institute of Technology	(716) 475-2411
One Lomb Memorial Drive	(716) 475-2810, TTY
Rochester NY 14623-5604	(716) 475-6500, fax
email: NTIDMC@rit.edu	
website: www.rit.edu/~418www/new/NTID.html	

Not Dead Yet

c/o Progress CIL	(708) 209-1500
7521 Madison Street	(708) 209-1735, fax
Forest Park, IL 60130	(708) 209-1826, TTY
website: www.notdeadyet.org	

Parent Training and Information Centers

To find the PTI in your state, contact:	(617) 482-2915, voice/TTY
Federation for Children with Special Needs	(617) 695-2939, fax
Technical Assistance for Parent Programs (TAPP)	
1135 Tremont Sreet, Suite 420	
Boston MA 02120	
email: fcsninfo@fcsn.org	
website: www.fcsn.org/	

Recording for the Blind and Dyslexic
20 Roszel Road
Princeton NJ 08540
email: info@rfbd.org
website: www.rfbd.org

800-803-7201, customer service
(609) 452-0606
(609) 987-8116, fax

RESNA
1700 N. Moore Street, Suite 1540
Arlington VA 22209-1903
email:info@resna.org
website: www.resna.org

(703) 524-6686
(703) 524-6639, TTY
(703) 524-6630, fax

SeniorNet
121 Second Street, 7th Floor
San Francisco CA 94105
email: sponsor@seniornet.com
website: www.seniornet.org

(415) 495-4990
(415) 495-3999, fax

Sensory Access Foundation
1142 West Evelyn Avenue
Sunnyvale CA 94086
website: www.sensoryaccess.com

(408) 245-7330
(408) 245-3762, fax

TASH (Association for Persons with Severe Handicaps)
29 West Susquehanna, Suite 210
Baltimore MD 21204
website: www.tash.org

(410) 828-8274
(410) 828-1306, TTY
(410) 828-6706, fax

Technology and Media (TAM)
Council for Exceptional Children
1920 Association Drive
Reston VA 22091-1589
email: yvetteh@cec.sped.org
website: www.tamcec.org/

(703) 620-3660
(703) 264-9446, TTY
(703) 264-9494, fax

Telecommunications for the Deaf Incorporated (TDI)
8719 Colesville Road, Suite 300
Silver Spring MD 20910
email: tdiexdir@aol.com

(301) 589-3786
(301) 589-3006, TTY
(301) 589-3797, fax

Through the Looking Glass
2198 Sixth Street, Suite 100
Berkeley CA 94710-2204
email: TLG@lookingglass.org
website: http://www.lookingglass.org

(510) 848-1112
(510) 848-4445, fax
(800) 804-1616, TTY

292

Computer
and Web
Resources
for People
with
Disabilities

Trace Research and Development Center
Waisman Center   (608) 262-6966
University of Wisconsin-Madison   (608) 263-5408, TTY
1500 Highland Avenue   (608) 262-8848, fax
Madison WI 53705
email: info@trace.wisc.edu
website: www.trace.wisc.edu

United Cerebral Palsy Associations
1660 L Street NW, Suite 700   (800) USA-5UCP (872-5827)
Washington DC 20036   (800) 872-5827, voice/TTY
email: ucpnatl@ucpa.org   (202) 776-0406
website: www.ucpa.org   (202) 776-0414, fax

United States Society for Augmentative and Alternative Communication (USSAAC)
P.O. Box 5271   (847) 869-2122
Evanston IL 60204-5271   (847) 869-2161, fax
email: aac-rerc@mc.duke.edu
website: www.aac-rerc.org/

University Affiliated Programs
American Association of University Affiliated Programs for Persons with
Developmental Disabilities   (301) 588-8252
8630 Fenton Street, Suite 410   (301) 588-3319, TTY
Silver Spring MD 20910   (301) 588-2842, fax
website: www.aauap.org/

National Conferences

The conferences listed here are key annual events that address technology and people with disabilities. This list is not exhaustive. There are literally hundreds of conferences each year that relate to this field. You can find out about numerous state, regional, and local conferences by contacting your community technology resources and the Tech Act project in your state.

Abilities Expo
ADVANSTAR Communications, Inc.   (203) 882-1300
440 Willis Farm Road   (203) 882-1800, fax
Milford CT 06460
website: www.tsnn.com/Advanstar/ae/sca

Alliance for Public Technology
PO Box 27146   (202) 263-2970, voice/TTY
Washington DC 20038-7146   (202) 263-2960, fax

email: apt@apt.org
website: www.apt.org/confer/

American Speech-Language-Hearing Association (ASHA)
10801 Rockville Pike   (800) 638-8255
Rockville MD 20852   (301) 897-5700
website: www.asha.org   (301) 571-0457, fax

American Occupational Therapy Association (AOTA)
4720 Montgomery Lane   (301) 652-2682
P.O. Box 31220   (800) 377-8555, TTY
Bethesda MD 20824   (301) 652-7711, fax
website: www.aota.org

Assistive Technology Industry Association
526 Davis Street, Suite 217   (847) 869-2842
Evanston IL 60201
website: www.ATIA.org

CAMA (Communication Aid Manufacturers Association)
P.O. Box 1039   (800) 441-CAMA (2262)
Evanston IL 60204-1039
email: cama@northshore.net
website: http://www.aacproducts.org

Closing the Gap
P.O. Box 68   (612) 248-3294
Henderson MN 56044   (612) 248-3810, fax
website: www.closingthegap.com

ConnSENSE
University of Connecticut–Center for Professional Development
One Bishop Circle, U-56D   (860) 486-0172
Storrs CT 06269-4056   (860) 486-0210, fax
website: www.ce.uconn.edu/connsnse.html
To register: 1-800-622-9905

Educational Computer Conferences
19 Calvert Court   (800) 255-2218
Piedmont CA 94611

International Society for Augmentative and Alternative Communication (ISAAC)
49 The Donway West, Suite 308   (416) 385-0351
Toronto ON M3C 3M9   (416) 385-0352 , fax
Canada
email: isaac_mail@mail.cepp.org

294

Computer
and Web
Resources
for People
with
Disabilities

website: www.isaac-online.org
For registration information and to join the mailing list, visit www.ISAA-conference.org

Learning Disabilities Association of America
4156 Library Road   (412) 341-1515
Pittsburgh PA 15234   (412) 344-0224, fax
email: ldanatl@usaor.net
website: www.ldanatl.org

President's Committee on Employment of People with Disabilities
1331 F Street NW, Suite 300   (202) 376-6200
Washington DC 20004   (202) 376-6205, TTY
email: info@pcepd.gov   (202) 376-6219, fax
website: www.pcepd.gov

RESNA
1700 N. Moore Street, Suite 1540   (703) 524-6686
Arlington VA 22209-1903   (703) 524-6630, fax
email:info@resna.org
website: www..resna.org

Technology and Media (TAM)
Council for Exceptional Children   (703) 620-3660
1920 Association Drive   (703) 264-9494, fax
Reston VA 22091-1589
website: www.cec.sped.org

Technology and Persons with Disabilities Annual Conference
California State University, Northridge (CSUN)
Center on Disabilities   (818) 885-2578, voice/TTY
18111 Nordoff Street   (818) 677-4929, fax
Northridge CA 91330-8340
email: ltm@csun.edu
website: www.csun.edu/cod/

Technology Expo
Center for Developmental Disabilities   (803) 935-5231
Midland Center, Educational Building   (803) 935-5250, fax
8301 Farrow
Columbia SC 29203
email: janetj@cdd.sc.edu
website: www.cdd.sc.edu

Technology, Reading & Learning Difficulties
Educational Computer Conferences   (888) 594-1249
19 Calvert Court   (510) 594-1249

Piedmont CA 94611
email: info@trld.com
website: http:// www.trld.com

(510) 594-1838, fax

295

Publications

Publications

The newsletters, magazines, and books listed here represent a wide range of subjects related to technology and are geared to a wide range of audiences. Most of the Alliance for Technology Access Centers, the Tech Act projects, and many of the other organizations cited in this book produce newsletters. Contact them directly for information about their various publications.

The roster of publications dealing with assistive technology changes weekly—new ones appear and older ones disappear. If you are having trouble locating any of the books listed here, or any other book related to the field, The Special Needs Project (a worldwide mail-order book company specializing in books on disability) can help you. They have an extensive catalog of books and can be reached at (800) 333-6867 or on the Web at www.specialneeds.com.

Newsletters and magazines

The Advance
650 Park Avenue West
King of Prussia PA 19406
email: advance@merion.com
website: www.merion.com

(610) 278-1400

Alternatively Speaking
Michael Williams
Augmentative Communication, Inc.
1 Surf Way, #237
Monterey CA 93940
email: sarablack@aol.com

(831) 649-3050
(831) 646-5428, fax

Assistive Technology Journal (RESNA)
RESNA
1700 N. Moore Street
Arlington VA 22209-1903
email: info@resna.org
website: www.resna.org

(703) 524-6686
(703) 524-6630, fax

Augmentative and Alternative Communication
International Society for Augmentative and Alternative Communication
(ISAAC)
49 The Donway West, Suite 308

(416) 385-0351
(416) 385-0352, fax

296

Computer
and Web
Resources
for People
with
Disabilities

Toronto ON M3C 3M9
Canada
email: isaac_mail@mail.cepp.org
website: www.isaac-online.org

Augmentative and Alternative Communication Journal
Decker Publishing   (905) 522-7017
4 Hughson Street South, LCD1   (905) 522-7839, fax
Hamilton ON L8N 3K7
Canada

Augmentative Communication News
Augmentative Communication, Inc.   (831) 649-3050
1 Surf Way, #237   (408) 646-5428, fax
Monterey CA 93940
email:sarablack@aol.com

CATALYST
Western Center for Microcomputers in Special Education, Inc.
1259 El Camino Real, Suite 275
Menlo Park CA 94025
email: catalystwc@aol.com

Closing the Gap Annual Resource Directory
Closing the Gap Newsletter   (507) 248-3294
P.O. Box 68   (507) 248-3810, fax
Henderson MN 56044
email: info@closingthegap.com
website: www.closingthegap.com

Communication Independence for the Neurologically Impaired, Inc.
CINI Resource Guide   (212) 385-8045
116 John Street, Suite 1304   (212) 385-9724, fax
New York NY 10038
email: cini@cini.org
website: www.cini.org

Communication Outlook
Artificial Language Lab   (517) 353-0870
Michigan State University
405 Computer Center
East Lansing MI 48823
email: artlang@pilot.msu.edu
website: www.msu.edu/~artlang

Communicating Together
ISAAC   (416) 385-0351
3-304 Stone Road West, Suite 215   (416) 385-0352, fax

Guelph ON N1G 4W4
Canada
email: isaac-mail@mail.cepp.org
website: www.isaac-online.org

Communication Matters
c/o Ace Centre
92 Windmill Road
Headington
Oxford OX 3 7DR
United Kingdom
email: isaac-mail@mail.cepp.org
website: www.isaac-online.org

Compuplay News (formerly Innotek News)
National Lekotek Center   (847) 328-0001
2100 Ridge Avenue   (847) 328-5514, fax
Evanston IL 60201-2796
email: lekotek@lekotek.org
website: www.lekotek.org

Connections
National Center for Youth with Disabilities   (612) 626-2825
University of Minnesota   (612) 626-2134, fax
Box 721
420 Delaware Street SE
Minneapolis MN 55455-0392
email: ncyd@gold.tc.umn.edu

CONNSense Bulletin
249 Glenbrook Road U-64   (860) 486-0172
Storrs CT 06269-2064   (860) 486-5037, fax
website: www.pappanikou.uconn.edu/CSBull.html

Counterpoint
National Association for Directors of Special Education   (215) 341-7874
LRP Publications—Education Department   (215) 784-9639, fax
747 Dresher Road, Suite 500
Horsham PA 19044

Directory of National Information Sources on Disabilities
National Rehabilitation Information Center (NARIC)   (800) 227-0216
8455 Colesville Road, Suite 935   (301) 588-9284, voice/TTY
Silver Spring MD 20910-3319   (301) 495-5626, TTY
email: naricinfo@kra.com   (301) 587-1967, fax
website: www.naric.com/

298

Computer
and Web
Resources
for People
with
Disabilities

Disability Resources Monthly
Disability Resources, Inc.   (516) 585-0290, voice/fax
Four Glatter Lane
Centereach NY 11720-1032
website: www.disabilityresources.org

Electronic Learning
Scholastic, Inc.   (212) 505-4900
555 Broadway   (212) 260-8587, fax
New York NY 10012

Exceptional Parent Magazine
P.O. Box 2079   (877) 372-7368
Marion OH 43306   (740) 302-5866, fax

Exceptional Parent Magazine—Resource Guide
555 Kinderkamack Rd   (800) 372-7368
Oradell NJ 07649   (201) 634-6550
website: www.eparent.com   (201) 634-6599, fax

Information Technology and Disabilities
Bobst Library, New York University   (212) 995-4583
70 Washington Square South   (212) 998-4980, TTY
New York NY 10012
email: tom.mcnulty@nyu.edu
website: www.rit.edu/~easi/itd.html
listserve: listserve@maelstrom.stjohns.edu

Issues and Updates
Newsletter of the California Deaf and Disabled Telecommunications Program   (510) 874-1410
505 14th Street, Suite 400   (510) 302-1101, TTY
Oakland CA 94612
email: kc@ddtp.org
website: http://ddtp.org

Journal of Special Education Technology
Council for Exceptional Children   (703) 620-3660
1920 Association Drive   (703) 264-9494, fax
Reston VA 22091-1589
email: service@cec.sped.org
website: www.cec.sped.org/

Journal of Visual Impairment and Blindness
American Foundation for the Blind   (800) 232-5463
11 Penn Plaza   (212) 620-2000
New York NY 10011   (212) 502-7771, fax
website: http://afb.org

Learning and Leading with Technology
International Society for Technical Education (800) 336-5191
480 Charnelton Street (541) 302-3778, fax
Eugene OR 97401-2626
email: cust_svc@ccmail.voregon.edu

Mainstream
P.O. Box 370598 (619) 234-3138
San Diego CA 92137-0598 (619) 234-3155, fax
email: subscribe@mainstream-mag.com
website: http//www.mainstream-mag.com

Mouth Magazine
P.O. Box 558 (785) 272-2578
Topeka KS 66601 (785) 272-7348, fax

New Mobility
Miramar Communications, Inc. (800) 543-4116
23815 Stuart Ranch Road (310) 317-4522
P.O. Box 8987 (310) 317-9644, fax
Malibu CA 90265
email: bcorbett@ix.netcom.com
website: www.newmobility.com

LD Resources
202 Lake Road (860) 868-3214 voice/fax
New Preston CT 06777
email: richard@ldresources.com or anne@ldresources.com
website: www.ldresources.com

Public Domain Software Catalogue
Colorado Easter Seal Society (303) 233-1666
5755 West Alameda Avenue (303) 233-1028, fax
Lakewood CO 80226-3500

Smiling Interface
PO Box 2792 Church Street Station
New York NY 10008-2792
email: mendelsohn@delphi.com

TAM Newsletter
Technology and Media (703) 620-3660
Editor: Susan Simmons (703) 264-9494, fax
Council for Exceptional Children
1920 Association Drive
Reston VA 22091-1589
email: service@cec.sped.org
website: www.cec.sped.org

300

Computer
and Web
Resources
for People
with
Disabilities

TeamRehab
P.O. Box 8987
Malibu CA 90265-8987

(310) 317-4522

Technology and Disability
Elsevier Science
655 Avenue of the Americas
New York NY 10010
email: usinfo-f@elsevier.com
website: www.elsevier.com

(212) 633-3750
(212) 633-3680, fax

Technology and Learning
P.O. Box 49727
Dayton OH 45449-0727

(800) 607-4410

Books

Adapting PCs for Disabilities—With CD-ROM. J. Lazarro. Reading, MA: Addison-Wesley, 1996.

Alternative Computer Access: A Guide to Selection. D. Anson, F.A. Philadelphia: Davis Company, 1997.

Assistive Technology: A Resource for School, Work and Community. K. Filippo, K. Inge, J. Barcus. Baltimore: Paul H. Brookes Publishing, 1997.

Assistive Technology for Persons with Disabilities: The Role of Occupational Therapy. Second Edition. William C. Mann and Joseph P. Lane. Rockville, MD: American Occupational Therapy Association, 1995.

Assistive Technology: Principles and Practice. A. Cook and S. Hussey. St. Louis, MO: Addison-Wesley, 1995.

Assistive Technology for Rehabilitation Therapists. J. Angelo, F.A. Philadelphia: Davis Company, 1997.

Assistive Technology for Young Children with Disabilities. Sharon Lesar Judge and Howard P. Parette. Cambridge, MA: Brookline, 1998.

Augmentative and Alternative Communication: Management of Severe Communication Disorders in Children and Adults. David Beukelman and Pat Mirenda. Baltimore: Paul H. Brookes Publishing, 1998.

Birth to Five: Early Childhood Special Education. Frank Bowe, Ph.D. Hempstead, NY: Hofstra University, 1999.

Book of Possibilities, Activities Using Simple Technology. Helen Canfield. Minneapolis: Ablenet, (phone: 800-322-0956), 1998.

Communication Skills in Children with Down Syndrome: A Guide for Parents. Libby Kumin. Rockville, MD: Woodbine House, 1994.

Communication Unbound: How Facilitated Communication Is Challenging Traditional Views of Autism and Ability/Disability. Douglas Biklen. New York: Teachers College Press, 1993.

The Complete Directory for People with Disabilities 1998/1999. L. Mackenzie. Lakeville, CT: Grey House, 1999.

Evaluating, Selecting and Using Appropriate Assistive Technology. Jan Galvin and Marcia Scherer, Ph.D. Gaithersburg, MD: Aspen Publishers, 1996.

Facilitated Communication Training. Rosemary Crossley. New York: Teachers College Press, 1994.

Family Guide to Assistive Technology. Katharin Kelker. PLUK (see ATA Resource Centers, Billings MT for contact information), 1997.

Financial Aid for the Disabled and Their Families 1998–2000. Gail Schlachter and R. David Weber. San Carlos, CA: Reference Service Press, 1999.

High Tech and Small Folks: Learning and Growing with Technology. Alice Wershing and Lois Symington. Lenoir City, TN: Little Tennessee Valley Educational Cooperative, 1995.

Learning Difficulties and Computers: Access to the Curriculum. David Hawkridge and Tom Vincent. Bristol, PA: Taylor & Francis, 1992.

Living in a State of Stuck: How Technology Affects Persons with Disabilities. Marcia Scherer. Cambridge, MA: Brookline Books, 1993.

Mindstorms: Children, Computers and Powerful Ideas. Seymour Papert. Scranton, PA: HarperCollins, 1980.

Reflections from a Unicorn. R. Creech. Greenville, NC: RC Publishing Company, 1992.

Silent Words. Margaret Eastham and David Eastham. Ottawa: Oliver-Pate, 1996.

Special Education Technology: Classroom Applications. Rena Lewis. Pacific Grove, CA: Brooks/Cole Publishing, 1993.

Spinal Network. 2nd Edition. Barry Corbett. Boulder, CO: Spinal Network, 1998.

Study on the Financing of Assistive Technology Devices and Services for Individuals with Disabilities: A Report to the President and the Congress of the United States. United Cerebral Palsy Association. Washington, DC: National Council on Disability, 1993.

Success for All Students: Technology for Children with Special Needs. Bob Glass. Armonk, NY: IBM Corporate Community Relations (email: ibmgives@ibm.com), 1999.

302

Computer
and Web
Resources
for People
with
Disabilities

Summary of Existing Legislation Affecting People with Disabilities. Washington, DC: U.S. Department of Education, Office of Special Education and Rehabilitative Services, 1992.

A Switch to Turn Kids On. Macomb Projects, Project ACTT. Macomb, IL: Western Illinois University, 1994.

Tax Options and Strategies for People with Disabilities. Second Edition. Steven Mendelsohn. New York: Demos Vermande Publications, Inc., 1996.

Technology in Early Intervention. James A. Blackman. Gaithersburg, MD: Aspen Publishers, 1995.

Technology for Inclusion: Meeting the Special Needs of All Students. Third Edition. Mary Male. Boston: Allyn & Bacon, 1996.

Technology for Students with Disabilities: A Decision Maker's Resource Guide. A collaborative production of the National School Boards Association and the Office of Special Education Programs, Office of Special Education and Rehabilitative Service, U.S. Department of Education. ISBN Number: 0-88364-207-7; 1997.

TRACE Cooperative Electronic Library, CO-NET, CD-ROM. Eleventh Edition. Winter 1998. Madison, WI: Trace Research & Development Center, University of Wisconsin, 1998.

Trace Resource Book: Assistive Technologies for Communication, Control and Computer Access. 1998–1999 Edition. Madison, WI: Trace Research & Development Center, 1999.

To keep informed on books in print related to disability and technology, be sure to visit these three websites: www.ldresources.com; www.amazon.com; and www.specialneeds.com.

Internet Resources

Internet services of specific interest to people with disabilities are increasing in number all the time. Many of the key commercial services offer resources for people with disabilities. Many organizations serving people with disabilities have developed their own webpages (or homepages), email capacity, and electronic bulletin board systems. The number of World Wide Web sites and other Internet resources focused on disability is extensive and expanding. The lists change often, and online addresses change often. As with every aspect of this field, the telecommunications scene changes rapidly, so the services and systems listed here are included to give you a sense of the scope of the field and where to begin exploring.

Commercial services with resources for people with disabilities

These services vary in cost and include per hour charges, flat rates for a specific number of hours, or a monthly rate for unlimited time. These rates change frequently due to heavy competition, so it pays to comparison shop before signing up.

America Online

AOL has a disABILITIES forum with a broad range of information, databases, chat rooms, software libraries, and presentations. You can get information on many topics of interest to people with disabilities, including ADA, job accommodations, and social security, to name a few. There is information about organizations you might want to know about and opportunities for interactive sessions with others. AOL will send you its proprietary graphic-interface along with an introductory offer if you call customer service at (800) 827-6364. It is also possible to access the AOL website with a browser at www.aol.com. Please note that there are issues in accessing this software with screen readers. .

CompuServe

CompuServe has a forum called Disabilities+ Forum. A wide range of topics are addressed, including information about mental health, learning disabilities, vision and hearing impairments, rights and legislation, and education and employment. There are areas ("rooms") for real-time chats, as well as libraries and discussion groups. You can call (800) 848-8199 for more information. Compuserve will provide you with its graphic interface (CIM), which makes the system easier to understand and navigate, but CIM does not work for those who need voice input or output. You can also connect to CompuServe using Internet browsers at www.compuserve.com.

Dimenet

Dimenet (Disabled Individuals' Movement for Equality Network) is an online service that provides access for communications and information sharing among individuals involved in the disability rights and independent living movements. The network is comprehensive and consumer controlled. Because it was designed with access in mind, it is easy to navigate. The phone numbers you must dial through your modem to reach Dimenet are: (508) 880-5412 in Taunton, Massachusetts; (508) 820-3376 in Framingham, Massachusetts; (513) 341-5205 in Dayton, Ohio; and (724) 223-6160 in Washington, Pennsylvania. Once you are connected, the first thing you do is type "dime" in lowercase letters and press <ENTER>. To create an account, type "new" and press <ENTER>. Once you have signed on to Dimenet, you can "TELNET" from other systems by entering "Dimenet.org."

304

Computer
and Web
Resources
for People
with
Disabilities

SeniorNet

SeniorNet is an organization dedicated to building a community of computer-using seniors. It has over 10,000 members and 55 learning centers. For more information, contact SeniorNet at (415) 495-4990 (fax, (415) 495-3999) or write to the organization at 121 Second Street, 7th Floor, San Francisco CA 94105. Email: sponsor@seniornet.org. Website: www.seniornet.org.

Prodigy Online

Prodigy is another popular online service. It hosts various chat rooms and bulletin boards of interest to people with disabilities. There is an introductory exploration period. Call (800) 776-3449 for more information and to receive the software you will need to connect to Prodigy's service.

Using the Internet

Commercial services, such as those described above, now provide an easy way to get onto the Internet. The advantages of this approach are ease in getting started as well as low cost. Another advantage is the substantial amount of disability-related content on the commercial services. Almost all now have an area for software, resources, sharing, and support.

If you are planning to spend a significant amount of time on the Internet, however, you may want to consider using an Internet Service Provider (ISP). These companies provide direct unlimited access to the Internet via local numbers for a monthly rate. This approach may be a bit daunting at the beginning, as you configure your system and find a Web browser, but connecting directly to the net is a very cost-effective and often faster approach for serious Internet users.

Yahoo, Hot Mail, and Juno represent new options in low-cost or no-cost Internet and email access. This access is generally free because you are exposed to advertising from the provider. Competition for Internet exposure will continue to rapidly change the options for Internet access.

What's on the Internet

The Internet is often described as a "network of networks." This means you can access information and resources on computers across the world as easily as the one on your desk by using your computer, modem, and telephone line. There are a variety of formats people typically use to get information. A couple of the most popular ways to use the Internet include:

World Wide Web

The World Wide Web (WWW) offers extensive information and resources in a format that is comfortable and intuitive for many people. Reviewing this information requires software known as a browser. Some popular browsers are Netscape, Microsoft Internet Explorer, Mosaic, and Lynx, among many. Browsers are graphics oriented, which creates potential barriers for users who rely on text-based material. Websites developed in accordance with the accessibility guidelines developed by the Web Accessibility Initiative (www.w3.org/WAI/) are accessible to all individuals, including those using text-based browsers and screen readers.

Each website has an address known as its URL (Uniform Resource Locator). Typing in the URL allows you to visit the website you have indicated. There are hundreds of disability-related websites and the number is constantly growing. The following organizations and their URLs will help you get started on the Web. Happy surfing!

Alliance for Technology Access
www.ATAccess.org

Deaf World Web
http://deafworldweb.org/dww/

The Disability and Medical Resources Mall
http://disabilitymall.com

EASI (Equal Access to Software and Information)
www.isc.rit.edu/~easi

Families and Advocates Partnership for Education
(communication exchange and resources to promote implementation of the IDEA amendments of 1997)
www.fape.org

Trace Research and Development Center
www.trace.wisc.edu/

Yahoo's Disability Resources
www.yahoo.com/yahoo/Society_and_Culture/Disabilities/

Job Accommodation Network
http://janweb.icdi.wvu.edu/

UCPA Assistive Technology Funding and Systems Change Project
www.ucpa.org/html/innovative/atfsc/index.html

RESNA
www.resna.org

University of Washington
www.washington.edu/doit/

Webable-Directory of Websites for People with Disabilities
http://webable.com/

Visit your favorite websites frequently, as they are updated often and will provide valuable and current information.

306

Computer
and Web
Resources
for People
with
Disabilities

In addition to World Wide Web sites, there are many other formats on the Internet that offer innumerable resources on virtually any topic of interest to you. Different formats include news groups, bulletin boards, list serves, and discussion lists. Your local library will no doubt have many books available that more thoroughly describe the different parts of the net. Some sample sites to visit are listed below. Remember, this is only a starter list. As with the Web, the numbers of new resources are growing rapidly, bringing unbelievable amounts of information and connections with helpful, knowledgeable people.

Sample List Serves

EASI (Equal Access to Software and Information) deals with issues related to technology and people with disabilities. To join, send a message with a blank subject line to listserv@stuvm.stjohns.edu. In the body of the message type "subscribe easi firstname lastname." To post to the list, send a message to easi@sjuvm.stjohns.edu.

The BlindFam mailing list is for discussions of all aspects of family life as they are affected by the blindness of one or more family members. All family members are invited to join, and people are encouraged to send descriptions of themselves and their families. To subscribe to BlindFam, send an electronic mail message to listserv@sjuvm.stjohns.edu.

The Deaf Discussion List provides *Deaf Magazine* to subscribers. Send an electronic mail message to deaf-request@clark.net. Leave the subject line blank and type in the body of the message, "SUB DEAF firstname lastname."

Handicap Digest is an electronic journal for individuals interested in disability-related issues. An electronic journal is the computer network equivalent to a printed magazine. To subscribe to *Handicap Digest*, send an electronic mail message to: wtm@bunker.shel.isc-br.com and request a subscription to *Handicap Digest*.

LD-List (Learning Disability Discussion List) is an open, unmoderated, international forum that provides information for individuals interested in learning disabilities. Subscribers include people with learning disabilities, family members and friends, educators and administrators, researchers, and others wishing to know more about the subject. To subscribe to LD-List, send an electronic mail message to: ld-list-request@east.pima.edu. In the body of the message type only, "SUBSCRIBE."

Sample Discussion Lists

Act is an EASI Digest list for Adaptive Computer Professionals. To subscribe, send a message with a blank subject line to listserv@maelstrom.stjohns.edu. In the body of the message type "subscribe act Firstname Lastname."

AToutcomes supports the development and use of reliable, valid, and sensitive outcome measures in assistive technology. To subscribe, send a message with a blank subject line to majordomo@snow.utoronto.ca. In the body of the message type "subscribe atoutcomes email-address."

Axslib-l focuses on issues surrounding access to libraries by people with disabilities. To subscribe, send a message with a blank subject line to listserv@maelstrom.stjohns.edu. In the body of the message type "subscribe axslib Firstname Lastname."

Blind-DEV is dedicated to the discussion of issues concerning the development of computer products and adaptive equipment for blind and visually impaired computer users. To subscribe, send a message with a blank subject line to listserv@maelstrom.stjohns.edu. In the body of the message type "subscribe blind-dev Firstname Lastname."

Crt-focus is for discussion of assistive technology for people with disabilities. To subscribe, send a message with a blank subject line to listproc@ smash.gatech.edu. In the body of the message type "subscribe crt-focus Firstname Lastname."

Design-for-all provides an electronic platform for people who are interested in design for all. To subscribe, send a message with a blank subject line to mailserv@rc.tudelft.nl. In the body of the message type "subscribe design-for-all."

EASI (Equal Access to Software and Information) deals with issues related to technology and the disabled. To subscribe, send a message with a blank subject line to listserv@maelstrom.stjohns.edu. In the body of the message type "subscribe easi Firstname Lastname."

Ibm-srd is for sharing information about using IBM ScreenReader software. To subscribe, send a message with a blank subject line to listserv@ vm1.nodak.edu. In the body of the message type "subscribe ibm-srd Firstname Lastname."

Information, Technology and Disabilities is a quarterly electronic journal devoted to computer use by people with disabilities. To join the list, which sends out complete issues, send a message with a blank subject line to listserv@maelstrom.stjohns.edu. In the body of the message type "SUB itd-jnl Firstname Lastname."

JFW is a discussion group for Jaws for Windows users. To subscribe, send a message with a blank subject line to majordomo@yoyo.cc.monash.edu.au. In the body of the message type "subscribe JFW."

308

Computer
and Web
Resources
for People
with
Disabilities

Kenx is a list for users of Ke:nx software, which provides alternatives to keyboard access for Mac users with special needs. To subscribe, send a message with a blank subject line to kenx-request@gospel.iinet.net.au. In the body of the message type "subscribe kenx Firstname Lastname."

Libacc is a list to help librarians provide people with disabilities access to library resources and services. To subscribe, send a note to the list owner, Dick Banks, at rbanks@uwstout.edu.

TecHabla deals with all aspects of speech technology in its official language, Spanish. To subscribe, send a message with a blank subject line to listserv@listserv.rediris.es. In the body of the message type "sub techabla Firstname Lastname."

Uaccess-l is for discussion of universal access to information systems. To subscribe, send a message with a blank subject line to listproc@trace. wisc.edu. In the body of the message type "subscribe uaccess-l Firstname Lastname."

Voice-users is a discussion list for people using, or planning to use, voice recognition software. To subscribe, send a message with a subject line "SUBSCRIBE" to voice-users-request@cuckoo.hpl.hp.com.

Sample Newsgroups

alt.education.disabled includes information regarding the education of people with disabilities.

alt.comp.blind-users includes information about computer use for people with blindness.

alt.support.arthritis includes information of interest about arthritis.

Bit.listserv.easi duplicates the EASI discussion list.

Bit.listserv.axslib-l duplicates the Axslib-l list.

Bit.listserv.l-hcap duplicates the L-hcap list.

Technology Vendors

The following list indicates vendors and developers in the field today. This list is not exhaustive but represents many of the products currently available. Contact vendors directly for a full list of their products. Many of the vendors included on this list are members of the Alliance for Technology Access (indicated by an asterisk). The Alliance for Technology Access is a growing organization with new vendor members joining regularly. If you are interested in becoming a vendor member of the Alliance for Technology Access, please contact it for information and an application.

Ability Research, Inc.
P.O. Box 1721
Minnetonka MN 55345
email: ability@skypoint.com
website: www.skypoint.com/~ability/
  • Assistive Communication Products
  • Dedicated Communication Devices
  • Electronic Pointing Devices
  • Switches and Switch Software

(612) 939-0121
(612)890-8393, fax

*AbleNet, Inc.
1081 Tenth Avenue SE
Minneapolis MN 55414
email: marykay_walch@ablenetinc.com
website: www.ablenetinc.com
  • Assistive Communication Products
  • Environmental Controls
  • Interface Devices
  • Switches

(800) 322-0956
(612) 379-0956
(612) 379-9143, fax

*Academic Software, Inc.
331 West 2nd Street
Lexington KY 40507
email: asistaff@acsw.com
website: www.acsw.com
  • Interface Devices
  • Switch Software

(800) VIA-ADLS (842-2357)
(606) 233-2332
(606) 231-0725, fax

*Access First!
P.O. Box 2990
Glen Allen VA 23058-3990
email: access1st@aol.com
website: access1st.net
  • Switches and Switch Software
  • Environmental Controls
  • Assistive Communication Devices
  • Interface Devices

(888) 606-6769
(804) 935-6739, fax

ACS Technologies
1400 Lee Drive
Coraopolis PA 15108
  • Assistive Communication Products
  • Environmental Controls

(800) 227-2922
(412) 269-6656
(412) 269-6675, fax

TECHNOLOGY VENDORS / A

310

Computer
and Web
Resources
for People
with
Disabilities

ADAMLAB
3350 Van Born Road
Box 807
Wayne MI 48184
email: kaminsk@wcresa.k12.mi.us
website: www.wcresa.k12.mi.us/adamlab
  • Assistive Communication Products

(734) 334-1415
(734) 334-1432, fax

Adaptability
P.O. Box 515
Colchester CT 06415
email: service@snswwide.com
website: www.snswwide.com
  • Arm and Wrist Supports

(800) 228-9941
(800) 566-6678, fax

*Adaptivation, Inc.
2225 W. 50th Street, Suite 100
Sioux Falls SD 57105
email: adaptaac@aol.com
website: http://users.aol.com/adaptaac
  • Assistive Communication Products
  • Switches and Switch Software

(605) 335-4445
(605) 335-4446 , fax

Adlib, Inc.
5142 Bolsa Avenue, Suite 106
Huntington Beach CA 92649
  • Pointing and Typing Aids

(714) 895-9529

Advanced Gravis Corporation
2855 Campus Drive
San Mateo CA 94403
email: custserv@gravis.com
website: www.gravis.com
  • Joysticks
  • Gaming Devices

(800) 235-6708
(650) 572-9675 , fax

Advanced Ideas, Inc.
591 Redwood Highway, Suite 2325
Mill Valley CA 94941
website: www.gallaudet.edu/~kkurlych/0352.html
  • Reading Comprehension Programs

(415) 388-2430
(415) 388-6575, fax

Ai Squared
P.O. Box 669
Manchester Center VT 05255-0669
email: zoomtext@aisquared.com

(802) 362-3612
(802) 362-1670, fax

website: www.aisquared.com
  • Screen Enlargement Programs

Aicom Corporation
2381 Zanker Road, Suite #160   (408) 577-0370
San Jose CA 95131   (408) 577-0373, fax
  • Speech Synthesizers

*ALVA Access Group, Inc.
5801 Christie Avenue, Suite 475   (510) 923-6280
Emeryville CA 94608   (510) 923-6270, fax
email: info@aagi.com
website: www.aagi.com
  • Screen Readers
  • Braille Displays
  • Screen Enlargement Programs
  • Graphics to Braille Representations Software
  • Browser Access

American Printing House for the Blind, Inc.
1839 Frankfort Avenue   (800) 223-1839
P.O. Box 6085   (502) 899-2274, fax
Louisville KY 40206
email: info@aph.org
website: www.aph.org
  • Notetakers
  • Screen Readers
  • Speech Synthesizers
  • Talking Software

*American Thermoform Corporation
2311 Travers Avenue   (800) 331-3676
City of Commerce CA 90040   (323) 723-9021
email: ATC@brleqp.com   (323) 728-8877, fax
website: www.ATCbrleqp.com
  • Braille Embossers, Translators
  • Refreshable Braille Displays
  • Tactile Graphics Production

*Antarq
Fernando No. 90, Col. Alamos   (525) 530-2077
C.P. 03400
Mexico, D.F.
website: www.antarq.com.mx
  • AT Products in Spanish, Portugese, and English

312

Computer
and Web
Resources
for People
with
Disabilities

*Apple Computer, Inc.
Worldwide Disability Solutions   (800) 800-2775 and (800) 767-2775
1 Infinite Loop MS 301-3ED   (800) 755-0601, TTY
Cupertino CA 95014   (408) 974-1478, fax
email: appledsg@applelink.apple.com
website: www.apple.com/disability/
  • Access Utilities
  • Menu Management Programs
  • Screen Enlargement Programs
  • Voice Recognition

*Apt Technology, Inc./DU-IT Control Systems
236 A N. Main Street   (330) 567-2001
Shreve OH 44676   (330) 567-3073, fax
email: apt2duit@valkyrie.net
website: www.valkyrie.net/~apt2duit
  • Environmental Control Units
  • Switches and Switch Software

*Arkenstone, Inc.
NASA Ames Moffett Complex, Building 23   (650) 603-8880
P.O. Box 215   (650) 603-8887, fax
Moffett Field CA 94035-0215   (800) 833-2753, TTY
email: info@arkenstone.org
website: www.arkenstone.org
  • Electronic Reference Tools
  • Reading Systems
  • Reading Software

Artic Technologies
55 Park Street, Suite 2   (248) 588-7370
Troy MI 48083   (248) 588-2650, fax
email: info@artictech.com
website: www.artictech.com
  • Screen Enlargement Programs
  • Screen Readers
  • Speech Synthesizers

*AssisTech
P.O. Box 137   (888)ASISTEK (274-7835)
Stow NY 14785
email: info@assisttech.com
website: www.assisttech.com
  • Early Childhood
  • Educational Technology

*Assistive Technology, Inc.
7 Wells Avenue   (800) 793-9227
Newton MA 02459
email: customercare@assistivetech.com
website: www.assistivetech.com
- Alternative and Augmentative Communication
- Authoring Software
- Speech Synthesizers
- Alternate Input
- Processing Aids

AT&T Accessible Communication Products
(see Lucent Technologies)
- TTYs

*Atlantis Corporation
804 Westham Parkway   (804) 673-7242
Richmond VA 23229   (804) 673-7168, fax
email: jcavera@atlantiscorp.com
website: www.atlantiscorp.com
- Custom Design of Accessible Control Systems

*Aurora Systems, Inc.
Box 43005   (888) 290-1133
4739 Willingdon Avenue   (604) 291-6310
Burnaby BC V5G 3H0
Canada
email: aurorasw@direct.ca
website: www.djtech.com / aurora
- Alternative and Augmentative Communication
- Processing Aids

A/V Concepts Corporation
30 Montauk Boulevard   (888) 553-3266
Oakdale NY 11769   (516) 567-7227
email: info@edconpublishing.com   (516) 567-8745, fax
website: www.edconpublishing.com
- Educational Software

Berkeley Systems, Inc.
(see Knowledge Adventures)
- Screen Enlargement Programs
- Screen Readers

314

Computer
and Web
Resources
for People
with
Disabilities

BEST
63 Forest Street
Chestnut Hill MA 02167   (617) 277-0179
     (617) 277-1275, fax
- Interface Devices

Beyond Sight, Inc.
26 East Arapahoe Road   (303) 795-6455
Littleton CO 80122   (303) 795-6425, fax
email: bsistore@beyondsight.com
website: www.beyondsight.com
- Braille Embossers and Translators
- CCTVs
- Screen Enlargement Programs
- Screen Readers
- Speech Synthesizers

Biolink Computer Research and Development, Ltd.
140 W. 15th Street, Suite 305   (604) 984-4099
North Vancouver BC V7M 1R6   (604) 985-8493, fax
Canada
email: 72604.367@compuserve.com
website: http://biz.bctel.net/biolink
- Screen Readers

*Blazie Engineering, Inc.
105 E. Jarrettsville Road   (410) 893-9333
Forrest Hill MD 21050   (410) 836-5040, fax
email: info@blazie.com
website: www.blazie.com
- Braille Embossers
- Braille Translation Software
- Notetakers

Blissymbolics Communication International
1630 Lawrence Avenue West, Suite 104   (416) 242-9114
Toronto ON M6L 1C5   (416) 244-6543, fax
Canada
email: ortckse@oise.on.ca
website: http://home.istar.ca/~bci
- Writing Composition Programs

*Braille Planet
(see Duxbury Systems)

Brain Actuated Technologies, Inc.
139 E. Davis Street
Yellow Springs OH 45387
email: support@brainfingers.com
website: www.brainfingers.com

(937) 767-2674
(937) 767-7366, fax

- Electronic Pointing Devices

BrainTrain, Inc.
727 Twin Ridge Lane
Richmond VA 23235
email: info@braintrain-online.com
website: www.braintrain-online.com

(804) 320-0105
(804) 320-0242, fax

- Cognitive Training Software

*Brøderbund Software, Inc. (a division of The Learning Company)
500 Redwood Boulevard, Box 6121
Novato CA 94948-6121
website: www.broder.com

(800) 825-4420, ordering
(415) 382-4400
(415) 382-4582, fax

- Educational Software

Bytes of Learning
60 Renfrew Drive, Suite 210
Markham ON L3R OEI
Canada
email: custservice@bytesoflearning.com
website: www.bytesoflearning.com

(800) 465-6428
(905) 475-8650, fax

- Talking Word Processors
- Educational Software

Cables to Go
1501 Webster Street
Dayton OH 45404
website: www.cablestogo.com

(800) 225-8646
(937) 496-2266, fax

- Monitor Additions

Caere Corporation
100 Cooper Court
Los Gatos CA 95032
email: custsupp@caere.com
website: www.caere.com

(800) 654-1187
(408) 395-1994, fax

- Optical Character Recognition Software

Carolyn's Products for Enhanced Living
1415 57th Avenue West
Bradenton FL 34207

(800) 648-2266
(941) 739-5503, fax

- CCTVs

316

Computer
and Web
Resources
for People
with
Disabilities

- Keyboard Additions
- Visual Aids

*Center for Applied Special Technology (CAST)
39 Cross Street   (978) 531-8555
Peabody MA 01960   (978) 531-0192, fax
email: cast.org
website: www.cast.org
  - Educational Software
  - Reading Comprehension Programs
  - Talking and Large-Print Word Processors

CE Software, Inc.
1801 Industrial Circle   (800) 523-7638
West Des Moines IA 50265   (515) 221-1801
email: sales@cesoft.com   (515) 221-1806, fax
website: www.cesoft.com
  - Abbreviation Expansion and Macro Programs

*Closing The Gap, Inc.
P.O. Box 68   (507) 248-3294
Henderson MN 56044   (507) 248-3810, fax
email: info@closingthegap.com
website: www.closingthegap.com
  - Information Resources

Colorado Easter Seal Society, Inc.
(see Easter Seals Colorado)
  - Switch Software

Compusult Limited
P.O. Box 1000   (888) 388-8180
Mt. Pearl NF A1N 3CP   (709) 745-4914
Canada A1N 3CP   (709) 745-7927, fax
email: hear-it@compusult.nf.ca
website: www.hear-it.com
  - Speech Synthesizers

*Compu-Teach
16541 Redmond Way, Suite 137C   (425) 885-0517
Redmond WA 98052   (800) 448-3224
email: cmpteach@compu-teach.com   (425) 883-9169, fax
website: www.wolfnet.com/~cmpteach
  - Educational Software
  - Reading Comprehension Programs

Computers to Help People, Inc.
825 E. Johnson Street   (608) 257-5917
Madison WI 53713
  • Switch Software

Conover Company
1050 Witcel Avenue   (800) 933-1933
Oshkosh WI 54901   (920) 231-4809, fax
email: conovercompany@execpc.com
website: http:www.conovercompany.com
  • Software: Work Skills

*Consultants for Communication Technology
508 Bellevue Terrace   (412) 761-6062
Pittsburgh PA 15202   (412) 761-7336, fax
email: ConCommTech@compuserv.com
website: www.ConCommTech.com
  • Environmental Controls
  • Interface Devices
  • Speech Synthesizers
  • Switch Software

Continental Press, Inc.
520 East Bainbridge Street   (800) 233-0759
Elizabethtown PA 17022   (717) 367-1836
email: edcsr@continentalpress.com   (717) 367-5660, fax
website: www.continentalpress.com
  • Reading Comprehension Programs

*Creative Communicating
P.O. Box 3358   (435) 645-7737
Park City UT 84060
email: mail@creative-comm.com
website: www.creative-comm.com
  • Early Learning Products
  • Literacy Materials
  • Educational Software

Creative Switch Industries
P.O. Box 5256   (800) 257-4385
Des Moines IA 50316   (515) 287-5748
  • Switches

Crestwood Company
6625 N. Sydney Place   (414) 352-5678
Milwaukee WI 53209-3259   (414) 352-5679, fax

318

Computer
and Web
Resources
for People
with
Disabilities

email: crestcomm@aol.com
website: www.communicationaids.com
- Assistive Communication Products
- Pointing and Typing Aids

Curtis Computer Products
2210 Second Avenue
Muscatine IA 52761
website: www.curtis.com
- Computer Accessories
- Monitor Mounts

(800) 272-2366
(800) 272-2382, fax

Data Cal Corporation
531 East Elliot Road, #145
Chandler AZ 85225-1118
email: sales@datacal.com
website: www.datacal.com
- Keyboard Additions

(800) 223-0123
(602) 813-3100
(602) 545-7212, fax

Davidson & Associates, Inc.
(see Knowledge Adventure)
- Educational Software
- Reading Comprehension Programs
- Talking and Large-Print Word Processors
- Writing Composition Programs

*Dolphin Computer Access
100 South Ellsworth Avenue
San Mateo CA 94401
email: sales@dolphinusa.com
website: www.dolphinusa.com.com
- Alternate Output for Visually Impaired Users
- Braille Output
- Speech Output
- Screen Enlargement

(650) 348-7401

*Don Johnston, Inc.
26799 W. Commerce Drive
Volvo, IL 60073
email: info@donjohnston.com
website: www.donjohnston.com
- Alternate Keyboards
- Assistive Communication Products
- Interface Devices
- Keyboard Additions
- Reading Comprehension Programs

(800) 999-4660
(847)740-0740
(800) 859-5242, fax

- Switches and Switch Software
- Talking and Large-Print Word Processors
- Word Prediction Programs
- Writing Composition Programs

*Don Johnston Special Needs
c/o NW SEMERC   (44) 1925 241 642
18 Clarendon Court—Calver Road
Windwick Quay
Warrington WA2 8QP
United Kingdom

*Dorling Kindersley Family Learning
14614 N.E. 82nd Street   (888) 225-3535
Vancouver WA 98682
- Literacy Technology
- Educational Software

Dragon Systems
320 Nevada Street   (800) 825-5897
Newton MA 02160   (617) 965-5200
email: info@dragonsys.com   (617) 630-9707, fax
website: www.dragonsys.com
- Voice Recognition

*DU-IT Control Systems Group, Inc.
(see Apt Technology)
- Environmental Control Units
- Switches and Switch Software

*Dunamis, Inc.
3423 Fowler Boulevard   (800) 828-2443
Lawrenceville GA 30244   (770) 932-0485
email: dunamis@aol.com   (770) 279-0809, fax
- Alternate Keyboards
- Communication Skills Software
- Educational Software
- Alternate Input

Duxbury Systems, Inc.
270 Littleton Road, Unit 6   (978) 692-3000
Westford MA 01886   (978) 692-7912, fax
email: info@duxsys.com
website: www.duxburysystems.com
- Braille Embossers and Translators

320

Computer
and Web
Resources
for People
with
Disabilities

*DynaVox Systems (formerly Sentient Systems Technology, Inc.)
2100 Wharton Street, Suite 630   (800) 344-1778
Pittsburgh PA 15203   (412) 381-4883
email: sstsales@sentient-sys.com   (412) 381-5241, fax
website: http://sentient-sys.com
 • Assistive Communication Products

Easter Seals Colorado
5755 W. Alameda   (800) 875-4732
Lakewood CO 80226   (303) 233-1028, fax
email: escinfo@cess.org
website: www.eastsealsco.org
 • Educational Software
 • Switch Software

EBM Corporation
2249 S. Grout Road   (800) 815-5719
Gladwin MI 48624   (517) 426-7354, fax
 • Accessible Furniture

*Echo Speech Corporation
6460 Via Real   (800) DSP-ECHO (377-3246)
Carpinteria CA 93013   (805) 684-4593
 • Speech Synthesizers   (805) 684-6628, fax

*Edmark Corporation
6727 185th Avenue NE   (800) 362-2890
P.O. Box 97021   (425) 556-8400
Redmond WA 98073   (425) 556-8402, TTY
email: edmarkteam@edmark.com (425) 556-8430, fax
website: www.edmark.com
 • Educational Software
 • Menu Management Programs
 • Reading Comprehension Programs
 • Switch Software
 • Touch Screens

Educational Activities, Inc.
P.O. Box 392   (800) 645-3739
Freeport NY 11520   (516) 223-4666
email: learn@edact.com   (516) 623-9282, fax
website: www.edact.com
 • Reading Comprehension Programs
 • Educational Software

*Educational Press/Learning Well
(see Learning Well)
- Educational Software

*Education TURNKEY Systems, Inc.
256 North Washington Street   (703) 536-2310
Falls Church VA 22046
email: turnkey@ix.netcom.com
- Consulting Services

EduQuest
2929 North Central Avenue   (800) 426-4338
Phoenix AZ 85012   (800) 214-1436, fax
website: www.solutions.IBM.com/K12
- Educational Software
- Large-Print Word Processors

EKEG Electronics Company, Ltd.
P.O. Box 46199, Station D   (604) 857-0820
Vancouver BC V6J 5G5   (604) 857-2726, fax
Canada
email: richmush@direct.ca
website: www.catscan.com/ekeg
- Alternate Keyboards

Enabling Technologies Company
1601 Northeast Braille Place   (800) 950-3687
Jensen Beach FL 34957   (561) 225-3687
email: enabling@brailler.com   (561) 225-3299, fax
website: www.brailler.com
- Braille Embossers and Translators

*Exceller Software Corporation
2 Graham Road West   (607) 257-1665
Ithaca NY 14850
email: exceller@aol.com
website: www.exceller.com
- Linquistic and Reference Software
- Bilingual Software in Spanish, Portugese, German, and Italian

Exceptional Computing, Inc.
450 NW 58th Street   (352) 331-8847
Gainesville FL 32607   (352) 331-4164, fax
email: rhm@exceptionalcomputing.com
- Alternate Keyboards
- Switches and Switch Software
- Educational Software

TECHNOLOGY VENDORS / E

322

Computer
and Web
Resources
for People
with
Disabilities

Extensions for Independence
555 Saturn Boulevard #B-368   (619) 423-1748
San Diego CA 92154
email: aheyer@mouthstick.net
website: www.mouthstick.net
  • Alternate Keyboards
  • Pointing and Typing Aids

EyeTech Digital Systems, Inc.
1705 East McLelland Road   (480) 610-1899
Mesa AZ 85203   (602) 728-9907
email: info@eyetechds.com
website: www.eyetechds.com
  • Alternative Pointing

Fellowes
1789 Norwood Avenue   (800) 945-4545
Itasca IL 60143   (630) 893-1600
  • Trackballs   (800) 955-9329 , fax
  • Accessible Furniture and Office Supplies

*FileMaker, Inc. (formerly Claris Corporation)
5201 Patrick Henry Drive, C-56   (408) 987-7000
P.O. Box 58168   (408) 987-3002, fax
Santa Clara CA 95052-8168
email: jeff_orloff@claris.com
website: www.claris.com
  • Home and Business Software

Fliptrack OneOnOne Computer Training
2055 Army Trail Road, Suite 100
Addison IL 60101
  • Audio Training Tapes

Florida New Concepts Marketing, Inc.
P.O. Box 261   (800) 456-7097
Port Richey FL 34673   (727) 842-3231
email: compulenz@gte.net   (727) 845-7544, fax
website: http://gulfside.com/compulenz/
  • Monitor Additions

Franklin Electronic Publishers, Inc.
One Franklin Plaza   (609) 386-2500
Burlington NJ 08016   (609) 387-7420, fax
email: customer_service@franklin.com
  • Electronic Reference Tools

Fred Sammons, Inc.
(see Sammons Preston)
- Pointing and Typing Aids

*FutureForms
903 Chicago Avenue   (616) 475-0236
Grand Rapids MI 49509
email: info@futureforms.com
website: www.futureforms.com
- Electronic Forms
- Electronic Reference Tools

Global Computer Supplies
2318 Del Amo Road   (800) 8-GLOBAL (845-6225)
Compton CA 90220   (310) 637-6191, fax
on the East Coast:
11 Harbor Park Drive   (516) 625-4388
Port Washington NY 11050
website: http://www.globalcomputer.com
- Keyboard Additions

*The Great Talking Box Company
22458 Fortune Drive   (408) 456-0133
San Jose CA 95131   (408) 456-0134, fax
email: sys_sym@pacbell.com
website: www.gtb-sym.com
- Assistive Communication Products

Great Wave Software
5353 Scotts Valley Drive   (831) 438-1990
Scotts Valley CA 95066   (831) 438-7171, fax
email: robertas@greatware.com   (800) 423-1144
website: www.greatwave.com
- Reading Comprehension Programs
- Educational Software

*Gus Communications
1006 Lonetree Court   (360) 715-8580
Bellingham WA 98226   (360) 715-9633, fax
email: gus@gusinc.com
website: www.gusinc.com
- Abbreviation Expansion and Macro Programs
- Access Utilities
- Alternate Keyboards
- Assistive Communication Products
- Environmental Controls

324

Computer
and Web
Resources
for People
with
Disabilities

- Speech Synthesizers
- Switch Software
- Talking and Large-Print Word Processors
- Touch Screens
- Word Prediction Programs

GW Micro

725 Airport North Office Park   (219) 489-3671
Fort Wayne IN 46825   (219) 489-2608, fax
email: support@gwmicro.com   (219) 489-5281, BBS
website: www.gwmicro.com

- Braille Embossers and Translators
- Screen Enlargement Programs
- Screen Readers
- Speech Synthesizers
- Browser Access

Hach Associates, Inc.

P.O. Box 11754   (800) 624-7968
Winston Salem NC 27116   (919) 744-7280
email: kelgreen@computersforkids.com   (800) 410-7282, fax
website: www.computersforkids.com

- Alternate Keyboards
- Interface Devices
- Switches
- Touch Screens

Handykey Corporation

141 Mount Sinai Avenue   (800) 638-2352
Mt. Sinai NY 11766   (516) 474-4405
email: handykey@mcimail.com   (516) 474-3760, fax
website: www.handykey.com

- Alternate Keyboards

HARC Mercantile Ltd.

P.O. Box 3055   (800) 445-9968, voice/TTY
Kalamazoo MI 49003-3055   (800) 413-5248, fax
email: home@hacofamerica.com
website: www.harcmercantile.com

- TTYs
- Assistive Listening Devices

Harris Communications, Inc.

15159 Technology Dr.   (800) 825-6758
Eden Prairie MN 55344-2277   (800) 825-9187, TTY
email: mail@harriscomm.com   (612) 906-1099, fax

website: www.harriscomm.com
- TTYs
- Amplifiers
- Accessible Pagers
- TTY Modems

*Hartley/Jostens Learning
9920 Pacific Heights Boulevard
San Diego CA 92121-4330
email: mjbradley@jlc.com
website: www.jostenslearning.com

(800) 247-1380
(619) 587-0087, voice / TTY
(619) 622-7873, fax

- Reading Comprehension Programs
- Software Features: Built-in Utilities
- Talking and Large-Print Word Processors
- Educational Software

Hear More, Inc.
P.O. Box 3413
Farmingdale NY 11735

(516) 752-0738, voice / TTY
(516) 752-0689, fax

- TTYs

Hear You Are, Inc.
4 Muscontcong Avenue
Stanhope NJ 07874

(201) 347-7662, voice / TTY / fax

- TTYs and TTY Modems

*Henter-Joyce, Inc.
11800 31st Court N.
St. Petersburg FL 33716-1805
email: info@hj.com
website: www.hj.com

(800) 336-5658
(727) 803-8000
(727) 803-8001, fax

- Screen Readers
- Screen Enlargement
- Browser Access

HITEC Group International
8160 Madison Street
Burr Ridge IL 60561
website: www.hitech.com

(800) 288-8303
(708) 654-9219, fax

- TTYs
- Telecommunications Equipment

Hooleon Corporation
411 South 6th Street, Building B
Cottonwood AZ 86326
email: sales@hooleon.com

(800) 937-1337
(520) 634-7515
(520) 634-4620, fax

326

Computer
and Web
Resources
for People
with
Disabilities

website: www.hooleon.com
- Keyboard Additions

Houghton Mifflin School Division
222 Berkeley Street (800) 758-6762
Boston MA 02116-3764 (617) 351-5000
email: susan_retik@hmco.com (617) 351-1121, fax
website: www.eduplace.com
- Reading Comprehension Programs
- Educational Software

*Humanities Software
P. O. Box 950 (800) 245-6737
408 Columbia Street (541) 386-6737
Hood River OR 97031 (541) 386-1410, fax
email: Hinfo@humanitiessoftware.com
website: www.humantiessoftware.com
- Writing Composition Programs
- Educational Software

HumanWare, Inc.
6245 King Road (800) 722-3393
Loomis CA 95650 (916) 652-7253
email: info@humanware.com (916) 652-7296, fax
website: www.humanware.com
- Braille Embossers and Translators
- CCTVs
- Notetakers
- Refreshable Braille Displays
- Screen Enlargement Programs
- Screen Readers
- Speech Synthesizers

*IBM Special Needs Systems/
Independence Series Information Center
Building 904, Internal Zip 9448 (800) 426-4832
11400 Burnet Road (800) 426-4833, TTY
Austin TX 78758 (512) 838-9367, fax
website: www.software.ibm.com (800) 465-7999, Canada
- Access Utilities
- Keyboard Additions: Keyguards
- Reading Comprehension Programs
- Screen Readers
- Talking Internet Browsers
- Talking and Large-Print Word Processors

- TTYs
- Voice Recognition
- Writing Composition Programs

Imaginart
307 Arizona Street
Bisbee AZ 85603
email: imaginart@compuserv.com
website: www.imaginartonlin.com
- Communication Aids
- Keyboard Additions

(800) 828-1376
(520) 432-5741
(800) 737-1376, fax

Index Braille Printer Company
Box 155, S-954
23 Gammelstad
Sweden
email: info@indexbraille.com
website: www.indexbraille.com
- Braille Embossers and Translators

+46 (0) 920-203080
+46 (0) 920-203085, fax

Infogrip, Inc.
1141 E. Main Street
Ventura CA 93001
email: infogrip@infogrip.com
website: www.infogrip.com/infogrip
- Alternate Keyboards

(800) 397-0921
(805) 652-0770
(805) 652-0880, fax

*Information Services, Inc.
Genesis Center, Suite 3008
St. Johns NF A1B 3X5
Canada
email: sales@is-inc.com
website: www.is-inc.com
- Writing Composition Software

(888) 492-4925
(709) 737-2539

Information Strategies Incorporated
1200 E. Campbell, #108
Richardson TX 75081
email: windows!mail1john@isio1.attmail.com
- Touch Screens

(214) 234-0176
(214) 234-5936, fax

Infra-Link, Inc.
P.O. Box 1008
Portland OR 97207-1008
email: zygo@zygousa.com
website: www.zygousa.com
- Environmental Controls

(800) 395-3596
(503) 598-7531, fax

328

Computer
and Web
Resources
for People
with
Disabilities

*Innocomp
26210 Emery Road, Suite 302
Warrensville Heights OH 44128
email: Innocomp@sayitall.com
website: www.sayitall.com
- Augmentative Communication
- Electronic Pointing Devices
- Switches

(800) 382-VOCA (382-8622)
(216) 464-3636
(216) 464-3638, fax

Innovation Management Group, Inc.
21550 Oxnard Street, Suite 300
Woodland Hills CA 91367
email: cservice@imgpresents.com
website: www.IMGPresents.com
- Mouse Alternatives
- Alternate Keyboard

(818) 346-3581
(818) 346-3973, fax
(800) 889-0987

Innovative Designs
2464 El Camino, Suite 245
Santa Clara CA 95051
email: 70502.2003@compuserv.com
website: www.spies.com / finishline
- Word Prediction Programs

(408) 985-9255
(408) 247-6624, fax

*Innovative Products
830 South 48th Street
Grand Forks ND 58201
email: jsteinke@iphope.com
website: www.iphope.com
- Mobility Products for Children

(701) 772-5185
(701) 772-5284, fax

Innoventions
5921 S. Middlefield Road, Suite 102
Littleton CO 80123-2877
- Monitor Additions

(303) 797-6554
(303) 797-1320, fax

Inspiration Software
7412 SW Beaverton Hillsdale Highway, Suite 102
Portland OR 97225
website: www.inspiration.com
- Writing Composition Programs

(800) 877-4292
(503) 297-3004
(503) 297-4676, fax

Institute on Applied Technology

850 Boylston Street, Suite 106　　　　　　(617) 731-6466
Chestnut Hill MA 02167　　　　　　　(617) 731-5201, fax
  - Large-Print Word Processors
  - Speech Synthesizer
  - Switch Software

Intelligent Peripheral Devices

20380 Town Center Lane, Suite 270　　　　(408) 252-9400
Cupertino CA 95014　　　　　　　　(408) 252-9409, fax
email: info@alphasmart.com　　　　　　(888) 274-0680
website: www.alphasmart.com
  - Notetakers

*IntelliTools

55 Leveroni Court, Suite 9　　　　　　(800) 899-6687
Novato CA 94949　　　　　　　　(415) 382-5959
email: info@intellitools.com　　　　　(415) 382-5950, fax
website: www.intellitools.com
  - Access Utilities
  - Alternate Keyboards
  - Keyboard Additions
  - Switch Software
  - Talking and Large-Print Word Processors
  - Educational Software

*In Touch Systems

11 Westview Road　　　　　　　　(800) 332-6244
Spring Valley NY 10977
email: susan@magicwandkeyboard.com
website: www.magicwandkeyboard.com
  - Alternate Keyboards

Jostens Learning

9920 Pacific Heights Boulevard, Suite 500　　(619) 622-5096
San Diego CA 92121-4430　　　　　　(619) 622-7877, fax
  - Talking and Large-Print Word Processors

*Judy Lynn Software

P.O. Box 373　　　　　　　　　　(732) 390-8845
East Brunswick NJ 08816
email: judylynn@castle.net
website: www.castle.net/~judylynn
  - Switch Software

TECHNOLOGY VENDORS / I-J

330

Computer
and Web
Resources
for People
with
Disabilities

K-12 MicroMedia Publishing
16 McKee Drive
Mahwah NJ 07430
email: k12mmp@aol.com
website: www.k12mmp.com
  • Educational Software
  • Reading Comprehension Programs

(800) 292-1997
(201) 529-4500
(201) 529-5282, fax

Kare Products/Ergo Kare, Inc.
1644 Conestoga Street, Suite 2
Boulder CO 80301
website: www.kareproducts.com
  • Arm and Wrist Supports
  • Ergonomic Products

(800) 927-5273
(303) 443-2522, fax

Kensington Microware
2855 Campus Drive
San Mateo CA 94403
  • Monitor Additions: Anti-Glare Filters
  • Trackballs
  • Mouse Alternatives/Emulators

(800) 535-4242
(650) 572-2700
(650) 572-9675, fax

*Keyboard Alternatives & Vision Solutions
537 College Avenue
Santa Rosa CA 95404-4102
email: keyalt@keyalt.com
website: www.keyalt.com
  • Screen Enlargement
  • Ergonomic Products
  • Alternate Input
  • Braille Output

(707) 544-8000

Keytec, Inc.
1293 N. Plano Road
Richardson TX 75081
email: sales@magictouch.com
website: www.MAGICTOUCH.com
  • Touch Screens

(972) 234-8617
(972) 234-8542, fax
(800) 624-4289

Kidsview Software
P.O. Box 98
Warner NH 03278
email: kidsview@iamnow.net
website: http://iamnow.net/gfs4/kvsinc.html
  • Enlarged Text Software
  • Large-Print Word Processors

(800) 542-7501
(603) 927-4428
(603) 972-4428, fax

KidTECH/SoftTouch
4182 Pinewood Lake Drive
(805) 396-8676
Bakersfield CA 93309
(805) 396-8760, fax
- Adaptivation
- Assistive Communication Products
- Switch Software

Kinetic Designs, Inc.
14231 Anatevka Lane SE
(800) 244-8882
Olalla WA 98359
- Access Utilities

KLAI Enterprises
P.O. Box 43
(313) 425-1165
Garden City MI 48136
(313) 425-9033, fax
- Arm and Wrist Supports

Knowledge Adventure, Inc.
1311 Grand Central Ave.
(800) 542-4240
Glendale, CA 91201
(818) 246-4400
email: info@adventure.com
(818) 246-5604, fax
website: www.knowledgeadventure.com
- Screen Enlargement Programs
- Screen Readers
- Educational Software
- Reading Comprehension Programs
- Talking and Large-Print Word Processors
- Writing Composition Programs

Kurzweil Educational Systems, Inc.
(see Lernout & Hauspie, Kurzweil Educational Systems Group)
- Voice Recognition

KY Enterprises
3039 E. 2nd Street
(310) 433-5244
Long Beach CA 90803
(310) 433-3970, fax
email: kyenterprises@juno.com
- Environmental Controls
- Joysticks
- Switches

*Laureate Learning Systems, Inc.
110 East Spring Street
(800) 562-6801
Winooski VT 05404
(802) 655-4755
- Educational Software
- Reading Comprehension Programs

332

Computer
and Web
Resources
for People
with
Disabilities

- Switch Software
- Writing Composition Programs

*Lawrence Productions
1800 South 35th Street   (800) 421-4157
Galesburg MI 49053   (616) 665-7075
  - Educational Software   (616) 665-7060, fax
  - Independent Living Software

LC Technologies, Inc.
9455 Silver King Court   (800) 393-4293
Fairfax VA 22031   (703) 385-7133
email: jlahoud@lctinc.com   (703) 385-7137, fax
  - Environmental Controls

*LD Resources
202 Lake Road   (860) 868-3214 voice/fax
New Preston CT 06777
email: richard@ldresources.com or anne@ldresources.com
website: www.ldresources.com
  - Consulting Services
  - Educational Software

The Learning Company
6493 Kaiser Drive   (800) 852-2255
Fremont CA 94555   (510) 792-2101
website: www.learningcompanyschool.com
  - Educational Software
  - Reading Comprehension Programs
  - Writing Composition Programs

*Learning Well
111 Kane Street   (800) 645-6564
Baltimore MD 21224   (800) 413-7442, fax
email: dealers@wclm.com
  - Educational Software

*Lernout & Hauspie, Kurzweil Educational Systems Group
52 Third Avenue   (800) 894-5374
Burlington, MA 01803   (781) 203-5033, fax
email: education.info@lhsl.com
website: www.lhsl.com/education/
  - Speech Recognition
  - Reading Tools
  - Reading System Software

Less Gauss, Inc.
187 East Market Street   (914) 876-5432
Rhinebeck NY 12572
- Arm and Wrist Supports
- Monitor Additions: Magnifiers

Lexia Learning System, Inc.
114 Lewis Street   (800) 435-3942
Lincoln MA 01773
- Reading Comprehension Programs

Lexmark
740 New Circle Rd.   (888) LEXMARK (539-6275)
Lexington KY 40511   (606) 232-2380, fax
email: solutions@lexmark.com
website: www.lexmark.com
- Printers
- Information Services

*Little Planet Publishing/Applied Learning Technologies, Inc
P.O. Box 158427   (800) 974-2248, voice
Nashville TN 37215   (615) 385-9496, fax
website: www.littleplanet.com
- Early Childhood Education
- Language Arts

Logitech, Inc.
6505 Kaiser Drive   (510) 795-8500
Fremont CA 94555
- Trackballs

Looking Glass Learning Products, Inc.
3858 Hull   (800) 545-5457
Skokie IL 60076
- Reading Comprehension Programs

*LS&S
P.O. Box 673   (800) 468-4789
Northbrook IL 60065   (847) 498-9777
email: lssgrp@aol.com   (847) 498-1482, fax
website: www.lssgroup.com
- CCTVs
- Visual Aids

334

Computer
and Web
Resources
for People
with
Disabilities

Lucent Technologies
5 Woodhollow Road
Parsippany NJ 07054
website: www.telephones.att.com
• TTYs

(888) 708-0874
(973) 581-4113, fax

Luminaud, Inc.
8688 Tyler Boulevard
Mentor OH 44060
• Assistive Communication Products
• Switches and Switch Software

(216) 255-9082
(800) 255-3408, fax
(216) 255-2250, fax

Maddak, Inc.
661 State Route 23
Wayne, NJ 07470-6814
email: custservice@maddak.com
website: www.maddak.com
• Pointing and Typing Aids

(800) 443-4926
(973) 628-7600
(800) 541-3311, fax

*Madentec, Limited
3022 Calgary Trail South
Edmonton AB T6J 6V4
Canada
email: techsup@madenta.com
website: www.madenta.com
• Alternate Keyboards
• On-screen Keyboards
• Environmental Controls
• Switch Software
• Word Prediction Programs

(800) 661-8406
(780) 450-8926
(800) 852-0815, fax
(780) 988-6182, fax

*MarbleSoft
12301 Central Avenue NE
Blaine MN 55434
email: mail@marblesoft.com
website: www.marblesoft.com
• Early Childhood Software
• Reading Comprehension Programs
• Switch Software

(612) 755-1402
(612) 755-1402, fax

The Matias Corporation
600 Rexdale Boulevard, Suite 1204
Rexdale ON M9W 6T4
Canada
email: ematias@dgp.toronto.edu

(888) 663-4263
(416) 749-3124
(416) 740-4132, fax

website: www.dgp.toronto.edu/matias
- Access Utilities

*Mayer-Johnson Company
P.O. Box 1579   (800) 588-4548 or (858) 550-0084
Solana Beach CA 92075   (858) 550-0449, fax
email: mayerj@mayer-johnson.com
website: www.mayerjohnson.com
- Alternate Keyboards
- Assistive Communication Products
- Speech Synthesizers

McIntyre Computer Systems Division
22809 Shagbark   (810) 645-5090
Birmingham MI 48025   (810) 645-6042, fax
- Alternate Keyboards
- Joysticks
- Word Prediction Software

MECC (a division of The Learning Company)
6160 Summit Drive, N.   (800) 685-MECC (685-6322)
Minneapolis MN 55430   (612) 569-1500
website: www.learningco.com   (612) 569-1551, fax
- Educational Software
- Reading Comprehension Programs
- Writing Composition Programs

Med Labs, Inc.
28 Vereda Cordillera   (800) 968-2486
Goleta CA 93117   (805) 968-2486, fax
email: medlabsinc@aol.com
website: http://members.aol.com/medlabsinc/
- Environmental Controls
- Switches

Microflip
11211 Petworth Lane   (301) 262-6020
Glenn Dale MD 20769   (301) 262-4978, fax
email: info@microflip.com
website: www.microflip.com
- TTY Modems

*Microsoft Corporation—Accessibility and Disabilities Group
1 Microsoft Way   (800) 426-9400, voice
Redmond WA 98052   (800) 892-5234, TTY
website: www.microsoft.com

TECHNOLOGY VENDORS / M

336

Computer
and Web
Resources
for People
with
Disabilities

- Access Utilities
- Menu Management Programs
- MS-DOS Updates
- Trackballs
- Voice Recognition

*Microsystems Software, Inc. (a division of The Learning Company)
(see Henter-Joyce, Inc.)
- Access Utilities
- Assistive Communication Products
- Environmental Controls
- Screen Enlargement Programs
- Switch Software
- Word Prediction Programs

*MicroTalk
3039 Aubert Aveenue   (502) 897-5789
Louisville KY 40206   (502) 721-6083, fax
website: www.microtalk.com
- Braille Translators
- Screen Readers
- Speech Synthesizers

MicroTouch Systems, Inc.
300 Griffin Brook Park   (978) 659-9000 and (800) 642-7686
Methuen MA 01844   (978) 659-9100, fax
email: webtouch@microtouch.com
website: www.microtouch.com
- Touch Screens

*Millenium Software
3155 Fujita Street   (310) 530-0356
Torrance CA 90505
email: peaupeu@aol.com
website: http://members.aol.com/peuapeu
- Cognitive Training Software

Milliken Publishing Company
P.O. Box 21579   (800) 325-4136
1100 Research Boulevard   (314) 991-4220
St. Louis MO 63132   (314) 991-4807, fax
email: mpwebmaster@millikenpub.com
website: www.millikenpub.com
- Educational Software
- Reading Comprehension Programs

Mindplay

160 W. Fort Lowell Road
Tucson AZ 85705
email: mindplay@rtd.com
website: www.mindplay.com

(800) 221-7911
(520) 888-1800
(520) 888-7904, fax

- Educational Software
- Reading Comprehension Programs
- Writing Composition Programs

Mindscape (a division of The Learning Company)

88 Rowland Way
Novato CA 94945
website: www.mindscape.com

(415) 895-2000
(415) 895-2102, fax

- Educational Software

Mobius Corporation

405 N. Henry Street
Alexandria VA 22314
email: Kidware@prodigy.net
website: www.kidware.com/mobius

(800) 426-2710
(703) 684-2919, fax

- Early Childhood Software

Mouse Systems

41660 Boscell Road
Fremont CA 94538
email: info@mousesystems.com
website: www.mousesystems.com

(510) 656-1117
(800) 886-6423
(510) 656-4409, fax

- Trackballs

NanoPac, Inc.

4823 South Sheridan Road, Suite 302
Tulsa OK 74145-5717
email: info@nanopac.com
website: www.nanopac.com

(918) 665-0329
(918) 665-0361, fax

- Switch Software
- Voice Recognition
- Braille Products
- Augmentative Communications Software
- Alternate Keyboards
- Environmental Controls

Nisus Software, Inc.

P.O. Box 1300
Solana Beach CA 92075
email: info@nisus-sost.com
website: www.nisus-sost.com

(858) 481-1477
(800) 890-3030
(858) 481-7485, fax
(858) 481-6154, fax

- Access Utilities

338

Computer
and Web
Resources
for People
with
Disabilities

North Coast Medical, Inc.
18305 Sutter Boulevard
Morgan Hill CA 95037
email: custserv@ncmedical.com
website: www.ncmedical.com
  • Pointing and Typing Aids

(800) 821-9319
(877) 213-9300, fax

NXI Communicators
4505 S. Wasatch Boulevard, Suite 120
Salt Lake City UT 84124
email: nxi@nxicom.com
website: www.nxicom.com
  • TTY Modems

(801) 274-6001
(801) 274-6004, TTY
(801) 274-6002, fax

Okay Vision-Aide Corporation
67-555 East Palm Canyon Drive, Building C-103
Cathedral City CA 92234
website: http://ovac.com
  • CCTVs

(760) 321-9220
(760) 321-9711, fax

*OMS Development
3631 S. Wallace, Suite 1F
Chicago IL 60609
email: ebohlman@omsdev.com
website: www.omsdev.com
  • Screen Readers
  • Word Prediction Programs

(773) 268-4688
(773) 268-4699, fax

Optelec USA, Inc.
6 Lyberty Way
P.O. Box 729
Westford MA 01886
website: www.optelec.com
  • CCTVs
  • Screen Enlargement Programs

(800) 828-1056
(978) 692-6073, fax

Optimum Resources, Inc.
18 Hunter Road
Hilton Head Island SC 29926
email: stickyb@stickybear.com
website: www.stickybear.com
  • Educational Software
  • Reading Comprehension Programs

(888) 784-2592
(843) 689-8000
(803) 689-8008, fax

ORCCA Technology

462 East High Street
Lexington KY 40507
website: www.orcca.com
- Switches

(606) 226-9625
(606) 226-0936, fax

Origin Instruments Corporation

854 Greenview Drive
Grand Prarie TX 75050
email: sales@orin.com
website: www.orin.com
- Electronic Pointing Devices

(972) 606-8740
(972) 606-8741, fax

*PageMinder

3623 South Avenue
Springfield MO 65807
email: pageminder@pageminderinc.com
website: www.pageminderinc.com
- Mobility Products
- Paging Systems

(888) 882-7787

Parrot Software

P.O. Box 250755
West Bloomfield MI 48325
email: support@parrotsoftware.com
website: www.parrotsoft.com
- Cognitive Training Software

(800) 727-7681
(248) 237-7282
(248) 788-3224, fax

*Pathways Development Group, Inc.

17409 57th Avenue W
Lynnwood WA 98037
- Adaptive Controls
- Game Controls

(877) 742-4604
(425) 742-4674
(425) 745-9279, fax

Penny and Giles Computer Products, Ltd.

163 Pleasant Street, Suite 4
Attleboro MA 02703
- Joysticks
- Trackballs

(508) 226-3008
(508) 226-5208, fax

Personal Data Systems, Inc.

100 West Rincon Avenue, #103
Campbell CA 95008
email: info@personaldatasystems.com
website: www.personaldatasystems.com
- Speech Synthesizers

(408) 866-1126
(408) 866-1128, fax

340

Computer
and Web
Resources
for People
with
Disabilities

Phone TTY, Inc.
1246 Route 46 West   (973) 299-6627
Parsippany NJ 07054   (973) 299-6626, TTY
email: phonetty@aol.com   (973) 299-7768, fax
website: www.phone-tty.com
  • TTYs and TTY Modems

Phonic Ear, Inc.
3880 Cypress Drive   (800) 227-0735
Petaluma CA 94954   (707) 769-1110
website: www.phonicear.com
  • Assistive Communication Products

Power Plus: The Accessories People
4100 Caven Road
Austin TX 78744
email: pplus@io.com
  • Monitor Additions

*Prentke Romich Company
1022 Heyl Road   (800) 262-1984
Wooster OH 44691   (330) 262-1984
email: Service@prentrom.com   (330) 263-4829, fax
Sales@prentrom.com
website: http://www.prentrom.com
  • Alternate Keyboards
  • Assistive Communication Products
  • Electronic Pointing Devices
  • Environmental Controls
  • Joysticks
  • Keyboard Additions
  • Switches
  • Word Prediction Programs

Productivity Software International, Inc.
(see Sunflower Software)
  • Abbreviation Expansion and Macro Programs

The Productivity Works, Inc.
7 Belmont Circle   (609) 984-8044
Trenton NJ 08618   (609) 984-8048, fax
email: info@prodworks.com
website: www.prodworks.com
  • Accessible Browsers
  • Telecommunications Access

Psychological Corporation
Communication Skill Builders
P.O. Box 839954
San Antonio TX 78283-3954
website: www.psychcorp.com
- Writing Composition Programs

(800) 211-8378
(800) 232-1223, fax

*Raised Dot Computing, Inc.
(see Duxbury Systems)
- Braille Editing Software
- Braille Embossers, Translators
- Screen Readers
- Speech Synthesizers

Reading Technologies
9269 Mission Gorge Road, PMB
Santee CA 92071
email: readtech@concentric.net
- Braille Embossers and Translators
- Optical Character Recognition Software and Scanners
- Screen Enlargement Programs
- Screen Readers
- Speech Synthesizers

(619) 685-7323

Reasonable Solutions
1535 E. University Drive
Mesa AZ 85203
- Menu Management Programs

(800) 876-3475
(202) 668-9425, fax

*Rhamdec, Inc.
Mydesc Division
P.O. Box 4296
Santa Clara CA 95056
website: www.mydesc.com or www.rhamdec.com
- Computer Mounting Products

(800) 4-MYDESC (469-3372)
(408) 496-5590

*Richard Wanderman
(see LD Resources)
- Consulting Services
- Educational Software

*R. J. Cooper and Associates
24843 Del Prado #283
Dana Point CA 92629
email: rj@rjcooper.com
website: www.rjcooper.com

(800) RJ COOPER (752-6673)
(949) 661-6904
(949) 240-9785, fax

TECHNOLOGY VENDORS / P-R

342

Computer
and Web
Resources
for People
with
Disabilities

- Alternate Keyboards
- Interface Devices
- Joysticks
- Switches and Switch Software

*Roger Wagner Publishing, Inc.
(see Knowledge Adventure)
- Authoring Software

Sammons Preston, Inc.
P.O. Box 5071   (800) 323-5547
Bowlingbrook IL 60440-5071   (800) 325-1745, TTY
- Pointing and Typing Aids   (800) 547-4333, fax
- Switches

*Saltillo Corporation
2143 TR112   (330) 674-6722
Millersburg OH 44654   (330) 674-6726, fax
email: aac@saltillo.com
- Assistive Communication Products

SaundersErgo Source
4250 Norex Drive   (800) 456-1289
Chaska MN 55318   (800) 375-1119, fax
- Arm and Wrist Supports

Schamex Research
19201 Parthenia Street, Suite H   (818) 772-6644
Northridge CA 91324   (818) 993-2496, fax
- Reading Machines

Scholastic Software
2931 East McCarty Street   (949) 240-9785
Jefferson City MO 65102   (800) 541-5513
website: www.scholastic.com   (800) 724-6527, orders
- Reading Comprehension Programs   (573) 635-5881, fax
- Writing Composition Programs

Seeing Technologies, Inc.
42 Executive Boulevard   (800) 462-3738
Farmingdale NY 11735   (516) 752-0234, voice/TTY
website: http://maxiaids.com   (516) 752-0689, fax
- CCTVs
- Visual Aids

*Seiko Instruments USA, Inc.
2990 W. Lomita Boulevard   (877) 344-4040

Torrance CA 90505
email: sii_usa_readingpen@bigfoot.com
- Reading Tools

(310) 517-7793, fax

Semerc/ProMedia
57 Lakeview Avenue
Clifton NJ 07011
email: promedia@mtlakes.csnet.net
website: www.promedia-semerc.com
- Educational Software
- Switch Software

(800) 462-0930
(973) 253-7600, voice
(973) 253-5601, fax

*Sentient Systems Technology, Inc.
(see DynaVox Systems)
- Assistive Communication Products

Shea Products
1721 W. Hamlin
Rochester Hills MI 48309
- Assistive Communication Products

(810) 852-4940
(810) 852-5298, fax

*Simtech Publications
134 East Street
Litchfield CT 06759
email: switchdon@hsj.com
website: www.hsj.com
- Educational Software
- Switch Software

(860) 567-1173, voice and fax

Skills Bank Corporation
(see The Learning Company)
- Reading Comprehension Programs
- Writing Comprehension Programs

SkiSoft Publishing Corporation
28 Fairlawn Lane
Lexington MA 02420
email: info@skisoft.com
website: www.skisoft.com
- Large-Print Word Processors

(800) 662-3622
(617) 861-0086, fax

SmartStuff Software
2100 SE 10 Avene
Portland OR 97214
email: info@smartstuff.com
website: www.smartstuff.com
- Menu Management
- Desktop and Internet Security Utilities

(800) 671-3999
(503) 231-4300
(503) 231-4334, fax

344

Computer
and Web
Resources
for People
with
Disabilities

SoftTouch/KidTECH
4182 Pinewood Lake Drive   (805) 873-8744
Bakersfield CA 93309
  • Educational Software
  • Switch Software

Span-America Medical Systems, Inc.
P.O. Box 5231   (864) 288-8877
Greenville SC 29606   (800) 888-6752
website: http://spanamerica.com   (864) 288-8692, fax
  • Keyboard Additions
  • Seating and Positioning

*Special Needs Project Worldwide
324 "H" State Street   (805) 962-8087
Santa Barbara CA 93105   (800) 333-6867
website: www.specialneeds.com   (805) 683-2341, fax
  • Books
  • Electronic Reference Tools

*Spinoza Company
1876 Minnehaha Avenue West   (800) 282-2327
St. Paul MN 55104-1029   (651) 644-7251
email: spinoza@spinozabear.com
website: www.spinozabear.com
  • Adapted Toys

SSK Technology, Inc.
5619 Scotts Valley Drive, Suite 280   (800) 775-0759
Scotts Valley CA 95066   (800) 775-1630, TTY
email: writalk@aol.com   (408) 461-8909, fax
  • TTYs

*Sunburst Communications
101 Castleton Street   (800) 321-7511
Pleasantville NY 10570   (914) 747-3310
email: service@nysunburst.com   (914) 747-4109, fax
support@nysunburst.com
website: www. sunburst.com
  • Alternate Keyboards
  • Educational Software
  • Large-Print Word Processors
  • Math Software
  • Reading Comprehension Programs
  • Writing Composition Programs

Sunflower Software
211 East 43rd Street, Suite 2201   (212) 818-1144
New York NY 10017   (212) 818-1197, fax
Website: www.sunflowersoft.com
- Abbreviation Expansion and Macro Programs

*Sun Microsystems Accessibility Group
901 San Antonio Road MS UCUPO2-103   (415) 863-3151
Palo Alto CA 94303
email: access@sun.com
website: www.sun.com/tech/access
- Internet Accessibility
- Internet Developer Products

SVE and Churchill Media (formerly Society for Visual Education, Inc.)
6677 N. Northwest Highway   (800) 829-1900
Chicago IL 60631   (773) 775-9550
website: www.svemedia.com   (800) 624-1678 and (773) 775-5091, fax
- Electronic Reference Tools

Switch In Time
172 Harvard Avenue   (978) 486-9433
Littleton MA 01460
email: adams@switchintime.com
website: www.switchintime.com
- Switches and Switch Software

Switch Kids
8507 Rupp Farm Drive   (513) 860-5475
West Chester OH 45069   (513) 860-5475, fax
website: www.switchkids.com
- Switches and Switch Software

Symantec
10201 Torre Avenue   (800) 441-7234
Cupertino CA 95014-1232   (541) 984-8020, fax
website: www.symantec.com
- Menu Management Programs

Sym Systems/The Great Talking Box Company
(see The Great Talking Box Company)
- Assistive Communication Products

Synergy
412 High Plain Street   (508) 668-7424
East Walpole MA 02081   (508) 668-4134, fax
email: synergy@ma.ultranet.com

346

Computer
and Web
Resources
for People
with
Disabilities

website: www.speakwithus.com
  • Switches and Switch Software
  • Augmentative and Alternative Communications Products

Syntha-Voice Computers, Inc.
800 Queenson Road, Suite 304   (800) 263-4540
Stony Creek ON L8G 1A7   (905) 662-0565
Canada   (905) 662-0568, fax
email: help@synthavoice.on.ca
website: www.synthavoice.on.ca
  • Screen Enlargement Software
  • Screen Readers

*TASH International, Inc.
Unit 1–91 Station Street   (800) 463-5685
Ajax ON L1S 3H2   (905) 686-4129
Canada   (905) 686-6895, fax
email: tashcan@aol.com
website: www.tashint.com
  • Abbreviation Expansion and Macro Programs
  • Alternate Keyboards
  • Assistive Communication Products
  • Environmental Controls
  • Interface Devices
  • Joysticks
  • Keyboard Additions
  • Switches and Switch Software

Taylor Associates Communications, Inc.
200-2 E. 2nd Street   (800) 732-3758
Huntington Station NY 11746   (516) 549-3000
email: ifo@ta-comm.com   (516) 549-3156, fax
website: www.ta-comm.com
  • Reading Comprehension Programs

Teacher Support Software
3542 N Street   (800) 228-2871
Gainesville FL 32605   (904) 332-6404
  • Reading Comprehension Programs   (904) 332-6779, fax
  • Talking and Large-Print Word Processors
  • Writing Composition Programs

**Tech-Able/Member Toy Adaptation Network for
Children with Disabilities**
1112 A Brett Drive SW   (770) 922-6768
Conyers GA 30094   (770) 992-6769, fax

email: techable@america.net
website: www.gatsl.org
- Keyguards (custom)
- Switches

Technology for Language and Learning
P.O. Box 327   (516) 625-4550
East Rockway NY 11518-0327   (516) 621-3321, fax
- Switches and Switch Software

Technos America, Ltd.
386 Quartz Circle   (877) 816-0495
Bailey CO 80421   (303) 816-0495
email: carl@mctos.com   (303) 816-9619, fax
website: www.mctos.com
- Electronic Pointing Devices

Teledyne Brown Engineering/Interact Plus Division
35805 Sparkman Drive   (800) 944-8002
Huntsville AL 35807   (205) 726-1743, fax
website: www.teledynebrownengineering.com
- Environmental Controls

*Telesensory
520 Almanor Avenue   (800) 804-8004
Sunnyvale CA 94086   (408) 616-8700
email: smiller@telesensory.com   (408) 616-8720, fax
website: www.telesensory.com
- Braille Embossers, Translators
- CCTVs
- Notetakers
- Reading Machines
- Refreshable Braille Displays
- Screen Enlargement Programs
- Screen Readers
- Speech Synthesizers
- TTYs
- Browser Access

Texas School for the Deaf
Denise Hazelwood   (512) 462- 5416 or (512) 462-5200
1102 South Congress Avenue   (512) 562-5313, fax
P.O. Box 3538
Austin TX 78764
email: deniseh@tsd.state.tx.us
website: www.tsd.state.tx.us/
- Educational Software

348

Computer
and Web
Resources
for People
with
Disabilities

textHELP! Systems, Ltd. (formerly Lorien Systems)
Enkalon Business Centre   011-44-1849-428105, voice
25 Randalstown Road   011-44-1849-428574, fax
Antrim BT41 4LJ
United Kingdom
email: info@texthelp.com
website: www.texthelp.com
  • Reading and Writing Software

TFI Engineering
529 Main Street   (617) 242-7007
Boston MA 02129   (617) 242-2007, fax
email: tfi@netcom.com
  • Notetakers

Tom Snyder Productions
80 Coolidge Hill Road   (800) 342-0236
Watertown MA 02172-2817   (617) 926-6000
email: ask@tomsnyder.com   (617) 926-6222, fax
website: www.tomsnyder.com
  • Educational Software
  • Reading Comprehension Programs
  • Writing Composition Programs

Toucan Press (formerly Pelican Software)
Queue, Inc.   (800) 232-2224
338 Commerce Drive   (203) 336-2481, fax
Fairfield CT 06430
email: queueinc@aol.com
website: www.queueinc.com
  • Educational Software
  • Writing Composition Programs

Toys for Special Children, Inc.
385 Warburton Avenue   (800) 832-8697
Hastings on Hudson NY 10706   (914) 478-0960
website: www.enablingdevices.com   (914) 478-7030, fax
  • Adapted Toys
  • Environmental Controls
  • Switches and Switch Software

Trace Research and Development Center
Room S-151, Waisman Center   (608) 262-6966
1500 Highland Avenue   (608) 263-5408, TTY
University of Wisconsin   (608) 262-8848, fax
Madison WI 53705
email: web@trace.wisc.edu

website: http://trace.wisc.edu
- Information Resources

Troll Touch
25510 Avenue Stanford, Suite 106   (661) 257-1160
Valencia CA 91355-1131   (661) 257-1161, fax
email: info@touchproducts.com
website: www.trolltouch.com
- Touch Screens

Turning Point Therapy & Technology, Inc.
P.O. Box 310751   (803) 608-9812
New Braunfels TX 78131-0751
website: www.turningpointtechnology.com
- Key Guards

*UCLA Microcomputer Project
1000 Veteran Avenue, Room 23-10   (310) 825-4821
Los Angeles CA 90095-1797   (310) 206-7744, fax
email: twebb@pediatrics.medsch.ucla.edu
- Alternate Keyboard Software
- Early Childhood Software
- Intellikeys Software
- Switches and Switch Software

Ultratec
450 Science Drive   (800) 482-2424, voice/TTY
Madison WI 53711   (608) 238-5400, voice/TTY
website: www.untratec.com   (608) 238-3008, fax
- Pay Phone Attachments
- Signaling Equipment
- TTYs

Varatouch Technologies, Inc. (formerly Presentation Electronics)
7325 Roseville Road   (916) 331-6300
Sacramento CA 95842   (916) 338-8255, fax
email: vti@varatouch.com
website: www/varatouch.com
- Remote controls

Visionware Software, Inc.
P.O. Box 1676   (617) 738-4757, voice and fax
Brookline MA 02146   (508) 692-6073, fax
email: dan@largeprint.com
website: www.largeprint.com
- Screen Enlargement Programs

350

Computer
and Web
Resources
for People
with
Disabilities

Visuaide, Inc.
841 Jean-Paul Vincent Boulevard   (450) 463-1717, accepts collect calls
Longueuil PQ J4G 1R3   (450) 463-0120, fax
Canada
email: info@visuaide.gc.ca
website: www.visuaide.com
  • Switches and Switch Software

Visual Tech Connection
P.O. Box 898   (614) 899-9989
Westerville OH 43081
  • Monitor Additions: Magnifiers

*Voice Communications
P.O. Box 29   (203) 775-3204
Wilton CT 06897
email: keghtesadi@aol.com
  • Voice Recognition

*VoiSys International
34 Linnell Circle   (508) 667-8145
Nutting Lake MA 01865
email: voisys@tiac.net
website: www.voisys.com
  • Assistive Communications Products

Volunteers for Medical Engineering
2301 Argonne Drive   (410) 243-7495
Baltimore MD 21218   (410) 467-3873, fax
email: vme@toad.net
website: www.toad.net/~vme
  • Computer Loan Closet for State of Maryland
  • Environmental Controls
  • Rehab Engineering Services

WCI Technology
2716 Ocean Park Boulevard, Suite 1007   (800) 233-9130, voice/TTY
Santa Monica CA 90405
website: www.weitbrechtcom.com
  • TTY's

*WesTest Engineering Corporation
810 W. Shepard Lane   (801) 451-9191
Farmington UT 84025   (801) 451-9393, fax
email: mary@westest.com
website: www.westest.com
  • Interface Devices

*William K. Bradford Publishing
16 Craig Road
Acton MA 01720
email: wkb@wkbradford.com
website: www.wkbradford.com
- Reading Comprehension Programs
- Writing Composition Programs

(800) 421-2009
(508) 263-6996
(508) 263-9375, fax

Words+, Inc.
1220 West Avene J
Lancaster CA 93534-2902
website: www.words-plus.com
- Access Utilities
- Alternate Keyboards
- Assistive Communication Products
- Electronic Pointing Devices
- Environmental Controls
- Interface Devices
- Keyboard Additions
- Switches and Switch Software
- Word Prediction Programs

(800) 869-8521
(661) 723-6523
(661) 723-2114, fax

*World Communications
245 Tonopah Drive
Fremont CA 94539
- Access Utilities
- Alternate Keyboards
- Assistive Communication Products
- Switches and Switch Software
- Word Prediction Programs

(800) 352-1979
(510) 656-0911
(510) 656-3005

Wynd Communications Corporation
75 Higuera Street, Suite 240
San Luis Obispo CA 93401
email: info@wynd.com
website: www.wynd.com
- Accessible Pagers

(800) 549-9800, voice
(800) 549-2800, TTY
(805) 781-6001, fax

X-10 (USA) Inc.
91 Ruckman Road
Closter NJ 07624
website: www.x10.com
- Environmental Controls

(800) 675-3044
(201) 784-9700
(201) 784-9464, fax

352

Computer
and Web
Resources
for People
with
Disabilities

Xerox Imaging Systems, Inc.
9 Centennial Drive   (800) 343-0311
Peabody MA 01960   (508) 977-2000
website: www.xerox.com   (508) 977-2148
  • Optical Character Recognition Software
  • Reading Machines

XYBIX Systems, Inc.
8160 Blakeland Drive, Unit G   (800) 788-2810
Littleton CO 80125   (303) 683-5454, fax
email: barrycowen@xybix.com
  • Arm and Wrist Supports
  • Adaptable Furniture

Zygo Industries, Inc.
P.O. Box 1008   (800) 234-6006
Portland OR 97207   (503) 684-6006
website: www.zygo-usa.com   (503) 684-6011, fax
  • Alternate Keyboards
  • Assistive Communication Products
  • Environmental Controls
  • Switches and Switch Software

Index

Names of commercial programs, services, and assistive hardware are indicated by®.

A

abbreviation expansion software, 55, 212–214
ABLEDATA®, 159
academic skills, acquiring, 28
Access Board, 67
access utilities, 54, 162, 163, 171, 179–181; cost, 180; features, 179–180; potential users, 179; related products, 181; uses for, 179; vendors, 180
accessories, computer, 121
ADA *see* Americans with Disabilities Act
Adaptive Device Locator System, 159
ADB connections, 48
advocates, disability, 84
Alabama, Alliance for Technology Centers, 265; Tech Act programs, 272
Alaska, Tech Act programs, 272
Alliance for Technology Access, xi, xii, xiii, 3, 72, 75; centers, 108, 148, 265–271; mission, 3–4; services, 4–5; website, 6
alternate output systems, 228–245
America Online®, 139, 141, 303
American Printing House for the Blind, 283, 287
Americans with Disabilities Act (ADA), 35, 66–67, 84, 100–101, 149; implementation resources, 283–286
Apple computers, 46
Apple Plain Talk®, 195
Arc, The, 72, 78, 147, 287
Architectural and Transportation Barriers Compliance Board, 70
Arizona, Alliance for Technology Centers, 265; Tech Act programs, 272–273
Arkansas, Alliance for Technology Centers, 265–266; Tech Act programs, 273
arm and wrist supports, 54, 162, 208–209
assistive technologies, 52–62; and setting goals, 29–42; future of, 149–153; guidelines for, 61–62; Internet resources, 302–308; organizations, 286–292; people's use of, 12–26; publications, 295–302; vendors, 81, 309–352
Assistive Technology Act, 67–68, 149
Assistive Technology Funding and Systems Change Project, 105
Assistive Technology Industry Association, 108
Attorney General's Office, 67
augmentative communication aids, 13, 37, 58–61, 246–250
Authorware®, 172
autism, 31, 37

B

backing up work, 130
Biggy, 143
books, assistive technology, 295–300

354

Computer
and Web
Resources
for People
with
Disabilities

356

Computer
and Web
Resources
for People
with
Disabilities

358

Computer
and Web
Resources
for People
with
Disabilities

National Federation of the Blind, 14

National Institute on Disability and Rehabilitation Research, 104

national programs, 93–101

National Service Program, 103

Nebraska, Tech Act programs, 278

Netscape®, 141, 143

Nevada, Tech Act programs, 278

New England Disability and Business Technical Resource Center, 284

New Hampshire, Tech Act programs, 278

New Jersey, Alliance for Technology Centers, 269; Tech Act programs, 279

New Mexico, Tech Act programs, 279

New York, Alliance for Technology Centers, 269; Tech Act programs, 279

newsgroups, 305–308

newsletters, assistive technology, 295–300

nonverbal disability, assistive technologies for, 12–13

North Carolina, Alliance for Technology Centers, 270; Tech Act programs, 279

North Dakota, Tech Act programs, 279

Northeast Disability and Business Technical Resource Center, 284

Northwest Disability and Business Technical Resource Center, 286

notetakers, 15, 254–256

Office of Civil Rights, 67

Office of Program Management of Federal Transit Administration, 67

Office of Special Education Programs (U.S. Department of Education), 65–66

Office of the Americans with Disabilities Act, 284

Ohio, Alliance for Technology Centers, 270; Tech Act programs, 280

Oklahoma, Tech Act programs, 280

online services, 139, 141, 303

operating system software, 15, 46–47, 117

optical character recognition and scanners, 54, 165, 167, 196–198; cost, 197; features, 196–197; potential users, 196; related products, 198; uses for, 196

Optimists, 13

Oregon, Tech Act programs, 280

organizations, assistive technology, 286–292

output devices, 114, 228–243; conventional, 52; assistive, 55, 57–58

Overlay Maker®, 85

P

Pacific Disability and Business Technical Resource Center, 286

Papert, Seymour, 149, 151

parallel ports, 48

parent support, 71, 77

Parents, Let's Unite for Kids, 77

360

Computer
and Web
Resources
for People
with
Disabilities

362

———

Computer
and Web
Resources
for People
with
Disabilities

364

Computer
and Web
Resources
for People
with
Disabilities

THE PLEASURE PRESCRIPTION: To Love, to Work, to Play—Life in the Balance by Paul Pearsall, Ph.D. *New York Times Bestseller!*

This bestselling book is a prescription for stressed-out lives. Dr. Pearsall maintains that contentment, wellness, and long life can be found by devoting time to family, helping others, and slowing down to savor life's pleasures. Pearsall's unique approach draws from Polynesian wisdom and his own 25 years of psychological and medical research. For readers who want to discover a way of life that promotes healthy values and living, THE PLEASURE PRESCRIPTION provides the answers.

288 pages ... Paperback $13.95 ... Hard Cover $23.95

WRITE YOUR OWN PLEASURE PRESCRIPTION: 60 Ways to Create Balance & Joy in Your Life by Paul Pearsall, Ph.D.

For the many readers who have written asking for ways to translate the harmony of Oceanic life to their own lives, Dr. Pearsall offers this companion volume. It is full of ideas for bringing the spirit of aloha—the ability to fully connect with oneself and with others—to everyday life. Pearsall emphasizes that pleasure is healthy balance. He encourages readers to disengage from the rush and frenzy of life in order to feel the pleasure that comes from the deep joy that can be part of each day.

224 pages ... Paperback ... $12.95

WRITING FROM WITHIN: A Unique Guide to Writing Your Life's Stories by Bernard Selling

Any writer can create vivid autobiographical stories and life narratives using the techniques taught in this book, which are based on Selling's widely followed classes and workshops. This program enables everyone interested in writing to explore their lives, rediscover forgotten experiences, and discover hidden truths about themselves, their parents, and their family histories.

"Anyone who has ever lost the opportunity to find out what really mattered to an important friend or relative will respond instantly to this book." — *Booklist*

288 pages ... Paperback $17.95 ... Revised 3rd edition

Hunter House
HEALTH

CANCER—INCREASING YOUR ODDS FOR SURVIVAL: A Resource Guide for Integrating Mainstream, Alternative and Complementary Therapies
by David Bognar

This book describes all the current conventional, alternative, and complementary treatments for cancer. Each listing covers the treatment and its success rates, and gives contact information for experts, organizations and support groups, and book, video and Internet resource listings. Full-length interviews with leaders in the field of healing, including Joan Borysenko, Stephen Levine, and Bernie Siegel, cover the powerful effect the mind has on the body and the therapies that strengthen the connection, spiritual healing, and issues of death and dying.

352 pages ... Paperback $15.95 ... Hard Cover $25.95

ALZHEIMER'S EARLY STAGES: First Steps in Caring and Treatment
by Daniel Kuhn, MSW

This is the only book to focus on early-stage Alzheimer's disease—often the most difficult time for caregivers, who may not know much about the disease, or how they can best be of help. The book addresses the wide range of medical, emotional, and practical concerns, and includes extensive resources for obtaining additional help. Straightforward and pragmatic yet compassionate and encouraging, this book is invaluable for anyone with a loved one in the early stages of Alzheimer's.

288 pages ... Paperback $14.95 ... Hard Cover $24.95

ALTERNATIVE TREATMENTS FOR FIBROMYALGIA AND CHRONIC FATIGUE SYNDROME: Insights from Practitioners and Patients
by Mari Skelly and Andrea Helm, Foreword by Paul Brown, M.D., Ph.D.

If you or someone you love suffers from FM and CFS, you know that conventional medicine may not always help. This book describes a wide range of alternative therapies from acupuncture to massage to yoga and more. It includes interviews with treatment professionals and personal stories from sufferers, who describe the individual drug, diet, and activity regimens that help them. Information on legal issues, such as obtaining Social Security disability, and a comprehensive resource section are also included.

288 pages ... Paperback $15.95 ... Hard Cover $25.95

To order books see last page or call (800) 266-5592

ORDER FORM

10% DISCOUNT on orders of $50 or more —
20% DISCOUNT on orders of $150 or more —
30% DISCOUNT on orders of $500 or more —
On cost of books for fully prepaid orders

NAME _____

ADDRESS _____

CITY/STATE _____ ZIP/POSTCODE _____

PHONE _____ COUNTRY (outside of U.S.) _____

TITLE	QTY	PRICE	TOTAL
Computer Resources, 3rd ed....(paperback)		@ $20.95	
Computer Resources, 3rd ed....(spiral)		@ $27.95	

Prices subject to change without notice

Please list other titles below:

		@ $	
		@ $	
		@ $	
		@ $	
		@ $	
		@ $	
		@ $	

Check here to receive our book catalog ❏   FREE

Shipping Costs:
First book: $3.00 by book post ($4.50 by UPS, Priority Mail, or to ship outside the U.S.)
Each additional book: $1.00
For rush orders and bulk shipments call us at (800) 266-5592

	TOTAL	_____
	Less discount @_____%	(_____)
	TOTAL COST OF BOOKS	_____
	Calif. residents add sales tax	_____
	Shipping & handling	_____
	TOTAL ENCLOSED	_____

Please pay in U.S. funds only

❏ Check ❏ Money Order ❏ Visa ❏ Mastercard ❏ Discover

Card # _____ Exp. date _____

Signature _____

Complete and mail to:
Hunter House Inc., Publishers
PO Box 2914, Alameda CA 94501-0914
Orders: (800) 266-5592   email: ordering@hunterhouse.com
Phone (510) 865-5282 Fax (510) 865-4295
❏ Check here to receive our book catalog

CTS3 3/00